W9-DGL-757

Women's Work in Britain and France

Women's Work in Britain and France

Practice, Theory and Policy

Abigail Gregory
Lecturer in French
University of Salford

and

Jan Windebank
Senior Lecturer in French Studies
University of Sheffield

First published in Great Britain 2000 by
MACMILLAN PRESS LTD
Houndmills, Basingstoke, Hampshire RG21 6XS and London
Companies and representatives throughout the world

A catalogue record for this book is available from the British Library.

ISBN 0–333–68306–4 hardcover
ISBN 0–333–68307–2 paperback

First published in the United States of America 2000 by
ST. MARTIN'S PRESS, INC.,
Scholarly and Reference Division,
175 Fifth Avenue, New York, N.Y. 10010

ISBN 0–312–23105–9

Library of Congress Cataloging-in-Publication Data
Gregory, Abigail, 1962–
Women's work in Britain and France : practice, theory and policy / Abigail
Gregory, Jan Windebank
p.   cm.
Includes bibliographical references and index.
ISBN 0–312–23105–9 (cloth)
1. Women—Employment—Great Britain.   2. Women—Employment—France.
3. Sex discrimination in employment—Great Britain.   4. Sex discrimination in
employment—France.   5. Women—Great Britain—Economic conditions.
6. Women—France—Economic conditions.   I. Windebank, J. (Janice)   II. Title

HD6135 .G74   1999
331.4'0941—dc21

99–052334

This book is printed on paper suitable for recycling and made from fully managed and sustained
forest sources.

10   9   8   7   6   5   4   3   2   1
09   08   07   06   05   04   03   02   01   00

Printed and bound in Great Britain by
Antony Rowe Ltd, Chippenham, Wiltshire

To Colin and Shaun, Elizabeth, Eve and Toby who give us hope that progress in gender relations is being made

Contents

List of Tables

List of Figures

Acknowledgements

This book, doubtless like many others before it, is the result not only of academic endeavour but much personal sacrifice. Indeed, the analyses, theorizations and progress under discussion within the covers of this volume are all intensely felt in the everyday experience of both authors. As women with both full-time employment and caring responsibilities for young children, as well as partners in full-time employment, the challenges which we document here are far from abstract to us. Indeed, the fact that we have managed to complete this book seems a small miracle in itself and a signifier that things must be starting to change. In this regard, we would like to thank Colin and Shaun, Elizabeth, Eve and Toby who give us hope that progress in gender relations is being made.

Besides such personal acknowledgements, there are also a number of people who we would like to thank who freely gave their time to read and make incisive comments on both the structure of the book and draft versions of chapters, namely Shirley Dex, Linda Hantrais, Pat Walters and Colin Williams as well as anonymous reviewers of papers and articles which have been fed into the book. Without their help, this book would have been much more difficult to write. Abigail Gregory would like to thank Marie-Thérèse Letablier at the Centre D'Etudes de l'Emploi in Paris, who has supported her research over many years by giving her access to the resources at the Centre, and the European Studies Research Institute at the University of Salford for helping to free up time to research and write this book. Jan Windebank would also like to thank the University of Sheffield for providing funding to conduct the study on motherhood in Britain and France presented in this book, along with all of the participants in the research who gave up a good deal of their scarce time to be interviewed and provided great insight into the similarities and differences of women's work and motherhood in Britain and France.

Of course, the normal disclaimers apply: any omissions or faults are the authors' alone.

1
Introduction

The evaluation of women's work has increasingly taken centre-stage in the study of gender, work and the family. This is the case across a wide range of disciplines, including sociology, social policy, economics and human geography. On an international scale, such evaluations have identified national differences in women's employment rates across Western, and especially European countries, and highlighted the effect that differing national social and labour market policy exerts on women's employment opportunities. The assertion has often been, therefore, that social and labour market policy can and does make a difference to the configuration of women's work. In this respect, Britain and France are countries that have proven to be particularly illuminating when compared. These are nations that have similar levels of women's employment, but highly different patterns of women's participation in the labour force, all set in the context of divergent policy environments. As such, at one level, Anglo-French comparisons reinforce the notion that policy is highly influential in women's working lives. As we shall see in this book, however, one should not accept such an idea too hastily, primarily because it is based on an over-emphasis of the importance of paid work.

Much research on women's working lives, cross-national or otherwise, has been founded upon the assumption that the rate of full-time employment among women is the principal barometer of progress in gender relations and that more employment for women equals liberation and gender equality. Such an assumption, however, is somewhat ironic. Early feminist studies achieved widespread acceptance that work is more than employment and thus re-valued much of women's unpaid work. Nevertheless, much contemporary

1

cross-national gender research has focused upon women's paid work, with unpaid work either being ignored, given secondary status or only considered in narrow terms, doubtless due to the difficulties involved in comparing unpaid work cross-nationally. Indeed, where women's unpaid work is discussed in cross-national terms, studies have essentially analysed the extent to which the state in different countries has assumed some of women's familial and caring responsibilities rather than assessing national differences concerning the division of unpaid work between men and women (for example, see the contributors to the volume by Willemsen *et al.*, 1995). The aim of this book, therefore, is to be one of the first within cross-national comparative literature on women's work to investigate in equal depth all forms of work and the ways in which unpaid work is divided between men and women, and not just between women and the state. This, however, is not an end in itself. By presenting a more comprehensive account of all women's work within a cross-national perspective than has hitherto been the case, the further objective is to bring a fresh insight into both theorizations of women's work and the policies required if more equitable gender divisions of work are to come about. Evaluating in cross-national perspective the impact of social and labour market policy on gender relations within the private as well as the employment sphere, we intend not only to assess the influence of state policy on women's work but also to re-evaluate the nature of such social policy in the context of the overarching economic changes taking place in these nations. The result will be a critical evaluation of current social and labour market policy and suggestions about the direction and nature of the changes required if progress in gender relations is to occur.

To provide the groundwork for such an analysis, this chapter commences by defining women's work and providing a brief rationale for the book in the context of previous cross-national studies of women's work. Following this, we then provide an overview of the structure of the book.

Defining women's work

The conventional conceptualization of economic life has been based upon the view that work equals employment. Indeed, this view of the economy still prevails in some circles. One has only to glance along the bookshelves of any academic library to see that the vast majority of texts focus upon employment. Moreover, the national accounting systems of the advanced economies relate to paid work and its products alone. This narrow and historically specific conceptualization of work was first questioned by the feminist movement and women's studies researchers when they introduced to the social sciences the concept that work is more than employment during the 1970s (Dupont, 1970; Oakley, 1974). For these analysts, if the major contributions of women to socio-economic life were to be recognized, the vast amount of unpaid economic activity, mostly undertaken by women, would have to be given heightened status in the study of work and welfare both theoretically and in terms of policy-making. Based on this reconceptualization of work, much theory-building ensued which attempted both to explain women's disadvantaged position in the labour market, particularly within a Marxist framework, and to provide empirical accounts of the gender division of labour.

Here, therefore, we deal with three principal forms of women's work: paid work, on the whole formal employment but also encompassing undeclared paid work or 'informal' employment and self-employment; 'domestic work', which is unpaid work undertaken by household members for themselves and each other; and third, a category which is perhaps most often forgotten, 'community work', which is work exchanged within the extended family or neighbourhood.

As we shall see throughout this book, defining work in this manner to incorporate all economic activity into analyses allows some significant insights to be gained not only concerning women's work and position in contemporary society but also concerning the role of social and labour market policy in shaping gender relations and the changes required if more equitable gender divisions of labour are to come about. The vast majority of cross-national analyses of gender relations, although having taken on board domestic labour to varying degrees, have looked primarily at employment when discussing progress in gender relations. By taking this wider approach to cross-national analysis of women's work, we will see that new light is cast on both gender relations, the role of social and labour market policy in mitigating women's position and the alterations needed to construct more equitable gender divisions of labour. Locating women's work at the cross-roads of both the formal and informal spheres, or what is often referred to as the spheres of production and reproduction (Chabaud *et al.*, 1985), allows a discussion of how women's changing responsibilities in one sphere impacts on the other, as well as of how policy with regard to one sphere can sometimes have unintended impacts on the other. Moreover, it enables the importance of women's 'caring' and 'emotional' activity, as distinct from more concrete activities that can easily be defined as 'work', to be taken into account in discussions of what constitutes progress in gender relations.

Rationale for the book

In order to situate this book and understand its rationale, it is first necessary to understand the cross-national comparisons that have been undertaken of women's work in Britain and France (for example, Beechey, 1989; Crompton *et al.*, 1990; Dex and Walters, 1989; Garnsey, 1985; Gregory, 1989; Gregory and O'Reilly, 1996; Hantrais, 1990; Hantrais and Letablier, 1996; Lane, 1993; Marsden, 1989) as well as cross-national studies of women's work more generally (for example, Crompton, 1997; Kamerman and Kahn, 1978).

As Glover (1996) has highlighted in an excellent review article of cross-national studies of women's work, there have traditionally been two main approaches. First, there is the 'indicators' approach and second, the 'societal' approach. The former seeks to establish convergence between countries, while the latter aims to explain difference by reference to social, cultural, historical and political features of each country. In the 'indicators' approach, therefore, the principal aim of cross-national comparison is to advance theory by seeking evidence of relationships that recur in more than one nation which can be done by establishing similarities among and between countries. For this approach, therefore, replication of a relationship between two or more variables in more than one nation makes for a more powerful finding than when it is established in one nation alone for it displays that this finding is not nationally specific. To do this, such studies often involve a large number of countries and use economic and social indicators, usually nationally aggregated, to create 'league tables' of nations on particular variables (for example, Kiernan, 1992; Merritt and Rokkan, 1966).

In contrast, other cross-national studies adopt a 'societal' approach, seeking to explain the differences between nations by reference to the societal factors in each country which structure economic and social organization. Rubery (1988), building on Maurice *et al.* (1982), argues that it is the intersection of political, economic and social factors within nations that provides the explanations for differences between countries; too much stress is put on the similarities between nations in the indicators approach. Such a societal approach has also been taken up in geography in the postmodernist slant towards identifying difference (see McDowell, 1991). However, Rubery (1992) cautions against the dangers as well as the benefits of this approach. These are first, that we may lose sight of the universality of gender inequality in the exploration of national differences, leading to a false view that specific policy measures have solved problems of gender equality. Second, the relationship of gender relations to the societal system may lead, almost by definition, to a focus on the harmony between the current gender order and the societal arrangements, with the danger that the inequalities which the system imposes on women are played down. Third, there is the danger that a societal-based approach will emphasize nationally specific differences between women but neglect differences in the interest and fortunes of women within nations.

In this book, following on from the recent work of others such as Crompton with Le feuvre (1996), our intention is to provide a synthesis of these two approaches by analysing both differences and similarities in women's work in Britain and France. The aim, in doing so, is to display that the existence of the similarities reveals that certain aspects of gender inequality wrought by patriarchy and capitalism are common across these two nations, while the differences are intended to show how gender inequalities are manifested in particular ways due to the mediation of patriarchy by nationally specific factors, including, social, political, institutional and economic contexts. Our intention, moreover, is to identify the nature of these commonalities and particularities. Indeed, it is only by looking at all forms of work that this is possible.

In other words, we are not seeking either to highlight the similarities in women's work patterns so as to pinpoint some universal theorization of women's disadvantaged position, nor are we seeking to highlight the cross-national variations in women's experiences so as to point to the contribution that policy can make to progress in gender relations. For us, too much of the contemporary literature draws out universalist assumptions about women's work situation from single-nation studies without recognizing the national specificity of their findings while cross-national studies place too much emphasis on identifying difference which is put down to contrasting policy environments. Rather, this book situates itself within a paradigm which not only seeks to recognize the differences in women's work patterns, but also to relativize the importance of these national differences. Put another way, our intention is to discover the relative importance of policy in shaping women's economic position through cross-national analysis. In doing so, we address the very heart of many of the contemporary discussions of women's work. Can policy really influence women's economic position? What is the evidence that this has indeed occurred? To what extent and how has it influenced women's working lives? Are all of these changes progressive? Or are there unintended impacts that have not been fully addressed due to the narrow focus upon employment as the principal form of work in contemporary society? In asking such questions in the context of a cross-national analysis of Britain and France, we will show that a focus upon employment as the principal form of work leads to a narrow conceptualization of 'progress' in gender relations and that by redefining work in a broader manner, both the nature and source of 'progress' in gender relations as these concern women's working lives must be redefined in ways that have only just started to be addressed.

As such, we aim to show that there are both theoretical and policy lessons to be learned from comparing Britain and France. So far as Britain is concerned, the comparison will show that British women will not necessarily become 'liberated' if they are given more plentiful opportunities for full-time employment and more state welfare support since it will be seen that despite such opportunities, French women remain, like British women, confronted by a double/triple burden of employment, domestic and community work and that such policy does nothing to encourage men to participate more fully in taking responsibility for domestic work and caring functions. This is particularly relevant in the light of the desire of the new British government to develop child-care provision and encourage lone mothers into employment. Similarly, it shows the French that more of the same is not necessarily the route to gender progress.

It is important to make explicit at the outset, however, that in this book, we are focusing upon similarities and differences *between* Britain and France. Adopting this as our emphasis does not mean that we do not recognize the major differences and similarities between geographical areas and social groups *within* each nation. We are well aware of the fact that women's work patterns, family responsibilities and indeed, the nature of patriarchy, need to be examined by social group and at different spatial scales to solely that of the nation-state (for example, Duncan, 1991, 1994; McDowell, 1991; McDowell and Massey, 1984; Monk and Garcia Ramon, 1996; Perrons, 1997; Pratt and Hanson, 1993). Nevertheless, in this book, our emphasis remains on an overview of the nation state for it is at this level that so many assumptions persist and much of the policy in the two nations which can affect progress in gender relations is based.

Structure of the book

As the sub-title of this book suggests, our intention is to examine practice, theory and policy towards women's work in Britain and France. As such, Part I focuses upon the practice through an empirical analysis of the differences and similarities in the work situation of British and French women while Part II explores the theorizations and the resulting policy proposals. In order to map out the differences and similarities in the work situation of British and French women in Part I, Chapters 2, 3, and 4 provide an empirical evaluation of women's position in the contemporary period in the spheres of paid work, domestic work and community work respectively, providing a more comprehensive view of women's work situation than has conventionally been the case. With this empirical grounding in hand, Part II then first explores in Chapter 5 the alternative explanations and theoretical positions which have been adopted to account for women's position in both paid and unpaid work and asks how these deal with cross-national differences and similarities. This is followed in Chapter 6 with an analysis of the policy issues that arise from this empirical and theoretical analysis. Finally, in Chapter 7, we draw conclusions concerning the implications of examining all forms of work in cross-national perspective for our understanding of gender relations in the sphere of work.

.

Part I

Differences and Similarities in the Work Situation of British and French Women

2
Women's Paid Work

We will begin our empirical analysis of the differences and similarities in the contemporary work situation of British and French
women by examining women's paid work in the two countries. In
doing so, we will be building on the large body of Anglo-French
comparative research into women's paid work carried out since the
mid-1980s in both countries (Barrère-Maurisson *et al.*, 1989; Beechey,
1989; Benoit-Guilbot, 1989; Blackwell, 1998; *Comparaisons internationales*, 1989; Dex *et al.*, 1993; Gregory, 1987, 1989; Hantrais,
1990; Lane, 1993; O'Reilly, 1994).

Women's paid work in Britain and France has been the focus of
considerable interest in recent years. This is in part because the
two countries are geographically close and in part because women's
position in paid work in Britain and France, as in most industrialized countries, has been affected by a number of common industrial,
economic, cultural and social changes in the postwar period that
might lead us to expect strong similarities in the characteristics of
paid employment between the two countries. The demand for
women's paid employment in industrialized countries during this
time has been affected, as Hagan and Jenson (1988) have convincingly
argued, first by the development of mass consumerism and mass
production under Fordist regimes and second by Keynesian economic policies to develop education and the welfare state. Subsequently,
women's employment has been influenced by the development of
flexible accumulation under Post-Fordism and the impact of spreading
neo-liberal ideologies (Hagan and Jenson, 1988).[1] These industrial,
political and economic changes have contributed to a transformation
in the nature of employment in industrialized countries: a dominant
model of full-time permanent employment characteristic of the

immediate postwar period has been replaced with more extensive use of part-time, temporary and short-time working in economies where high levels of unemployment have been common after the oil crises of the 1970s. This transformation in the nature of employment has taken place against the backdrop of a shortening of working lives and annual working time (Bosch *et al.*, 1994). In addition, women's labour supply in Britain and France has been particularly influenced by common social and cultural changes which have affected industrialized countries in the postwar period: greater control over women's fertility, a fall in family size, rising divorce rates and changes in family form, notably the growth of one parent families (Rubery *et al.*, 1995). Other common influences include the increased importance of the state (Rubery, 1988) and the impact of the internationalization of social and political ideas and values such as feminism.

However, against the backdrop of these broad similarities seen in the postwar period, the large body of cross-national comparative work to date provides evidence of significant differences in certain features of women's paid work in Britain and France which has led many authors to seek explanations for these differences in terms of the impact of national social policy frameworks. We will, therefore, on the basis of aggregate national and comparative data and research monographs, examine a number of features of women's paid work that have been shown to be important indicators of the social construction of women's employment in these two countries: activity and unemployment rates, women's working hours, employment status and the degree of occupational segregation and pay inequality.

A few words should also be said about methodological issues. First, the chapter focuses on paid work in the formal economy, paid informal work being extremely difficult to chart accurately, particularly in a cross-national comparative perspective, and researchers on this subject being particularly 'gender-blind' (see Williams and Windebank, 1998a). Second, while this book, as the title states, is concerned with women's paid and unpaid work in Britain, reliable comparative statistics on employment are often only available from sources such as the European Labour Force Survey which use the United Kingdom rather than Britain in its comparative statistics. Throughout this chapter, therefore, statistics for the UK are taken to apply equally to Britain. Third, as Hantrais and Letablier (1996) point out, problems of comparison still arise from the use of the

Labour Force Survey primarily as a result of the use of differing definitions for labour market phenomena in the national surveys and as a result of external national features affecting measurements (such as training and education, retirement measures and legislation and working hours norms). We attempt to take into account these problems of comparison in our analysis below. Fourth, it should be noted that this account focuses principally on trends over the last fifteen years (as far as is allowed by statistical sources). However, where appropriate, we seek to offer an understanding of trends over a longer period. Lastly, and to reiterate what we stated in Chapter 1, we are neither seeking just to isolate differences in women's paid work in the two countries nor to focus only on similarities. Rather, we aim to examine *both* differences and similarities and to identify recent trends in the two countries in women's paid work situation.

Economic activity rates

Women's activity rates in Britain and France have risen steadily since the late 1960s, even through periods of recession, with women increasing their proportion of all employment compared with men (Hantrais, 1990). It may be dangerous, however, as Lewis (1992b) points out, to characterize this trend as revolutionary because many women earlier this century, in Britain at least, often worked part-time on a casual basis and were not included as employed by census enumerators. Hakim (1995) too has highlighted the difficulties of looking at the postwar period in isolation from levels of activity earlier this century and in the nineteenth century, because a number of indicators of women's economic activity (full-time employment rates, full-time equivalent rates) have remained relatively stable in the longer term. There have also been similar sectoral changes in women's paid employment in the postwar period: a fall in the proportion of all women employed in manufacturing and a rise in the proportion in services, although the UK started the century with a much lower proportion of women in agriculture than in France, a difference that, although reduced, remains today.[2]

By 1997, activity rates for women in the UK, defined as the total number of women in the labour force aged 15 or over as a percentage of the population of women of working age, were slightly higher than those of French women according to the Labour Force Survey, with levels at 53.2 per cent and 48.2 per cent respectively

(OOPEC, 1998: Table 003). These levels exceed the EU15 average (of 45.6 per cent) and place the UK and France among the countries with the highest women's activity levels in the European Union (EU). French levels must be considered to be particularly high given the very significant proportion of women in full-time education compared with the UK in the 15 to 24 age group (as discussed below). However, these figures relate to all women and do not reflect the considerable diversity in activity levels in both Britain and France by ethnic group. For example in 1995, activity levels for the population of women immigrants as a whole (aged 15+) in France, at 41.6 per cent, were below the national average of 47.2 per cent, according to the Enquête sur l'Emploi (Institut Nationale des Statistiques et des Etudes Economiques – INSEE, 1997). More specifically, for those aged 39 to 59, women's activity levels fluctuated widely by ethnic group. Spanish (61.3 per cent), Italian (51.8 per cent), Portuguese (74.5 per cent) and Black African (67.4 per cent) women's activity levels were well above the average for all ethnic minority women (55.7 per cent), while those for Algerian (40.0 per cent), Moroccan (37.8 per cent) and Tunisian (44.7 per cent) women were well below average. A similar situation exists in the UK. In the age group 16 and over activity levels were also lower overall for ethnic minority women according to the Labour Force Survey of Autumn 1995 (55 per cent compared with 71.8 per cent) (Sly, 1996). Women's activity rates are highest for Black, Indian and Chinese women (respectively 69 per cent, 61 per cent and 56 per cent) and are lowest for Pakistani/Bangladeshi women (22 per cent) (Sly, 1996).

Although the overall trend has been of rising activity rates for women in both countries since the early 1980s, activity rates have also risen faster in the UK than in France over this period and have affected all age groups (see Table 2.1). Latterly, nevertheless, there has been a slight fall in activity rates for the under 25s in the UK. In France, by contrast, activity rates have fallen significantly for women aged under 25, a trend which shows evidence of continuing (Gissot and Meron, 1996). On the other hand, for the under 60s, levels have fluctuated and risen in recent years. Furthermore, although activity levels are increasing in France, the proportion of women in the workforce is relatively stable. The consequence of the French mismatch is rising unemployment levels (Gauvin, 1995). On the other hand, in Britain both activity levels and the proportion of women in the workforce are increasing.

Table 2.1 Activity rates for women by age group, France and UK, 1983, 1993 and 1997

	1983[†]	1993[†]	1997*
15–25 years old			
UK	58.6	61	60.2
France	49.0	36.2	31.7
25–49 years old			
UK	63.1	74.4	75.6
France	68.4	77.3	78.6
50–64 years old			
UK	44.2	50.2	52.6
France	39.2	38.5	42.8

Source: [†] Eurostat, (1995: 106–8); * OOPEC, (1998: Table 004).

Table 2.1 shows that while activity levels are higher in France in the 25 to 49 age group they are higher in younger and older age groups in the UK. In part, this difference reflects considerably higher rates of participation by French women in education between the ages of 15 to 24 (63.1 per cent of women aged between 15 and 24 in 1997 were in education in France compared with 28.2 per cent in the UK [OOPEC, 1998: Table 002]), a disparity which is likely to continue into the next century (Hantrais, 1990). It also reflects particularly low participation rates among an older generation of women in France, which may be the consequence of the introduction of a series of early retirement measures (*Contrats de Solidarité – Réduction du temps de travail*) in the early 1980s and the imposition of a retirement age for men and women of 60 in 1983 which together had a considerable impact on activity rates in the over 60s,[3] whereas in Britain such measures have been limited and the retirement age for women has recently been increased to 65 for new retirees.

The trend both in the UK and in France over the last 15 years has been towards the concentration of work and family responsibilities for women in the 25 to 49 age group (Harrop and Moss, 1995; Letablier, 1995). This reflects in part a continuation of the postwar increase in activity levels among married women, and particularly among women with children, in the two countries (Hantrais, 1990). However, activity rates during the family formation period are higher in the 1990s in France than in Britain for women aged 25 to 49, although there is evidence that the extension of the *Congé Parental d'Education* (child raising allowance) to families with two or more children in 1994 (from those with three or more) has led to a fall in activity rates for mothers with two children (Afsa, 1996),

Figure 2.1 Women's employment continuity in France, 1963–82.

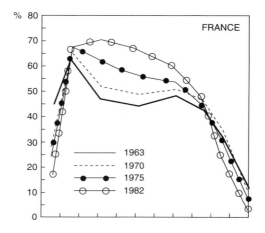

Source: OECD (1985: 34).

Figure 2.2 Women's employment continuity in the UK, 1963–82.

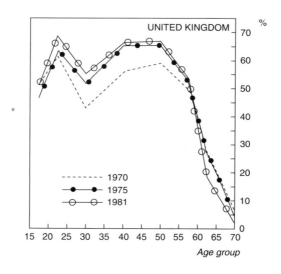

Source: OECD (1985: 34).

and to a polarization between lower and higher income families in their labour market behavior. This difference in continuity of employment across women's life cycles can be identified as early as the beginning of this century. At that time, although activity levels for young women aged 15 to 24 were higher in the UK than in France, after the age of 25, activity levels plummeted in the UK while they remained much higher in France. This feature may reflect the greater concentration of women in agricultural jobs and family businesses in France where combining work with family may have been easier.[4] This continuity in employment was broken somewhat in France in the immediate postwar period with French women temporarily developing a more discontinuous activity profile in the age group 25 to 39 between 1946 and 1954, with women leaving work in their early 20s and returning to work in their early 30s (Hantrais, 1990). By 1968, however, this pattern had begun to be eroded and a more continuous employment pattern emerged (see Figure 2.1).

In the 1990s the dominant model in France is one of high levels of participation for women independently of age, family circumstances, social background and region (Letablier, 1995). Nevertheless, labour force participation is strongly influenced by education levels (Coutrot *et al.*, 1997), as it is in Britain (Walby, 1997). Women with few or no educational qualifications are more likely to be out of the labour force while university graduates are more likely to be employed.[5] Recent research among young men and women in France has found that there is a greater commitment to employment among young women than men and an increased commitment to employment among young women who have traditionally worked discontinuously across their working lives and tended to give priority to family over employment (Nicole-Drancourt, 1996). The French literature is categorical in its view that women's entry into the labour force is an 'irreversible' fact (Commaille, 1992; Letablier, 1995; Nicole-Drancourt, 1996). Letablier (1995:11), for example, states that:

> social identity, for women as well as men, rests largely on work. French women's investment in the world of paid work has encouraged their commitment to work to the detriment of their commitment to politics or community life, which plays a greater role in Germany or the United Kingdom, in terms of the construction of social identity.

Table 2.2   Activity levels for women with children, by number of children and age of child, France and UK, 1990

| | Percentage economically active | |
	France	UK
No children	68.6	77.1
1 child	77.3	67.3
2 children	69.9	63.4
3 children +	39.6	46.7
Youngest child:		
2 years or less	61.5	46.5
>2 years and <7	69.4	61.6
7–<14	72.7	76.1

Activity rates for mothers relate to women who are married to the household head or are the household head.

Source: Labour Force Surveys, in *Bulletin on Women and Employment in the EC* (1992: 8).

In Britain, by contrast, it is still the case (see Table 2.2) that the continuity of employment of White women[6] is more likely to affected by the arrival of children than that of French women: they are less likely to be active when they have one or two children and their activity levels are particularly low when the youngest child is aged under seven.[7] Evidence from a Eurobarometer survey of women aged 22 to 60 in 1990 (Gauthier and Lelièvre, 1995) supports earlier work by Dex *et al.* (1993) in finding that although the proportion of women employed at least once in their lives was lower in France than in Britain (86 per cent compared with 96 per cent), all the indicators of continuity were less favourable for British women: they were more likely to have stopped employment at least once (60 per cent compared with 37 per cent), were more likely to state they had stopped employment for family reasons (80 per cent compared with 63 per cent) and less likely to say that they had been employed during the pre-school years of their first child (39 per cent compared with 59 per cent). This difference is also apparent among women in higher-status jobs. Dex *et al.* (1993) found that 63 per cent of mothers working as professionals and 60 per cent of mothers working as teachers in France were continuous workers compared with only 7 per cent and 9 per cent respectively in Britain. While continuity falls for French women in lower-status jobs, levels still remain considerably higher than in the UK: 22 per cent of mothers in France employed in semi and unskilled jobs were continuous workers compared with only 3 per cent in Britain (Dex *et al.*, 1993: 83–6).

As can be seen in Figure 2.2, the development of a more continuous activity pattern has been slower overall in the UK. First
evidence of a bi-modal pattern of activity was recorded in the 1961
Census for England and Wales, since in the immediate postwar period
women had followed a monotonic pattern by which they left the
workforce at the age of 21 and the level of activity decreased until
retirement age (Hantrais, 1990: 77). However, in contrast with the
postwar trends in France, in Britain the bi-modal pattern has not
disappeared despite the fact that there has been an erosion in the
traditional 'camel's back' found in British women's participation in
paid work over the family formation period. British women are now
returning to employment much more quickly after the birth of their
first child (Joshi and Hinde, 1993; Macran *et al.*, 1996; McRae, 1991)
and rates of full-time employment for mothers have increased in
recent years. This feature is considered to be very important by
Hakim (1991), for until recently, women's activity rates in the UK
had been rising only by means of replacing full-time jobs by part-
time ones. This reduction of the break in employment is cited as
the most important factor in explaining rising women's participation rates (Harrop and Moss, 1995).

The growth of British mothers' employment in the 1980s has
not, however, been uniform and there is evidence of a polarization
in women's experience of combining work with motherhood between a relatively privileged group of women high up the occupational
scale and another larger group who are likely to stay out of the
labour market after childbirth (see Glover and Arber, 1995; Harrop
and Moss, 1995; Macran *et al.*, 1996; McRae, 1991). Women higher
up the occupational scale are less likely to suffer occupational downgrading and more likely to retain their employment benefits because
they stay in their jobs or take only a short break. Also, working
part-time in professional/intermediate classes enables women to
maintain their continuity of employment and thereby protect their
employment rights (Glover and Arber, 1995). By contrast, women
lower down the occupational scale more often leave the labour market
after childbirth, returning later into low-status part-time employment, with negative effects for their labour-market position (Glover
and Arber, 1995; Macran *et al.*, 1991).

The disparity in the situation of single mothers[8] in the two countries
is particularly marked.[9] Single-parent households, along with single-
person households, are the most rapidly expanding household type
in Britain and France. Single-parent households remain, however,

more numerous in Britain than in France. In 1997, one-person households with children under 15 represented 5.1 per cent of household types in the UK compared with 2.7 per cent in France (OOPEC, 1998: Table 114). In France, the majority of single mothers (82 per cent) were economically active in 1992 (Bradshaw *et al.*, 1996) and rates of activity have been further increasing in the 1990s (Lefaucheur and Martin, 1995, 1997), although so too have their unemployment rates. Over half of family income in France in 1989 came from paid work in single parent families, compared with 70.7 per cent from partnered families (INSEE, 1997). Single mothers are not only more likely to be employed than partnered ones, they are also less likely to work part-time rather than full-time (15 per cent compared with 20 per cent in 1992 [Bradshaw *et al.*, 1996: 8]). In the UK, despite the fact that a similar proportion of lone mothers (about half) have no qualifications (Lefaucheur and Martin, 1995), activity levels are much lower. In 1990/2, just 41 per cent of lone mothers were economically active (Bradshaw *et al.*, 1996). Indeed, in 1993, lone parents received 63 per cent of their income from state benefits, mostly from Income Support. Only 24 per cent of average income was provided by earnings from paid employment. As in France, lone mothers are more likely to work full-time rather than part-time, but part-time levels remain higher in the UK than in France (24 per cent compared with 15 per cent), reflecting national differences (described below), while full-time levels remain considerably lower in the UK than in France (21 per cent compared with 49 per cent). In contrast with the situation in France, moreover, activity levels of single mothers in Britain have been falling since the 1970s (Lefaucheur and Martin, 1995), while those of partnered mothers have increased substantially to outstrip those of lone mothers (Duncan and Edwards, 1997b). Harrop and Moss (1995) suggest that the continuing fall in activity levels in the 1980s among lone mothers in the UK may, in particular, reflect the nature of the development of child-care provision in Britain over this period which has been primarily through the development of private child-care facilities which tend to be too expensive for lone parents.

The overall dissimilarity between lone mothers' position on the labour market in the UK and France would seem to relate, as Millar (1994) points out in her international comparison of lone mothers' labour market situation, to the gender roles which prevail in the two countries and to the state's support for those roles. In the UK, the association between a strong breadwinner state, characterized by a division between public and private responsibilities and a lack of support for women's work outside the home, and a benefit system which replaces the earnings of men with social assistance for those outside the labour market, has led to low employment rates for single mothers. In France, by contrast, where there is a modified breadwinner state, in which families with children are given financial assistance and in which there is support for working mothers, single mothers are given an incentive to work by the limitation of the period over which non-contributory benefits are paid, and by making subsequent benefits (such as the *Revenu Minimum d Insertion*) dependent on the willingness to actively seek employment (Hantrais, 1993).

Unemployment rates

While women's activity rates have been increasing over the past decade in both Britain and France, unemployment rates[10] have not followed a common trend: rates fell for British women aged 25 to 49 from 8.3 per cent to 5.1 per cent between 1983–97 while they rose from 7.5 per cent to 13.4 per cent over the same period in France (OOPEC, 1998: Table 009). Once again, the averaged figures mask considerable fluctuations according to women's marital status and ethnic group. Figures for 1992 (INSEE, 1994) found that lone mothers' unemployment rate in France was considerably higher than that of all women (17.4 per cent compared with 12.8 per cent), while in Britain (Bradshaw *et al.*, 1996) the disparity in 1990 was apparent but not so great (8 per cent compared with 7 per cent). Unemployment rates are much higher among ethnic minority populations in both countries. In France, the 1995 *Enquête Emploi* showed that unemployment rates were 21.8 per cent for ethnic minority women aged 15 and over but only 13.9 per cent for all women, although the rate had fallen somewhat since 1990 (INSEE, 1997). Unemployment rates were lowest for women from Spain, Italy and Portugal (respectively 11.3 per cent, 11.2 per cent and 8.9 per cent) and highest for women from Algeria (36 per cent), Morocco (43.3 per cent), Tunisia (38.5 per cent), Turkey (44.7 per cent) and among Black Africans (31.2 per cent). In the UK, the Labour Force Survey of Autumn 1995 (Sly, 1996) found that unemployment rates among women aged 16 and over were substantially higher for ethnic minority groups than for all women (17 per cent compared with 7 per cent) and rates had increased substantially

Table 2.3   Percentage of women unemployed by age group, France and UK, 1997

Age group	UK*	France
15–24	11.2	31.2
25–49	5.1	13.4
50+	3.9	9.0

*The UK definition of unemployment is claimants to unemployment benefit. This may significantly understate women's unemployment levels as many women may be excluded from claiming for benefit even if they are, in fact, looking for paid work.

Source: OOPEC, (1998: Table 008).

since 1990. Highest rates were found among Black (22 per cent) and Pakistani/Bangladeshi women (29 per cent) with the lowest levels for Indians (11 per cent) and Others (including Chinese) (15 per cent).

Part of the explanation for the divergent trends found in Britain and France when all women are considered would seem to lie in the fact that in France, women's employment in manufacturing was disproportionately concentrated in textiles which fared badly in the recession of the 1980s, whereas men's jobs in manufacturing were less concentrated and thus spared to some extent (Tomasini, 1994). Also, while jobs have been created in the service sector in France, many of these have been on a part-time basis, which are not generally seen as attractive (Barrère-Maurisson et al., 1987). By contrast, in Britain women have tended to be substituted for male workers, often in part-time jobs created after the wave of British privatizations in the 1980s by employers preoccupied with wage-cutting (Barrère-Maurisson et al., 1987).

The evidence suggests that it is now much harder for French women to find jobs than British women, particularly in younger age groups (see Table 2.3). Although there are some commonalities in women's unemployment in the two countries, notably that unemployment varies with qualification levels, creating a polarization between qualified and unqualified women,[11] a number of other significant differences remain. In the UK, women remain unemployed for shorter periods than men while the situation for French women is slightly worse than that of their male counterparts (OOPEC, 1998: Table 097). Although this Anglo–French difference may in part be explained by the tendency for women with family commitments to leave the labour market when they do not find a job, the relative similarity of the proportions of discouraged workers in the two countries (the proportion of economically active women discouraged from working was estimated as 0.3 per cent in France and 0.7 per cent in the UK in 1993 according to the OECD (Gauvin, 1995)) suggests that a more likely explanation might be the high incidence of part-time working in the UK (see below) and the much greater willingness of unemployed women in the UK to seek part-time work.[12] Barrère-Maurisson *et al.* (1989) argue that the explanation for this Anglo-French difference lies in the relationship between work and family in the two countries. They suggest that British women are less demanding and more flexible than their French counterparts because of their lower qualification levels and a need for working hours to suit child-care requirements.

In Britain, it may be that the model for women's employment is more akin to that of the US where low unemployment is associated with a polarization of the labour force and women's position in the labour market is primarily in secondary jobs defined by their responsibilities within the home (Hegewish, 1995). In France, by contrast, both men and women are competing for qualified full-time jobs. The differing location of unemployment in women's employment patterns in the two countries is revealed in the principal characteristics of women's unemployment. In 1997, only 35 per cent of unemployed women in the UK were seeking a job after job loss or leaving a job compared with 69 per cent of French women. By contrast over 48.2 per cent of women in the UK were seeking work after inactivity compared with only 14.7 per cent of women in France (OOPEC, 1998: Table 093). The disparity between women's reasons for seeking work in the UK and France has increased in recent years.

Another reason for the very high unemployment rates among French women is that they are no longer discouraged from seeking jobs during economic recession. Unemployment is also exacerbated by the already high levels of women in education and in early retirement which closes down some alternative routes out of the labour market in times of recession (Gauvin, 1995).

Working hours

Full-time work and working hours

Numbers of women working full-time in Britain and France increased over the 1980s although the proportion of full-time paid work fell in France and remained stable in Britain (see Table 2.4). The growth in Britain can be explained to a large extent by the growing proportion

Table 2.4 Numbers of women and men employed full-time, 1980/82, 1990, 1996 in Britain and France (thousands)

	Men	Women	Percentage full-time
Britain*			
1982	11 803	5 106	57.5
1990	10 766	6 346	57.7
1996	9 742	5 845	52.9
% change 1982–90	−8.8	+24.0	
% change 1990–96	−9.5	−8.0	
France			
1980	12 709	7 060	83.1
1990	12 206	7 159	76.4
1996	11 727	6 970	70.5
% change 1980–90	−4.0	+1.4	
% change 1990–96	−4.0	+2.6	

* Statistics by status of employment only available from 1982; Statistics relate to September for 1982 and 1990 and for December in 1996. Definitions of part-time work vary in the two countries (see note 13). Unadjusted figures.

Source: Employment Gazette, February, 1984, November, 1990: Table 1.4; *Labour Market Trends,* October, 1996: Table 1.1; Husson, 1996: 138; *Enquête sur L'Emploi,* 1996. All French statistics relate to March of each year.

of full-time employment among women with young children, especially since the mid-1980s (Walby, 1997). Over the period 1990 to 1996, this trend was reversed and numbers employed full-time fell in both countries (by 2.6 per cent in France and by 8 per cent in Britain) and the proportion of women working full-time also fell (from 76.4 per cent to 70.5 per cent in France and from 57.7 per cent to 52.9 per cent in Britain).

The UK distinguishes itself in the EU for having the highest proportion of employees (men and women) whose usual weekly working hours exceed 48 (Watson, 1992). Full-time hours for all employees increased between 1983 and 1993 by 1.1 hours (increasing their average to 43.4), compared with stability (+0.1 per cent) in France (from 39.7 to 39.8) and a falling average for the EU12 (Boisard, 1995). In 1997, 58.3 per cent of employed men in the UK usually worked 40 hours or more per week and 30.9 per cent more than 46 hours per week (see Table 2.5). This compared with respectively 36.3 per cent and 16.3 per cent in France. However, France and the UK have been following opposite trends over the period 1993 to 1997. There has been a significant rise in longer working hours in France (+17.8 per cent for over 40 hours a week) and a signifi-

Table 2.5 Persons in full-time employment, groups of hours usually worked in reference week (employees), France and UK, 1997

Hours Employed	Men France	UK	Women, France	UK
1–35	7.8	17.1	13.9	30.2
36–39	48.6	17.9	52.7	26.5
40	8.0	11.5	7.3	9.8
41–45	12.0	15.9	8.4	11.3
46+	16.3	30.9	8.0	12.8
% 40+	36.3	58.3	23.7	33.9

Note: use of employees in employment removes inconsistencies introduced by the working hours of the self-employed, which tend to be very long, particularly in France.

Source: OOPEC, (1998: Table 0.77).

cant fall in the UK (−21.6 per cent), although the proportion of men working between one and 35 hours in the UK has also increased between 1993 and 1997.

The length of full-time working hours for both men and women in the UK and France is clearly affected by the working-time regime in the two countries. The UK is characterized by a lack of regulation and a reliance instead on voluntary regulation and custom and practice. The consequence of this policy, combined with a lack of minimum-wage regulation and an active policy to encourage low pay, has been the development of very long full-time working hours, particularly for men. The working-time regime in France, by contrast, is characterized by relatively strict statutory regulation of working hours (a legal maximum working week and working day and controls over overtime use), and relatively weak collective regulation of working time (Rubery *et al.*, 1995). The more rigid working-time regime in France, linked to higher average wages deriving from the application of a minimum wage, has had the effect of limiting the growth of very long working hours for men and women, although it is still the case that significant proportions of men and women work over 46 hours a week.

Full-time working hours for women are also longer in the UK than in France, but the difference is smaller than for men. In 1997, 33.9 per cent of all women's usual working hours exceeded 40 hours per week in the UK compared with 23.7 per cent in France. However, as has been the case for men, this proportion has fallen significantly in the UK (−26.2 per cent) and increased significantly in France (+13.9), although in France at the same time the proportion

Table 2.6   Levels of part-time employment for women, France and UK, 1983 and 1997

| | Part-time as a percentage of all women employees in employment | |
	France	UK
1983	18.7	41.8
1997	30.9	44.9

Note: for an explanation of the difficulties in comparing part-time levels in France and the UK see note [13].

Source: Labour Force Surveys: Table 053; Hantrais (1990: Table 3.5).

working one to 35 hours has also increased. Furthermore, as is the case for men, women's full-time hours below 40 a week in France are more heavily concentrated in the 36 to 39 hours group than those in the UK. If working hours do appear to be lengthening in France, it is still the case that the disparity between the proportion of men and women working over 40 hours a week has increased over the period 1993 to 1997 (from 10 per cent to 12.6 per cent), while in the UK, in the context of falling full-time working hours, the opposite is true (the disparity falling from 28.5 per cent to 24.4 per cent).

Part-time work and working hours

Part-time work[13] has been the main vehicle for the growth in paid employment for women in Britain and France since the 1980s (Rubery and Fagan, 1996), as it has been in much of Europe (OECD, 1994) (see Table 2.6). In Britain the proportion of women working part-time, which was already relatively high, rose rapidly in the 1970s and early 1980s, slowing in the late 1980s when full-time levels climbed quickly. In the 1990s, the situation has reversed again with part-time employment rates growing and full-time rates declining. In France, although its growth also began in the 1970s, part-time rates rose gradually from 1982 to 1987 and, after stabilizing until 1992, rose steeply thereafter: two thirds of jobs created between 1994 and 1995 were on a part-time basis (Le Corre, 1995).

This growth in Britain and France, in common with all Western economies, has been driven by employers' demands for increased flexibility in work-time schedules and has been facilitated by technical innovation, increased unemployment and hence weaker union resistance in Western economies since the mid-1970s (Bosch *et al.*, 1994). Some authors also argue that there has been a parallel growth

in employees' aspirations for more leisure time and greater individual control over working hours or 'time sovereignty', stimulated
by the growing diversification in working time schedules (Fagan,
1998). The process of development of part-time work in Britain
and France has, however, shown a number of significant differences.[14]
In the UK, its growth during the 1980s has derived from labour-
market policies founded on a model of extensive employment growth
by which employment was created in low-paid, low-productivity
service sector jobs. This was achieved in part through the deregulation of the labour market which allowed a growing disparity in
wage rates and a weakening of the trades unions (Hoang-Ngoc and
Lefresne, 1994). In France, by contrast, the system of industrial
relations and the existence of pay minima prevented it from adopting
the same model of development for part-time work as in the UK.
Instead, pressures to create part-time jobs in France, deriving from
preoccupations with unemployment and/or worktime flexibility since
the 1980s,[15] have led to explicit government measures to encourage
the development of this form of work.[16] A greater decentralization in
negotiations over working time, encouraged by the government from
the early 1980s, has also played an important role in this process.[17]

Over recent years, part-time jobs in both countries have been
created primarily in the service sector, although significant differences remain between Britain and France in the levels of use of
part-time work in this and other sectors of the economy.[18] In both
countries it continues to be mostly women who work part-time
(82.9 per cent of all part-time employees in France were women in
1997 compared with 80.6 per cent in the UK), although levels have
risen rapidly for men in both countries (from 2 per cent to 5.5 per
cent in France over the period 1983 to 1997 and from 3.1 per cent
to 8.8 per cent in the UK) albeit from low levels (Commission of
the European Communities, 1997: Table 052).

Part-time levels, however, remain considerably higher in Britain
than in France. The reasons for this are complex and cannot be
dealt with in detail here. They include a historically more favourable legislative framework for the development of part-time work
in the UK (Garnsey, 1985; Gregory and O'Reilly, 1996; Hoang-Ngoc
and Lefresne, 1994) and differences in labour supply (notably the
impact of a lack of child-care benefits and facilities and lower levels of training for women in the UK (Barrère-Maurisson *et al.*, 1989)).
Other factors more recently identified include the relatively high
concentration of business ownership in the service sector in the

Table 2.7 Proportion working part-time, by age and gender, France and UK, 1989–1995

Percentage of men in each age group employed part-time					
	15–24		25–49		50–64	
	1989	1995	1989	1995	1989	1995
France	39.00	13.46	1.82	3.57	4.56	6.12
UK	10.08	21.24	1.40	2.69	4.61	8.07

Percentage of women in each age group employed part-time					
	15–24		25–49		50–64	
	1989	1995	1989	1995	1989	1995
France	25.96	35.20	22.06	27.73	28.02	30.34
UK	22.71	33.46	46.84	43.10	55.25	54.06

Note: See also note [13] for difficulties in comparing levels of part-time working in France and the UK.

Source: European Labour Force Survey, Special Tabulations.

UK, the deregulation of UK labour markets and production (Rubery and Fagan, 1996), the different approaches of the unions towards flexible working time (Gregory and O'Reilly, 1996) and the very long working hours of men which limit women's ability to work full-time (Rubery and Fagan, 1996).

In both Britain and France, the rate of part-time working varies over the lifecourse, although the importance of part-time working by age group differs significantly between the two countries. In the UK and France there has been a substantial increase in part-time working (see Table 2.7) over the period 1989 to 1995 among young people, particularly by women. This may be explained partly in the UK by the significant increase in the numbers of students working part-time since the mid-1980s: according to the Labour Force Survey numbers rose from 343 000 in 1984 to 960 000 in Spring 1997 (Hakim, 1998). The 1991 Census of Employment suggested that the proportions of students (aged over 16) with a job were in fact greater for women than for men. This increase may have been catalysed by the reduction in student grants in some cases but would seem to be driven principally by the rising percentage of young people in full-time education in the UK (Hakim, 1998). There would also seem to be an as yet unexplained increase in part-time working as a first job after full-time education in the UK (Burchell *et al.*, 1997). In France, growing numbers of young people, and particularly young women, are taking part-time jobs, often created as a result of government initiatives (Coutrot *et al.*, 1997). They do so as a means of obtaining their first employment and experience on a labour market which is particularly unwelcoming for them (Estrade and Thiesset, 1998), a feature explained in part by the dominance of the rules of the internal market for recruitment into French firms (Jeder-Madiot and Ponthieux, 1996; Marsden, 1989; Meron and Minni, 1996). The high rate of part-time employment for young women (and men) corresponds with occupational downgrading and the preponderance of temporary working during the time when they are trying to step onto a career ladder (Estrade and Thiesset, 1998).

In France, there has also been an increase in part-time levels for older women (50 to 64), one explanation for which being the implementation of early-retirement schemes in France. In the UK, by contrast, levels have fallen slightly between 1989 and 1995 for women in this age group while they have nearly doubled for men. They nevertheless remain highest in this age group in the UK and there is a strong correlation between age, level of occupation and propensity to work part-time: older women tend to be more heavily concentrated in unskilled jobs and working part-time than younger women (Walby, 1997).

In Britain, where the life cycle has a particularly strong influence on labour supply (Rubery and Grimshaw, 1994), part-time work is the principal socially acceptable means of enabling women to reconcile work with family (Brannen et al., 1994; Watson and Fothergill, 1993), even though it is still associated with poor conditions of employment: low pay and reduced pensions (Arber and Ginn, 1991; Ginn and Arber 1991, 1993, 1995; Joshi and Davies, 1992). Parental leave, which is available in France, is not a statutory right in the UK at the time of writing. In comparative research carried out in 1990 (Gauthier and Lelièvre, 1995), it was found that among women aged 22 to 60 in the UK, 73 per cent went from full-time to part-time jobs after their longest break from employment. Despite the increase in levels of part-time work among young women (and men) in both countries, levels of part-time working remain much higher in the middle-age group in the UK, and notably when women have heavy child-care responsibilities, although they are on a downward trend (see Table 2.7). In these middle-age groups, part-time work in the UK appears to be almost entirely voluntary (Watson and Fothergill, 1993).[19] The importance of part-time work in women's employment is greatest when they have children aged up to ten and falls thereafter (see Table 2.8). In Britain, therefore, part-time work continues to be used to adapt women's paid

Table 2.8 Levels of full- and part-time employment, by age of youngest child, UK, 1991

| | Percentage of mothers employed | | Percentage part-time/ part-time + full-time |
	Part-time	Full-time	
Age of youngest child:			
0–4 years	29	13	69
5–9 years	44	22	66
10+ years	40	35	53
All with dependent children	36	22	62

Note: part-time work is defined as work for under thirty hours a week.

Source: derived from OPCS (1996: Table 7.7) (cited in Walby, 1997: Table 2.19).

employment to the presence of children, although the degree to which part-time work is used in this way is mediated considerably by a woman's socio-economic group, with levels of part-time working lowest (and levels of full-time working highest) in the highest socio-economic group (professional/employer/manager) and increasing in lower socio-economic groups (Walby, 1997).

In France, part-time rates are relatively low in the years when women are likely to be carrying their heaviest child-care responsibilities (28 per cent), although rates of part-time working are rising. In the European Survey cited above (Gauthier and Lelièvre, 1995) only 33 per cent of French women aged 22 to 60 were found to have gone from full-time to part-time jobs after their longest break from employment. Indeed, Coutrot *et al.* (1997) found, on the basis of an analysis of women's movements in and out of part-time work over the lifecourse that, contrary to the situation in Britain, the switch to part-time work tended to occur at the same time as a change of employment and not during a given job, hence suggesting that labour-market strategies precede family events for French women. Nevertheless, French women do, as British women, adapt the extent of part-time working to the age of their youngest child (Dex *et al.*, 1993) (see Table 2.9), but the degree of part-time working is much less significant than in the UK when women have young children (Coutrot *et al.*, 1997). It should be born in mind, however, that in seeking to compare Tables 2.8 and 2.9 not only was the definition of part-time work used different in the two surveys but that also the sampling method differed. Nevertheless studies in France show that size of family has a greater effect than age of youngest child on levels of part-time work for mothers, with the

Table 2.9 Part-time employment levels of mothers, by age of youngest child, France, 1991

	<3 years (percentage)	3–5 years (percentage)
Full-time	36.3	41.6
Part-time	13.6	17.9
per cent part-time/ full-time + part-time	27.2	16.8

* Full-time employment rates increase when the youngest child reaches the age of 3 in part because the child raising allowance (*Allocation Parentale d'Education*) is no longer paid to eligible families after this age.
Note: part-time work has working hours one fifth shorter than the normal working time or the legally allowed maximum of 39 hours or any lesser number of hours specified in collective agreements.

Source: INSEE (1992: Section 3.2).

likelihood of working part-time rather than full-time increasing significantly for mothers with three or more children (Coutrot *et al.*, 1997). This is explained in part by the fact that as families get larger, it becomes less financially viable to work full-time given that child-care expenses need to be paid and that larger families often belong to the lower socio-economic groups (for a full explanation, see Gregory, 1989). Also, full-time employment becomes less attractive in larger families as non-income related family allowances are greater for such families with the benefit rate increasing sharply at the birth of the third and subsequent children.

The stage in the life cycle is not the only factor to be related to part-time work in the two countries. Burchell *et al.*'s (1997) analysis of the dynamics of part-time work experiences in Britain finds that more highly qualified women were significantly less likely to transfer into part-time work than women with lower qualifications. Only 14 per cent of full-time jobs held by women with degrees were followed by part-time jobs, compared to 29 per cent of jobs held by women without any formal qualifications. This finding has also been born out by Rubery and Grimshaw (1994), who found that increasing education levels counterbalanced the impact of dependent children, in terms of participation rates, employment rates and whether women worked full- or part-time. In France, there is also a correlation between educational levels and the incidence of part-time working. Women who have qualifications higher than the *baccalauréat* (equivalent of the British 'A' Levels) are 1.5 times more likely to work full-time than part-time. By contrast women with

Table 2.10   Persons in part-time employment, groups of hours usually worked in reference week (employees), France and UK, 1986, 1990, 1997

Hours employed	UK 1986	1990	1997	France 1986	1990	1997
01–10	23.8	34.0	21.2	12.2	20.5	10.1
11–20	23.8	38.4	41.7	45.6	36.0	39.1
21–24	11.8	10.2	12.9	9.7	8.4	9.5
25–30	16.1	12.2	17.9	19.8	21.2	22.4
31+	6.0	5.2	6.2	12.6	14.0	18.9

Source: Labour Force Surveys: Table 078

no qualifications are 1.6 times more likely to work part-time than full-time (Coutrot *et al.*, 1997). Ironically, women with higher education are more likely to work part-time than to be out of the labour force in France, while the reverse is true for women without higher education (Coutrot *et al.*, 1997). It appears then that for highly-qualified women in France, as in Britain, part-time work is something of a luxury, enabling them to stay in the labour force while devoting more time to other activities.

Part-time working hours are overall much longer in France than in Britain (see Table 2.10). The proportion of women working 20 hours or less in the UK was 62.9 per cent in 1997 compared with 49.2 per cent in France. In the UK, a very large proportion of women are working 1–10 hours a week, with levels increasing very rapidly between 1986 and 1990 (Hoang-Ngoc and Lefresne, 1994), although falling back after this date. The proportion of women employees working part-time hours of between 11 and 20 in the UK, by contrast, have increased continually over the period 1986 to 1997. Very short part-time hours for women and very long full-time hours for men have led to the UK having the greatest polarity in hours in the EU (Rubery and Fagan, 1996), although our analysis above suggests that this trend may be eroding somewhat. In France, by contrast, there is a much greater concentration of hours in the longer-hours categories (25 to 30 and 31+) and this trend has been accentuated in recent years (Hoang-Ngoc and Lefresne, 1994). At the same time as in the UK, however, there was a rapid increase in short-hours working in France between 1986 and 1990 which was attributed to the growth in the use of part-time work in low-skilled jobs in services (Hoang-Ngoc and Lefresne, 1994). The combination of long part-time hours with low levels of part-time working in France has led to women having a relatively high share of all working hours compared with other EU countries (*Bulletin on Women and Employment in the EU*, 1995). It also contributes to French women more often feeling harried and suffering from 'time famine' to a greater extent than British women (Hantrais, 1990),[20] despite the wider availability of child-care facilities in France. Another contributing factor is the relative lack of flexibility in working hours for French women: the Labour Force Survey clearly demonstrates the greater rigidity of working hours in France, with fewer women working Saturdays, Sundays and nights and involved in shift work than women in the UK. There is also a relative lack of flexible working-time options in France such as late-morning starts and early afternoon finishes, with little improvement over the period 1978 to 1991 (DARES, 1993; Wareing, 1992).

The varying length of part-time hours across the EU has been attributed to different employee preferences and collective and regulatory norms (Rubery *et al.*, 1996). Cross-national comparative research has shown that this provides a partial explanation for the differences found between Britain and France (see Chapter 5). Many French women are looking for four day part-time working so that they can take a Wednesday off to be with their primary and junior school-age children; British women, by contrast, prefer working hours which fit in with their child-care commitments which generally implies working shorter hours than French women. Also, the institutional framework in France has historically given an incentive to the development of longer working hours while the opposite has been the case in the UK.[21] However, Anglo–French comparisons of the use of part-time work in large-scale grocery retailing and in retail banking (Gregory and O'Reilly, 1996) also found that the length of working hours was related to the differing configuration of local, sectoral and national influences in collective bargaining and in the way in which businesses compete.

In France, discussion about part-time work has been overlaid by the issue of choice over taking up this form of work (INSEE-DARES, 1995; Rogerat and Senotier, 1996), in contrast to Britain where recent debate has focused on the degree to which part-timers are committed to paid work and how this is related to their occupational segregation (Ginn *et al.*, 1996; Hakim, 1991, 1995, 1996). The importance of the choice issue in France derives from the fact that women's paid work has traditionally been on a full-time basis and that part-time work is a recent phenomenon. As such, it has been resisted by trades union movements and sociologists (Coutrot *et al.*, 1997). Comparative statistics taken from the 1997 Labour Force Survey show that the proportions of women stating they were working part-time because they could not find a full-time job were indeed much higher in France than in Britain (38.8 per cent compared with 9.5 per cent) (OOPEC, 1998: Table 059) and this proportion has risen very rapidly in recent years in France (Eydoux *et al.*, 1996), while it has fallen in the UK.

The growth of part-time work in France appears to have developed in three ways (Letablier, 1995). First, it has to a limited extent been the result of an expansion of 'chosen' or 'voluntary' part-time work, developed to a large extent in the public sector, by women seeking to adapt work to their family commitments, and associated with good conditions of employment (see, for example, its development in banking in France (O'Reilly, 1994)). This would seem to be the 'individual strategy' part-time work identified by McRae (1995) and tends to be carried out by the higher paid, educated women described earlier who elect to work part-time. French women part-timers have a larger share of higher-grade jobs compared with UK part-timers (Blackwell, 1998; Dex *et al.*, 1993). Second, its growth also derives to a much greater extent from a trend towards greater flexibility in employment emanating from French companies, corresponding with McRae's (1995) 'corporate strategy' part-time work. These part-time jobs would seem more akin to the part-time work seen in Britain: they are concentrated mainly in the private sector (cleaning, retailing, child care), and have been associated with poor working conditions (notably short working hours and changing working patterns) and a greater casualization of employment. In France they have been thought to be carried out mainly on an involuntary basis (Belloc, 1986; Coutrot *et al.*, 1997; Galtier, 1998; Gregory, 1989; Maruani and Nicole, 1989), constituting therefore under-employment. Nevertheless, Bouffartigue *et al.*'s (1992) longitudinal survey of two cohorts of women in the Cote d'Azur region suggested that part-time work, although not preferable to direct entry into full-time work, represents a halfway house for some women, helping them to exit from unemployment or a discontinuous employment trajectory. Third, much of the more recent growth of part-time work, resulting from the French government's programmes to reduce unemployment[22] would seem to be 'non-voluntary' or 'imposed', affecting young women above all. This pattern of development of part-time work in France has led to the view that a polarization is taking place in France (Letablier, 1995) between women in full-time or permanent part-time jobs with associated good conditions of employment,[23] and those in casual part-time jobs with little chance of integration into the full-time workforce. Echoes of a similar polarization are also found in Britain where the distinction has been applied specifically to mothers in employment (Rubery and Fagan, 1996).

There is also evidence in France (Maruani and Decoufle, 1987; Nicole-Drancourt, 1989), as in the UK (Beechey and Perkins, 1987) and across Europe (*Bulletin on Women and Employment in the EU*, 1995) that the development of flexibility in working time is a gendered process. Women have been occupying new flexible forms of working time created in the late 1980s – notably part-time work – which have often not been negotiated and have been exempt from payment bonuses whereas the opposite has been true for men (shift work, compressed working weeks etc.). In addition, in France the process of the reduction of working time also appears to be gendered: recent reductions of working time are being achieved partly by the development of part-time contracts, applying particularly to women, rather than by collective reductions in working time. Furthermore, the ceding of control over the development of working-time patterns to collective bargaining, and particularly to company-level bargaining, seems to be leading to a segmentation of the labour market for women which is not necessarily to their advantage.

This gendered process of change in working hours in France is now leading to concern over the growing disparity between women's and men's working hours. Although the difference is much less than in Britain, the trend is seen to be undermining women's traditionally full-time position in the workforce (de Singly, 1991; Letablier, 1996) and reinforcing their position as carers in the home (Rogerat and Senotier, 1996), a finding supported by both the trends in working hours outlined in this chapter and the fact that the 1993 '*Loi Quinquennale sur L'Emploi*', which allowed annualized working, has led to more women to adapt their working hours explicitly to child-care commitments by taking annualized part-time work with time off during school holidays (Letablier, 1996).

Temporary work

Women are more likely to be on temporary contracts than men in both the UK and France, akin to all EU countries (Rubery *et al.*, 1996). However, levels of temporary work are considerably higher for French than UK women (see Table 2.11) and have increased

Table 2.11   Proportion of women in temporary work, France and UK, 1989 and 1994

	1989	**1994**
France	9.4	12.4
UK	7.4	7.5

Source: Rubery *et al.* (1996a: Table 2.3.6).

significantly over the 1989 to 1994 period (by 30 per cent), whereas in the UK they have remained stable. The lower rates of temporary contracts in the UK may reflect the fact that all employees have limited employment protection and labour market regulation is much more flexible (Rubery, 1989).

While the UK and France have shared a trend toward falling proportions of women working in permanent full-time jobs (of −1.2 per cent in France and −3.2 per cent in the UK [see Rubery *et al.*, 1996a: Table 2.3.7]), France saw a very rapid increase in temporary part-time jobs for women over the 1989 to 1994 period (+91.6 per cent), whereas in the UK levels fell (−16 per cent). In both countries, temporary work, while remaining a significant though minority form of employment, is disproportionately concentrated among the young (under 30 years). Nevertheless, the proportion of young women (and men) in temporary work is much higher in France than in the UK, approximately 55 per cent in France compared with 40 per cent in the UK (Rubery *et al.*, 1996a), suggesting that the shortage of permanent jobs for young people is particularly severe in France.

The rapid growth in temporary work in France reflects in part the French state's job-creation efforts beginning in the early 1980s as a response to a rapidly rising unemployment rate. It introduced measures in both the private and public sectors, many of which encouraged the creation of temporary often part-time jobs, frequently combining them with training.[24] The state was also responding to employers' demands for a more flexible labour market. This led it to increase the ease of use of different forms of temporary working (short-term contracts (*contrats à durée déterminée*), and temporary contracts (*l'intérim*)), while at the same time gradually improving the conditions of employment attached to this type of work.[25]

Observers of the French labour market have concluded that the growth of temporary jobs through the state's job creation schemes has had mixed effects (Belloc and Lagarenne, 1996; Letablier, 1996). On the one hand, they have helped women who are in one way or another disadvantaged on the labour market (for example single parents, women aged over 50 or long-term unemployed). On the other hand, they have increased the proportion of women working in jobs which are removed from the 'norm' of full-time permanent work: women represented 58 per cent of those in work experience and state-aided contracts (*stagiaires et contrats aidés*) in the private sector and 64 per cent in the public sector in 1995 (Belloc and Lagarenne, 1996), and 50 per cent of those in private sector short-term contracts (*contrats à durée déterminée*). These are jobs for which the chance of obtaining stable permanent employment after their completion is low (between 15 per cent and 27 per cent a year after completion) and has been falling since the 1990s (Belloc and Lagarenne, 1996).

Occupational segregation

Dex and Walters (1989), using data from the early 1980s, showed that French women were achieving higher occupational status than British women, with significantly higher proportions of women in more qualified occupations (professional, teaching, nursing and intermediary non-manual), and in skilled-manual occupations, whereas proportions of women in the lowest three occupational categories were twice as high in Britain. This finding has been born out by research into highly qualified women in the two countries, carried out by Hantrais and Walters (1994). Nevertheless, segregation indexes all give France and the UK similarly high levels of segregation in employment for women.

The increasing numbers of women entering more highly qualified jobs in the UK is not necessarily leading to a reduction in segregation.[26] In the UK, for example, between 1981 and 1990, while women were increasing their presence in the growing number of managerial jobs, men were taking a disproportionate share of them, hence increasing segregation within these jobs. Overall, however, the UK is seeing a slow decrease in segregation (Rubery *et al.*, 1996), although the overall trend is masking a complex pattern. For example, over the 1971 to 1991 period, Blackwell (1998) found there was relative stability in the segregation of part-time occupations and a fall in segregation in full-time occupations. In France, the trend over the 1982 to 1994 period (Eydoux *et al.*, 1996) is of a continued increase in the proportion of women employed in more highly-qualified occupations and a slowing in the increases in the proportion of women employed in traditionally women's occupations.

Table 2.12   Concentration of women full- and part-timers relative to all women in employment, France and UK, 1994

Socio-economic Group*	Full-time		Part-time	
	France	**UK**	**France**	**UK**
1+2+3	111.68	128.42	69.72	64.51
4	100.85	109.43	97.8	88.22
5+9	84.14	54.55	141.11	156.76
6+7+8	110.04	131.49	73.99	60.67

* 1 + 2 + 3 = managerial, professional and associate professional
   4 = clerical
   5 + 9 = service and elementary occupations
   6 + 7 + 8 = skilled agriculture, craft and operative occupations.
The regrouping of categories 1 + 2 + 3 overcomes the problem identified by Elias (1995) which is that in the UK women are categorized as corporate managers when in other countries they are more often categorized as 'professionals'.

Source: Rubery *et al.* (1996a: Table 2.1.13).

By contrast with the UK, there is evidence in France that in an increasingly competitive labour market men are beginning to threaten some of the traditional preserves of women such as primary school teaching (Eydoux *et al.*, 1996).

The two countries appear to have a fairly similar distribution of women's and men's employment between women-dominated, mixed and men-dominated occupations: in both Britain and France nearly 70 per cent of women are in workforces with less than 15 per cent of men, while mixed workforces (40–50 per cent women) attract a disproportionately low percentage of women and men in employment (12 per cent in France and 16 per cent in the UK), and in male-dominated workforces well over 70 per cent of men work with less than 20 per cent of women (Rubery *et al.*, 1996a: Table 2.1.2). However the proportion of women full-timers in women-dominated occupations would seem higher in France (64.4 per cent compared with 56.6 per cent) while the same is true for part-timers in the UK (79.2 per cent compared with 74.2 per cent) (Blackwell, 1998; Rubery *et al.*, 1996a: Table 2.1.12). In both countries, the proportions are higher for part-time work than for full-time work, revealing the distinctive feminization of part-time jobs. The negative impact of part-time working and positive effect of full-time working for occupational status in both France and the UK is apparent when looking at the concentration of women full-time and part-time by occupational status relative to all women in employment (see Table 2.12), although the impact of both seems particularly acute in the

UK. As Blackwell (1998: 112) points out: 'The association between part-time work and the secondary sector, characterised by low pay, low skills and poor promotion prospects, is stronger in the UK than France'.

Evidence from the UK (Rubery *et al*., 1992) would seem to suggest that part-time work plays an important role, associated with patterns of discontinuous working, in increasing women's segregation in employment over their life-cycle, although women's inequality should decrease as more women work full-time and adopt more continuous patterns of employment (McRae, 1991). While we might expect the opposite to be true in France given the lower levels of part-time working and greater continuity in employment, there is no evidence to date to support this hypothesis.

Inequality in pay

Despite the poor availability of comparable data relating to pay (Rubery *et al*., 1996a), it is clear that one of the most significant differences between France and the UK is in pay inequality. In both countries, women's pay is lower than that of men, but the difference appears to be greater in the UK (women earned 80.8 per cent that of men as manual workers in industry in 1993 in France compared with 68.4 per cent in the UK; non-manual workers earned 68.4 per cent of men's pay in France and 59.7 per cent in the UK in the same year), and is widening, while it has stayed more or less stable in France (INSEE, 1995). Explanations for this significant difference would seem to lie partly in the weaker system of wage protection in the UK and the impact of state labour market policies. The UK has had no national minimum wage and the removal of the wages councils in August 1993 has encouraged a low-wage economy. Pay has also been affected by the state's policy of deregulating the labour market during the 1980s, notably within the public sector. Here job conditions deteriorated significantly in services such as catering and cleaning, where women are concentrated, through the impact of measures such as competitive tendering (Rubery and Grimshaw, 1994). A contributory factor too has been the high levels of part-time working in the UK, where women's part-time wage levels are lower than those of full-timers (70 per cent of the full-time wage) and have fallen between 1989 and 1995.

Conclusion

This review of contemporary trends in women's paid work in the UK and France reveals a number of similarities in the two countries and notably support for the conception of women's employment in terms of integration (rising participation rates of women and gradual desegregation of occupations), differentiation (the continued gap between men's and women's pay in the UK and France), and polarization (between women in more highly qualified professions working full-time or who can negotiate part-time work with good working conditions, and less well-qualified women, or younger women in particular in France, who find themselves more often in part-time work with poor conditions of employment) (Brannen *et al.*, 1994; Eydoux *et al.*, 1996). The data presented supports the hypothesis (Rubery *et al.*, 1996a) that more highly qualified women's patterns of employment are showing increasing similarities across Europe.[27]

A number of recent national and supra-national measures in Britain and France would also suggest that the characteristics of women's paid work may show increasing similarities in years to come. In Britain, it is primarily the impact of supra-national regulation which is likely to affect these characteristics. First, the implementation of the EU Directive on the Protection of Pregnant Women at Work, (Council Directive 92/85/EEC of 19 October 1992) which extended a right to 14 weeks maternity leave to all women independently of hours worked and period of service, is likely to encourage greater continuity of employment. The Blair government has announced its intention to extend this leave to 18 weeks in the White Paper *Fairness at Work*. Second, part-time employment may become a less attractive option to employers as a number of part-time conditions of employment (redundancy and dismissal rights, pay benefits) have, as a result of appeals to European equal opportunities law, been harmonized with those of full-timers (see Gregory and O'Reilly, 1996). Equality in rights for part-timers (pro rata) will be enshrined in UK law when the Social Charter is applied to the UK from December 1999 and the European Directive on part-time work is implemented (*Liaisons Sociales*, 1998).

Third, and also following from the application of the Social Charter, the UK is due to implement the EU Parental Leave directive (Council Directive 96/34 EC of 3 June 1996 amended by Council Directive 97/75/EC of 15 December 1997) and introduce parental leave from

December 1999[28] which may be conducive to a greater continuity in women's employment over their life-cycle in the UK. A trend away from excessively long hours for men, which may put pressure on women to increase their hours, may be triggered by the application of the EC working time directive (Council Directive 93/104/ EC of 23 November 1993) which came into force on 1 October 1998. The directive's provisions may, however, be diluted as it gives considerable powers to derogate from them by means of collective bargaining. Furthermore, the maximum limit of 48 hours per week remains very long if major change is to be effected. The British government is also initiating a range of measures, many of which resemble French policies of long-standing, which may also impinge on women's conditions in Britain and increase the similarities between the women's work situations in Britain and France. These measures include the introduction of a minimum wage, the working parents' child-care allowance for lower income families, the development of nursery schooling for children aged three and four and out-of-school clubs for older children (DfEE, 1998) and the reinforcement of the UK Equal Opportunities legislation. The latter is planned to involve more monitoring of inequalities in women's pay, a requirement on public bodies to promote Equal Opportunities and an improved process for equal pay cases (Ward, 1998).

In France, changes in women's employment may be engendered by the reduced incentives for creating *emplois familiaux* (family jobs) Cealis and Zilberman, 1998), and the planned reduction of the working week to 35 hours which became law on 19 May 1998 and will be rolled out between the years 2000 and 2002 (*Libération*, 1998), although the impact of these measures remains as yet unclear. In addition, a growth in part-time work in all posts, including in posts of responsibility, may be the outcome in both Britain and France if the recommendations to employers contained in the European Directive on Part-time Work (Council Directive 97/81 of 15 December 1997 concerning the framework agreement on part-time work concluded between the UNICE, CEEP and CES) are acted on: these state that more part-time posts should be created at all levels of responsibility and that training should be offered to part-timers to facilitate their professional mobility (*Liaisons Sociales*, 1998).

However, at present a number of significant differences remain between patterns of women's employment: higher rates of full-time continuous employment for women in France, higher rates of unemployment for French women compared with British women, greater pay inequality in the UK, a greater penetration of women in France into higher occupational groups and a greater impact of full and part-time employment on occupational status in the UK. Moreover, very different patterns of employment for women in the two countries emerge across their life cycles. After spending longer in education than in the UK, young French women enter a labour market which is relatively hostile to young people, requiring many of them to pass through a number of trial, temporary, often part-time, jobs juggling these with periods of unemployment in order to obtain a full-time permanent post. In the UK, by contrast, young women often work part-time while in education but leave earlier to enter into full-time employment. When children arrive, British women, and lone mothers in particular, more often leave the labour market and then return into plentiful secondary part-time jobs where they no longer compete directly with men. Their lower qualification levels and need to fit in with child-care commitments make them a less demanding and more flexible labour force than women in France (Letablier, 1995) where, by contrast, women are more likely to stay in full-time employment competing directly with men for jobs, resulting in higher unemployment levels for them. For older age groups of women, patterns still diverge with women leaving the labour force earlier in France than in Britain, and those in activity more often full-time or unemployed.

Our findings from this overview suggest that greater progress in gender relations have to date been achieved in France than in Britain if women's position in paid work is taken as an indication of the degree of progress. In France, full-time participation rates are considerably higher than in Britain and, as a consequence, there is a less significant disparity between men's and women's working hours. French women's continuity in employment and employment status is also less affected by the arrival of children than those of British women. There is, however, evidence that in recent years French women's traditional full-time position in the labour force is being challenged. We will now see in Chapters 3 and 4 whether French women's 'progress' in gender relations in the employment sphere is also reflected in the division of unpaid work in the home and in the community.

3
Women's Domestic Work

As discussed in Chapter 1, the term 'domestic work' refers to the unpaid work carried out by household members for themselves and each other. This can include routine housework (for example, cooking, cleaning, washing and shopping); non-routine work (for example, gardening, do-it-yourself and car maintenance); and child care which is often considered to be the most onerous of women's contemporary domestic duties. The activities usually associated with domestic work are to be found in all societies with women being assigned to similar types of tasks in all contexts. However, although in pre-capitalist societies a strict gender division of tasks may have existed, productive and reproductive tasks were not separated in time and space. Consequently, women's domestic activities counted as work alongside subsistence agriculture and production for the market. It is only in industrial societies, such as Britain and France, where the employment-place became separated from the household temporally and spatially, that women's household activities became detached from the notion of work. Indeed, the concept of 'domestic work/labour' was originally developed within women's studies research and the feminist movement in the 1960s and 1970s in North America and Europe as part of a strategy to emphasize both the practical importance of women's work in the home to the functioning of society and the economy and, more importantly, the theoretical importance of women's responsibility for this labour in explaining their oppression (see Chapter 5). Indeed, one of the major contributions to the study of 'work' which feminist academics and theorists and women's studies researchers have made during the past 30 years is to challenge the dominant ideology that views work as synonymous with employment. A comparison of women's participation in domestic labour must, therefore, be central to any comparison of women's working lives in Britain and France as we highlighted in Chapter 1.

However, although much research has been carried out on women's domestic labour in the context of single-nation studies which conclude that the unequal gender division of domestic labour has far-reaching consequences for all aspects of women's lives (for example, Baruch and Barnett, 1987; Berk, 1985; Brannen *et al.*, 1994; Gershuny *et al.*, 1994; Gregson and Lowe, 1994; Morris, 1995; Pahl, 1984; Sofer, 1985), many of the existing cross-national comparisons of women's economic position have focused upon differences in employment patterns and highlighted the effect that contrasting social and labour market policies exert on women's opportunities for paid work. Consequently, if not necessarily intentionally, the principal barometer of progress in gender relations within such studies has been rates of women's full-time employment and the implicit conclusion has generally been that progressive social and labour market policies can and do challenge women's subjugated position. In this vein, countries are frequently placed on a spectrum of 'more' to 'less' progressive. If we retain this primary focus on paid work, such a conclusion is perhaps not unfounded, as we have seen in Chapter 2. However, do such conclusions still hold true when the gender division of domestic labour within and between households is taken into account? We must ask, therefore, if women are involved in paid work to a greater extent in France than in Britain, is there also a greater renegotiation of the domestic workload taking place in France? If not, then we must address the question of how the domestic work traditionally carried out by 'inactive' women is getting done. These are the questions raised and answered by this chapter.

To commence, therefore, this chapter reviews the contrasting methodologies that have been adopted to evaluate the extent and nature of domestic work so as to contextualize the findings on domestic labour in Britain and France presented in subsequent sections. Following this, we examine the magnitude and character of domestic labour in each country. On the one hand, we analyse the gender division of domestic labour in couple-based households, evaluating the amount of domestic work undertaken by men and women in each country, the types of tasks each undertakes, the question of responsibility for domestic labour and to conclude, the central and particular issue of child care. On the other hand, we examine domestic labour in single-person and single-parent households, an issue that despite the increasing prevalence of such household types in each country has not so far received much attention in the literature on domestic work.

Measuring and valuing domestic labour

Unlike paid work where there are regular national and cross-national evaluations of its magnitude and character, domestic labour has not until recently been considered a serious topic for investigation, reflecting the dominance of the ideology that employment is the principal form of work in contemporary society.[1] However, since the 1960s, there has been an international feminist campaign to have domestic work adequately recognized, based on the view that the ways in which unpaid work is measured and valued have significant implications for women and impact heavily on social policy-making (Chadeau and Fouquet, 1981; James, 1994; Luxton, 1997). Arguing that the national accounts are systematically skewed because they ignore the value of women's unpaid work, they have sought to change the ways in which international bodies and national governments measure economic activity. Indeed, this campaign has met with considerable success.

Of potential long-term significance to the revaluing of domestic work is a recommendation, made in 1993 by the UN after a review of the UN System of National Accounts, that 'satellite national accounts' be developed that incorporate the value of unpaid work. This became an obligation for Britain and France under the terms of the Final Act of the 1995 UN Fourth World Conference on Women in Beijing (United Nations, 1995: Section 209: f, g). These computations will be an adjunct to the standard national accounts that were roundly criticized for their silence on women's unpaid work. Although such accounts remain subsidiary, it is clear that they represent a step in the right direction. In more recent years, moreover, both the European Commission as well as the national governments of Britain and France have accepted this decision and sought to develop 'satellite' accounts of the value of unpaid work as part of wider redefinition of the relationship between the state, the market and the family.

The way in which governmental agencies have taken on board such recommendations in both Britain and France is by using time-budget studies to assess the extent of domestic labour for the national accounts (Murgatroyd and Neuberger, 1997; Roy, 1991). A time-budget study is a technique for data collection whereby the research participants complete diaries chronicling the number of minutes spent on a range of activities. From these, it is possible to calculate the time spent on domestic labour. Indeed, it is now widely accepted that measuring time use is as useful and accurate in assessing unpaid work as money is in measuring paid employment (Gershuny and Jones, 1986; Gershuny *et al.*, 1994; Juster and Stafford, 1985).

In Britain, there have been numerous time-budget studies conducted outside central government agencies such as in 1974 and 1984/5. However, the first national survey, conducted by the Office of National Statistics (ONS), only took place in pilot form in 1995 (Murgatroyd and Neuberger, 1997) and this is currently being implemented as a full-scale national time-budget study in a partnership venture with the ESRC and various other public agencies. In France, meanwhile, time-budget studies conducted in 1975 (Chadeau and Fouquet, 1981) and 1985 (Roy, 1991) by the INSEE as well as a nation-wide survey on 'Domestic Production' undertaken in the late 1980s all provide quantitative data on the gender division of domestic work.

The overwhelming finding of these studies is that the British and French population spend more time engaged in domestic labour than in employment (Chadeau and Fouquet, 1981; Gershuny *et al.*, 1994; Murgatroyd and Neuburger, 1997). To put a monetary value on this time, three techniques have been adopted: opportunity costs; housekeeper wage costs; and occupational wage costs. In each, monetary values from the market sector are used to impute values to unpaid domestic labour or its products (Luxton, 1997). The opportunity-costs model calculates the income the worker would have earned if s/he had been in the paid labour force instead of undertaking domestic labour. Second, the housekeeper wage-costs approach calculates how much a worker in paid employment doing similar work is paid. Third and finally, the occupational wage-costs approach measures the price of household inputs by calculating market equivalents for the costs of raw materials, production and labour and comparing it with market prices for each product and/or service. An extensive literature assessing the various approaches exists and methods have become increasingly sophisticated (Bittman, 1995; Ironmonger, 1996; Jenkins and O'Leary, 1996; Lutzel, 1989; Luxton, 1997; OECD, 1997).

However, the issue with all of these valuation methods is that they accept the existing gender divisions of labour and pay inequalities as normal and unproblematic. The result is that the valuations produced serve to reinforce gender inequalities rather than challenge them (Bryson, 1996; Chadeau and Fouquet, 1981). For example, child care is usually assessed at (low-paid) child-care worker rates rather than, for instance, at rates earned by psychologists, teachers and nurses with no questioning of why such child-care workers are so lowly paid. The result is that although more time is spent on unpaid than paid work in both Britain and France, when evaluated in monetary terms, it is worth less. In Britain, the ONS survey conducted in 1995 finds that using replacement costs assessed by input/output methods whereby time spent cooking is replaced by chefs, child care with nannies, DIY time with professional builders, etc., domestic work was worth 56 per cent of GDP because these sectors tend to be the lowest paid in the economy. However, if the time spent on unpaid work was valued at the same average wage rate as paid employment as a whole it would be 122 per cent of GDP (Murgatroyd and Neuburger, 1997). Meanwhile, unpaid work in France was worth only one half of GNP in 1975 according to the opportunity-cost and replacement methods (which on the whole use women's wage rates as a basis of calculation) and two thirds of GNP on the final method, which uses wage rates current for men as well as women (Chadeau and Fouquet, 1981).

Despite such problems, the importance of these large-scale surveys is that they provide solid statistical evidence that the family has not lost its productive functions under capitalism. For example, comparing the 1985–86 time-budget study in Britain with the study conducted in 1995 (Gershuny and Jones, 1986; Murgatroyd and Neuburger, 1997), domestic work occupied 48.1 per cent of people's total time spent working in 1985–86, but by 1995, this had risen to 58 per cent. Similarly, the 1975 French time-budget study revealed that domestic labour is a more time-consuming activity than professional work, occupying an average of 31 hours per person per week as opposed to 28 hours for professional work. In other words, domestic work occupied 52 per cent of total work time for that year (Chadeau and Fouquet, 1981). By 1986, moreover, domestic labour had risen to occupy 55 per cent of total working time, suggesting that in terms of its role in production, the household is becoming more important rather than less (Roy, 1991). Domestic work, therefore, appears to have been increasing rather than decreasing in importance relative to paid work in both Britain and France during the latter part of the twentieth century.

Indeed, time-budget studies may well under-estimate the time spent on domestic work compared with employment. On the one hand, this is because the time spent in employment may be over-estimated since the total time engaged in employment is usually counted when much of this time may include meal- and coffee-breaks, associated travel as well as socializing. On the other hand, this is because the time spent in domestic work may be under-estimated. First, time-budget studies only measure an individual's commitment in time to a concrete activity. They do not capture the time and effort involved in planning and managing one's own and others' activities which may often occur when one is watching television, lying in bed or undertaking some other supposedly leisure pursuit or indeed when one is engaged in one's employment (Haicault, 1984). Second, there is much evidence that unlike an employee's relationship to his/her company, women must be permanently available to their families so that time not actually spent in the service of the family may still be constrained time (Chabaud-Richter and *et al.*, 1985). Third and finally, there is the argument that much of women's work burden within the household and family derives from their caring duties for other household members. While time-budget studies can capture the practical aspects of this care-giving work, they cannot capture its emotional and affective side which either is ignored completely, or indeed, can be portrayed as leisure and socializing.

For these reasons, many have argued that if women's relationship to domestic work is to be more fully understood, there is a need to combine the results of such time-budget studies with other survey techniques which assess issues such as responsibility for managing and organizing domestic labour and emotional commitment (see, for example, Luxton, 1997). These other techniques include survey questions and in-depth interviews. They also include participant observation where researchers spend lengthy periods in households helping out and observing the labour process so as to compare what people say they do with what is actually done as well as understanding the configuration of the emotional work involved in the domestic sphere (Luxton, 1986). Indeed, some have argued that the ideal is to combine all four methods – survey questions, time use, in-depth interviews and participant observation if domestic work is to be more fully understood (Peters, 1997).

As we have already mentioned (see note 1), direct comparisons of domestic work between Britain and France are scarce and where they do exist, specific rather than general in nature (for example

Windebank, 1999). Therefore, for the most part, comparisons have had to be drawn using existing single-nation studies. Whether time-budget techniques or some other survey method is applied, it is important for cross-national analysis that studies using the same method, the same definition of domestic work at the same time on a similar sample of each population be compared. The problem, however, is that this is seldom possible since surveys employ different methods, adopt varying definitions and often conduct research on very different groups and/or places. For these reasons, although this chapter will use the results of single-nation surveys where necessary to compare the differences and similarities in women's domestic work in Britain and France, we will also give some emphasis to one of the very few known Anglo-French comparative studies on this subject, a cross-national comparison of child care and domestic strategies of 112 middle-income dual-earner families in two comparable localities conducted by one of the authors.

To commence, therefore, we examine the extent and nature of domestic labour and child care in couple-based households, the subject upon which most of the emphasis has been placed in the research on this form of work.

Domestic labour within couple-based households

In the 1960s and 1970s, it was assumed by some that the rise in the number of working wives would be accompanied by a corresponding increase in the husband's input into domestic work. Young and Wilmott (1975), for example, argued that the middle classes in particular were leading the way towards more egalitarian, 'symmetrical' marriage relationships in which the husband and wife shared the tasks of both wage earning and domestic labour. This was part of a much wider debate at the time that society was becoming more middle-class and that what the middle classes were currently doing would be replicated later by the working class. Here, with the fortune of historical hindsight, we examine whether such a shift towards more egalitarian marriage relationships has indeed taken place in Britain and France.

To do this, we examine first the amount of domestic work undertaken by men and women in the two countries; second, the types of domestic tasks that they perform and third, the division of responsibilities for such work. Finally, we examine the gender division of child care in couple-based British and French households since the presence of children in a household is important both in the sense that it significantly increases the amount of domestic and caregiving work undertaken by the household and leads to the greatest distinctions in gender work roles.

Amount of domestic work undertaken by men and women in Britain and France

If the assumptions of Young and Wilmott (1975) that more employment for wives would lead to a more 'symmetrical' division of domestic labour among married couples are founded, then one would expect that these symmetrical arrangements would be more in evidence in France, where women's full-time and continuous employment is historically deep-rooted, than in Britain where part-time and interrupted patterns of employment are more common among women. We will now discover whether the available evidence suggests that this is, in fact, the case.

As Table 3.1 displays, time-budget studies conducted in the mid-1980s in both Britain and France show a distinct similarity in the contributions of British and French men and women to the domestic workload. It reveals that men spent significantly less time working in total than women, whatever their employment status. For example, full-time employed men spent 56.4 and 61.4 hours engaged in work in the UK and France respectively compared with 59.0 and 67.8 hours for full-time employed women. For men, moreover, a greater proportion of their total time spent working is dedicated to employment than for women. Full-time employed men, for instance, spent longer hours in employment than full-time employed women, but this was insufficient in either the UK or France to compensate for the greater time that full-time employed women spent in domestic work. The result in both countries is that women had less free time than men, whatever their employment status. This echoes findings on men's and women's leisure time in the two countries (Hantrais, 1985; Hantrais *et al.*, 1984).

Such evidence, therefore, undermines the notion that more full-time employment for women necessarily leads to more domestic labour for men. Instead, it shows that more full-time employment for women means more work overall. As Gershuny *et al.* (1994: 175-6) put it:

Employed husbands of employed women work in total significantly less time than their wives. We find . . . a gradient: full-time

Table 3.1 Structure of time in Britain and France: by employment status

	Hours per week			
	Men		Women	
Employment Status	UK 1984	France 1986	UK 1984	France 1986
Full-time employed				
Personal time	73.5	71.0	73.9	72.5
Employment	43.4	44.9	40.1	40.1
Domestic work	13.0	16.5	18.9	27.7
Total work time	56.4	61.4	59.0	67.8
Free time	38.1	35.6	35.1	27.7
Part-time employed				
Personal time	74.0	74.0	75.0	74.1
Employment	27.6	33.3	20.1	25.8
Domestic work	18.1	13.4	36.9	36.0
Total work time	45.7	46.7	57.0	61.8
Free time	48.3	47.3	36.0	32.1
Non-employed				
Personal time	81.3	80.2	79.6	79.7
Employment	2.6	1.4	1.6	0.8
Domestic work	20.9	23.6	37.5	40.0
Total work time	23.5	25.0	39.1	40.8
Free time	63.2	62.8	49.3	47.5

Source: derived from Roy (1991: Figure 1).

employed husbands of non-employed women have the same work-time total as their wives; if their wives are part-time employed their total is a little smaller; if their wives are full-time employed, they do substantially less work. Plainly the inference to be drawn is that, as women increasingly enter the formal economy on a full-time basis, so the overall household division of labour will become increasingly unequal.

In other words, women employed full-time are working the longest total hours of any group in both nations due to the 'double burden' of their domestic work and employment responsibilities. On the basis of this time-budget data, we can calculate that a shift from no employment to 40 hours of employment per week resulted in a reduction in domestic work time of only 18.6 hours per week in the UK and 12.3 hours in France. In other words, for each extra hour of paid employment, full-time employed women were doing about 28 minutes less domestic work in the UK and 18 minutes less in France. Getting a job thus meant a substantial rise in their total (paid plus unpaid) work time. This fact that women reduce their unpaid work but not proportionate to their increase in paid work is because 'men hardly increase their domestic work when their wives go out to work' (Gershuny, 1992: 7).

Besides these similarities in the gender division of labour in Britain and France, there are nevertheless also some notable contrasts between the two nations. First, according to these time-budget studies, the French spent longer working in both employment and domestic work than their UK counterparts. The only exception is that part-time employed men and women in France spent less time on domestic work than their UK equivalents but this is due to the fact that part-time employees in France are generally employed for longer hours than in the UK, as we have discussed in Chapter 2, which reduces the time available for domestic work. Nevertheless, whether full- or part-time employed, or non-employed, French women had less free time than their equivalents in the UK. A second difference between the UK and France concerns the relative gender divisions in domestic work. Full-time employed French men spent only 59.5 per cent of the time that full-time employed French women used undertaking domestic work, while in the UK, such men spent 68.8 per cent of the time of their women equivalents. Similarly, part-time employed men in the UK spent just under half the time (49.1 per cent) that part-time employed women spent on domestic work, while in France this figure was 37.2 per cent. For employed people, therefore, the UK appears to show slightly greater tendencies towards equality in domestic work times than France. However, whether this is a significant difference, politically rather than statistically speaking, is debatable. In both countries, women spent considerably longer than men with equivalent employment status engaged in domestic work and thus had considerably higher total work times.

This data, nevertheless, is a snapshot of one particular period. It provides no clue as to whether there is an increasingly symmetrical egalitarian arrangement emerging over time in either or both of these nations. Table 3.2 displays that in both the UK and France, although husbands have increased the proportion of all unpaid work which they undertake (to around about a third of the total), their share of the total work undertaken is decreasing in both countries. The overall outcome, in other words, has been that wives' share of the total work time has increased with their entry into employment due to the fact that the renegotiation of the division of domestic labour has not kept pace with their entry into employment. Moreover,

Table 3.2   Change in work time in married couples in Britain and France, 1961–90

| | Men's time as a percentage of total for | | | | | | | |
| | all work-related activities (excluding commuting) | | | | all unpaid work | | | |
	1961–70	1971–77	1978–82	1983–90	1961–70	1971–77	1978–82	1983–90
France	54	52	–	–	25	28	–	–
UK	–	57	–	54	–	26	–	37

Note: paid work includes work breaks, unpaid work time excludes breaks, so men's total work time is overestimated

Source: Gershuny *et al.* (1994: Table 5.8)

and as Gershuny *et al.* (1994) note, the table misleadingly suggests that the aggregate of work time is substantially higher for husbands than wives due to the above-mentioned tendency of time-budget evidence to over-estimate time spent in paid work.

Gender variations in the types of domestic tasks undertaken

In both nations, similar variations exist in how domestic tasks are divided by gender. Women are primarily responsible for conducting the routine domestic tasks (for example, washing and ironing, preparation of the evening meal, household cleaning) and much of the rise in men's contribution to domestic work can be attributed to their increased engagement in non-routine domestic work (for example, DIY activities). Indeed, according to men's testimonies, and as Table 3.3 reveals, of those French men who said that they contributed to the domestic work, only between a quarter and a half said that they did various routine tasks. In Britain, similarly, only a slightly higher proportion of the men who contributed to domestic work engaged in routine domestic work. Once again, the important point of this data is perhaps the fact that so few British or French men claim to engage in domestic work of a routine nature, and that if any difference is to be discerned, it is the British men who are doing more and not the French. Indeed, in Britain, Gershuny *et al.* (1994) find that non-employed wives of employed husbands carried out 83 per cent of the total unpaid work of the household, full-time employed wives of full-time employed husbands carried out 73 per cent and part-time employed wives carried out 82 per cent of all unpaid household work.

Such inequalities are further reinforced by a cross-national study of 112 dual-earner married couples with children in Britain and

Table 3.3 Nature of the tasks undertaken by men 'who do something' according to their own and their partners' testimonies

	France	Britain
According to men's partners:		
Shopping	48	51
Washing up	48	72
Transporting children	49	26
Dressing children	38	37
Cooking	37	48
Household cleaning	35	42
According to men:		
Shopping	54	–
Washing dishes	44	–
Transporting children	49	–
Dressing children	31	–
Cooking	27	–
Household cleaning	24	–

Source: Eurobarometer, *Enquete Famille et Emploi dans L'Europe des Douze*, 1990 (cited in INSEE, 1995: Table 7.3.2)

France conducted by one of the authors. As Table 3.4 displays, although the British men in the study again did slightly more routine domestic work than French men according to the testimony of their partners – see Table 3.3 – except in the realms of vacuuming and dusting and cleaning, this difference should not hide the fact that in both countries it was most often women who conducted such routine household work. No routine domestic task was on average more likely to be undertaken by the father, whatever his employment status and this is despite the fact that women in all of the households surveyed were employed and had young children. Indeed, comparing women who were full- and part-time employed, we see that women's full-time employment status made little difference to the fact that they undertook the routine domestic work. This was particularly the case in France.

On the basis of this evidence, therefore, it would seem that routine domestic work is predominantly undertaken by women, even in dual-earner households. Men's contribution to the domestic workload in contrast, tends to be much more in the realm of non-routine domestic work. Warde and Hetherington (1993: 32), for example, in a study of Manchester found that gender-stereotyping of domestic tasks remains very strong with a wife being 'about

Table 3.4 Division of domestic labour between dual earner married couples with children, Britain and France, 1995

Average score*	Britain			France		
	Full-time employed mother	Part-time employed mother	Over-all	Full-time employed mother	Part-time employed mother	Over-all
Preparing evening meal	3.06	4.17	3.81	3.80	4.55	4.10
Household Shopping	3.00	3.71	3.48	3.60	4.24	3.94
Washing dishes	3.00	3.14	3.09	3.46	3.24	3.34
Ironing	3.93	4.56	4.37	4.86	4.50	4.66
Washing clothes	4.56	4.51	4.53	4.67	4.48	4.57
Vacuuming	3.60	4.06	3.91	3.67	3.88	3.79
Dusting and cleaning	3.94	4.12	4.06	3.90	3.96	3.94

* 1 = father only, 2 = father more than mother, 3 = shared, 4 = mother more than father, 5 = mother only

Source: Windebank survey

14 times more likely than her husband to have last done the ironing, almost 30 times as likely the washing, nine times the tidying up, seven times the cooking, twice the washing up. A husband was four times as likely to have done the painting or car washing, 20 times the plastering, three times cutting the lawn'. However, this should not lead one to think that all non-routine domestic work is undertaken by husbands. Although more husbands than wives 'usually' do the non-routine domestic work, 'the majority of non-routine domestic work time is still contributed by the wives. Only in the case of couples in which both spouses have full-time jobs does the husband's non-routine domestic work time exceed the wife's' (Gershuny and Jones, 1986: 32). It appears, therefore, that any notion of a shift towards a more 'egalitarian' and 'symmetrical' division of domestic labour is far from the reality, given the ways in which individual domestic tasks remain highly segregated. Nevertheless, some optimism that things are starting to change, at least in Britain, is provided by Gershuny *et al.* (1994: 176), who argue that 'while women's work has contracted fastest in the area of cooking and routine housework, it is precisely in these areas that their husbands' work has grown fastest', albeit from a very low base level. A key question, however, is who retains overall responsibility for domestic work and who helps out?

The gender division of responsibility for domestic labour

So far, we have seen that the increase in married women's employment has been accompanied to some extent by an increase in men's domestic involvement, albeit insufficient to compensate for women's increased involvement in paid work and on the whole, this increased participation is in a limited range of tasks. To find out whether men are taking the responsibility for domestic work, such as by managing, planning, organizing and supervising the housework, or whether they are merely helping out, we have to look to more qualitative studies conducted in each of the nations. All of these studies indicate that women retain the responsibility in both Britain (Brannen and Moss, 1991; Harris, 1987; Morris, 1990) and France (Chabaud *et al.*, 1985; Fougeyrollas, 1994; Haicault, 1984; Nicole-Drancourt, 1989) and that men's role is simply one of 'assistant' rather than 'equal partner'. The idea that it is a woman's responsibility to ensure that the domestic work gets done, which usually means doing it herself, especially the routine domestic work, thus appears to be firmly embedded in everyday life in both countries.

This fact that men generally tend to 'help out' rather than take responsibility for the domestic workload is well portrayed in the earlier-discussed cross-national survey of dual-earner couples with children in Britain and France conducted by one of the authors. When discussing the gender division of domestic work, women commonly made comments such as 'he helps out where he can' and 'he does a lot but it's more helping out than anything else'. As one of the British respondents commented:

> I think a lot of the reason's been not that he doesn't want to do it, but we've had so much work on the house. My husband's always trying to get things done. It's not that he doesn't want to help. Its rather that he's doing other things. I wouldn't like people to think that he doesn't help me. He'd be very upset. It's not a thing that he won't help . . .'

As a French respondent preferred to put it: 'My husband helps me out when I cannot manage everything and that's how it is'. Indeed, many of the women in the study did not have high aspirations of what they expected from their husbands. As a French respondent asserted, 'I have an indispensable husband. He does everything around the house. When I need him too, he will step in and replace me. If I am ill, he'll do things like the laundry. He isn't against doing such things. He'll do it'. Or as a British participant in the research claimed, 'He does an awful lot to help out, not so much during the week, but at the weekend, he does the vacuuming and dusting and he likes to cook Saturday tea'.

Indeed, a key finding of this research is that the division of the domestic workload is often closely associated with men tending to do things either which are closed- rather than open-ended in nature (for example cooking a meal) or engaging in pleasurable non-routine tasks rather than what they see as unpleasurable routine work. As a British woman asserted, 'He does not mind doing set things like the washing-up or giving Dee his bottle. He'll just get up and do it. But its the other things – like making sure that everything is clean – he doesn't think. So I spend the weekend working and he'll be messing around and doing nice things, like playing with Dee'. Similarly, many wives take responsibility for child care while the husband engages in the domestic work which he finds enjoyable. As a British wife and mother commented, 'I put Chloe to bed, but that is because he likes cooking – he won't eat what I cook, so I put her to bed and he makes dinner'. No significant differences between the British and French respondents, or between full- and part-time workers, were discovered in this respect.

Two final issues need to be considered here. The first is that there is a perception that women should be permanently available to their partners and children and the second is that if any emotional caring work is required, then it is women's responsibility. These two features extend the concept of responsibility to the wider realm of social support, an activity that is often a major component of women's investment within the household. Whatever women do in terms of hours of domestic work, and even if they do not carry out particular tasks themselves, the argument here is that it is always they who are responsible for the management of family life. For example, on the basis of fieldwork in France, Haicault (1984) developed the concept of the '*charge mentale*' (mental burden) to describe the way in which employed women must constantly balance two sets of responsibilities – for their homes and families and for their jobs – and that they carry these two sets of responsibilities in their heads wherever they are physically, that is, at work or home. Similarly, Chabaud *et al.* (1985) describe the relationship of women to their household tasks and families as one of 'permanent availability' since even when they are physically doing nothing, or engaging in a so-called leisure activity such as watching television at home, for many women this time is still constrained because they have to be 'on-call' to respond to the needs of the husbands and/or offspring. In a study of mothers with careers, Nicole-Drancourt (1989) came to much the same conclusion, stressing the fact that women in her study managed their family and work lives in spite of their male partners rather than because of them.

Indeed, Bryson (1996: 217) argues that to see how women remain responsible for domestic work, one needs look no further than the fact that despite men sometimes sharing the domestic labour, or even in extremely rare cases taking major responsibility for it (though usually only temporarily), there has been no transfer to women of a cultural acceptability to 'keep' a househusband, unlike men for whom it remains culturally acceptable so far as a housewife is concerned. As she puts it: 'The capacity to expropriate domestic labour is gender specific and the rights to it lie with men'. The way forward is not of course to extend this right to some or all women but to revalue the two forms of work and to ensure equal participation of men in such work. Nevertheless, how to achieve both of these things is a vexing question in a world where there is a dominant emphasis on paid work and little or no increase in men's contribution to unpaid domestic work. This issue will be revisited in later chapters.

In this section, we have seen that there is a relative lack of difference between British and French couples so far as the gender division of domestic labour is concerned. Women engage to a far greater extent than men in domestic work whatever their employment status, especially the routine domestic tasks, and take overall responsibility for planning and arranging the domestic workload as well as for the emotional and managerial aspects of such work. Indeed, if any minor difference exists between the two countries, it is that men in Britain engage in slightly more domestic work than French men.

Until now, we have spoken about domestic work in general and about the difference between routine and non-routine domestic work. However, as we discussed at the beginning of the chapter, one aspect of domestic labour which is often singled out for specific attention is that of caring for children. Indeed, it is frequently argued that it is now the presence or absence of children in the household which has the greatest impact on women's ability to engage in other activities since not only must small children be supervized 24 hours a day, but the number of tasks associated with their care increases the burden particularly of routine domestic tasks.

Furthermore, the presence or absence of alternative carers for small children to enable their mothers to enter paid work is of paramount importance to women's employment patterns. It is to the question of caring for children and child care which we now turn.

Child care in couple-based households

Britain and France are two countries with very diverse approaches towards child care. Although framed within a concern for demographic decline rather than gender equality, French policy has had the aim of helping women to be mothers and full-time workers whereas British policy has, until now at least, viewed mothers' employment as an individual choice whose costs must be borne by the individual (Hantrais, 1990; also see Chapter 6). Indeed, these policy differences are very well-documented (Crompton with Le feuvre, 1996; Dex *et al.*, 1993; Hantrais, 1990; Jenson, 1986; Lane, 1993; Lewis, 1992a; Windebank, 1996). It is not our intention in this chapter, therefore, to reiterate in detail this very thorough work but to outline the main policy thrusts in the two countries. Indeed, it is to be noted that in difference to domestic work *per se*, a realm into which state policy has not ventured, care functions, whether these be for children or dependent adults (see Chapter 4), have been a central feature of modern social policy. We then focus upon the gender division of child care in couple-based households. To do this, first, we review the more general literature on child-care strategies in Britain and France (see also Chapter 2) and second, we examine the results of an Anglo-French comparative study of child-care in couple-based households.

Starting with France, how do mothers manage their child-care needs and employment commitments, and what assistance do they receive from the state? France is often seen as a 'halfway house' between the 'woman friendly' states of Scandinavia and the liberal *laissez-faire* Anglo-Saxon nations, and has been termed a 'modified male breadwinner' state in that 'the nature of women's labour market participation has . . . been predominantly full-time and women have benefited . . . indirectly . . . from a social security system that has prioritised horizontal redistribution . . . between families with and without children' (Lewis, 1992a: 160) to assist women to combine motherhood and paid work. Parents in France have a right to parental leave for up to three years, but a replacement benefit only exists for those with two children or more (the *Allocation parentale d'éducation*). In the public sector, full-time employees have the opportunity to opt for part-time work, but this is decided not only on the basis of child-care responsibilities, but also operational requirements. Furthermore, leave to look after sick children is a feature of public sector employment agreements, but less so in the private sector. It is not a statutory right. Indeed, the choice for mothers in France between working on a full-time and fairly rigid basis and not working at all is more stark than in Britain (Windebank, 1996).

The corollary of this rigidity in the organization of employment for mothers is the subsidy and support given by the French state for non-home-based child care for pre-school age children. The state provides free nursery education for all three to six year-olds in the country. For the under three's, provision is more patchy. On average, 10 per cent of two year olds are in state nursery schools, a figure which rises to 20 per cent in certain large cities (Leprince, 1991). Furthermore, there are a limited number of crèche facilities provided by local authorities, but their geographical distribution is very uneven (Hatchuel, 1989). However, the state provides financial assistance to parents using a registered childminder via cash subsidies and the payment of the employers' social security contributions for these employees and this practice has increased in recent years (Flipo and Olier, 1996), as has the use of nannies (Flipo, 1996). Tax allowances are also available for child-care expenses up to a ceiling. For school-age children, schools often provide before and after school care at no or very low cost and both municipalities and employers may provide subsidized school holiday schemes. Once again, however, such provision differs geographically, as there is no requirement for local authorities to provide child-care facilities, with large metropolitan cities being best served.

As far as the under threes are concerned, the INSEE (1995:175) reports that in 1990, 54 per cent were looked after by mothers at home and 46 per cent were looked after by someone other than the mother either outside the home (39 per cent) or inside the home (7 per cent). Of those under threes not looked after by their mothers, 19 per cent were in free nursery school education, 14 per cent were in a crèche, 27 per cent were with registered childminders, 27 per cent with other family members (inside or outside the home, these carers often being grandmothers), 8 per cent with unregistered childminders/friends and 5 per cent with registered or unregistered nannies. Consequently, of those children cared for by someone other than their mother, 60 per cent were in state-funded, subsidized or regulated services and 40 per cent in informal (paid or unpaid) arrangements. These results are echoed to a certain extent by Hatchuel (1989) in his 1986 study of child care in dual-earner families and by Leprince (1991) in his survey of care for the under threes in 1989. Social class, nevertheless, mediates the type of child care used in France with those from the lower end of the occupational and educational spectrum turning more to informal and familial care than to collectivized and paid care (Beillan, 1991; Daune-Richard, 1988; Dechaux, 1990; Marpsat, 1991).

In terms of child-care arrangements, children in France from three to twelve years-old can be treated in the same way because almost all three year-olds and above attend free nursery school. However, for mothers of nursery and primary school children, there is the problem of Wednesday when there is no school. Furthermore, full-time, and even part-time, work hours tend to be relatively long in France (see Chapter 2), sometimes extended at each end of the day by a long lunch break. Relatively few part-time jobs are available which allow the possibility of starting late and finishing early, although the introduction of the 35-hour working week in France may improve this situation (see Chapter 2). Thus, even though school hours are also relatively long, many women have to find before- and after-school care. In both instances, it is often members of the extended family who are called upon (Beillan, 1991; Daune-Richard, 1988; Marpsat, 1991; Roussel and Bourguignon, 1979) or if these are not available, registered or, more often, unregistered childminders are used. For occasional care to cover illnesses, it is often parents themselves, and more often mothers (53 per cent) than fathers (13 per cent) who take time off, although there is no statutory right to take such time. However, in addition, relatives are called upon in 23 per cent of cases (de Singly, 1993).

Britain, in contrast, has been described by Lewis (1992a) as a 'strong male breadwinner' state in which a clear dividing line has traditionally been drawn between public and private responsibility. If women have entered the labour market, then no special provision has been made for their responsibilities as mothers and only minimal provision made for child care, maternity leave and pay and the right to reinstatement. Although the Blair government has accepted the EU directive on parental leave, it has not legislated to give parents rights to vary work hours to suit child-care arrangements or to take time off to care for sick children, proposals also made by the EU. Equally, the state has only provided or subsidized child care for the neediest families. Tax deductions have been available on workplace nurseries for employers only and not employees. There are, in any case, very few of these. Therefore, that child care which does exist is at present located mainly in the private market sector, in which parents must pay full market price for the care of their children, or within the community or extended family on an unpaid or informally paid and individual basis.

However, it should be noted that the bulk of this description refers to the Conservative administration of 1979 to 1997 which influenced the situation of all women participating in the studies reported in this book. At the time of writing, the new Labour government is in the process of expanding child-care provision. Nevertheless, rather than putting the emphasis on child care as a universal right and part of the national education system, the Blair government is approaching the question more from the point of view of the alleviation of poverty, with the emphasis on single-parents and low-income families.

As in other countries, social class and household income mediate the types of child care used, with market solutions being affordable for those women and households with higher earning potential and those with lower earning possibilities having nothing else to rely on but their own resources within the couple or family and friends. As Chapter 6 reveals, however, this is starting to change with some of the Blair government's proposals.

Given this lack of state support for working mothers, how in fact have they coped with their child-care needs in Britain up until now? In general, for all children under 12, the 1991 British Household Panel Survey finds that 61 per cent of households arranged care within the nuclear family (28 per cent of mothers engaged in their paid work while their children were at school, 4 per cent of children looked after themselves, 6 per cent of mothers worked from home and 23 per cent relied on their spouse); 13 per cent used outside paid care (4 per cent nursery; 9 per cent childminder); and 22 per cent used external unpaid care (16 per cent a relative; 3 per cent a friend/neighbour, 3 per cent others) (Dex *et al.*, 1995). This reliance on managing care within the couple, turning next to family and friends and only in a minority of cases relying on paid forms of care remains a general trend and is easily explicable by the high cost of child care and lack of subsidy in Britain. However, for the under-fives with mothers working full-time, whose number has been steadily rising despite such poor support (see Chapter 2), there is more reliance on external and paid forms of care: 38 per cent use childminders and 36 per cent rely on family and friends (Bridgwood and Savage, 1993: Table 7.5). For the more short-term occasional or secondary care needed for school-age children, Bridgwood and Savage (1993) find that for children aged 5–11, unpaid family and friends are the biggest category of minders for before and after school care and holidays.

Thus, in Britain until 1998 at least, child care has been a personal rather than a state concern. As DfEE (1996: 10) stated, the Major government's policy was 'for parents to decide whether they wish to combine work with their family responsibilities'. This means that the relationship between working mothers and those who provide child care has most often been personal in the sense either of being within the nuclear or extended family or of there being a direct monetary transaction taking place between mother and child carer. In contrast to France, many working mothers manage their child care by adapting their own work schedules. However, this occurs according to market demand for short hours part-time flexible labour rather than on the basis of statutory parental rights. Nevertheless, for those hours that cannot be covered by the mother, British women have had to turn to private market or family solutions, just as do French women in order to compensate for the rigidity of their work hours, despite more state support for child care.

These general surveys, however, only provide us with information concerning who minds children while their mothers are at work. They do not tell us anything about who in the household undertakes which of the tasks necessary to care for children nor who takes responsibility for the care of children. In order to provide a more in-depth examination of these issues in Britain and France, we here present the results of the Anglo-French study of child-care strategies conducted by one of the authors and discussed above. All the women interviewed for the study had at least one child aged under twelve, lived with the father of their children and were working full- or part-time in secretarial or clerical occupations. This group of women was chosen because these are heavily feminized occupations and those who work in them represent a 'middle mass' of women employees who have the skills and qualifications to work on a full-time and regular basis. This is an option which is perhaps not open to those with fewer skills and qualifications in either country, but whose earning capacity, in contrast to women working in professional occupations, does not give them unlimited choice as far as child-care arrangements are concerned.

Table 3.5 Division of child care tasks between dual-earner married couples with children, Britain and France, 1995

| Average score* | Britain | | | France | | |
	Full-time employed mother	Part-time employed mother	Over-all	Full-time employed mother	Part-time employed mother	Over-all
Bathing	3.61	3.56	3.58	3.83	3.89	3.86
Dressing/undressing	3.23	3.84	3.67	3.87	3.77	3.82
Nappy changing	3.67	3.38	3.43	3.50	4.00	3.67
Preparing food	3.31	4.20	3.79	4.00	4.50	4.15
Feeding	3.25	3.67	3.52	3.50	4.00	3.67
Taking to/from school	3.13	4.03	3.75	3.60	3.89	3.75
Play and educational activities	3.08	3.81	3.56	3.43	4.26	3.92
Tidying up	3.93	3.81	3.86	3.83	3.93	3.89
Seeing to child at night	3.59	3.09	3.26	3.79	3.77	3.78

* 1 = father only, 2 = father more than mother, 3 = shared, 4 = mother more than father, 5 = mother only

Source: Windebank survey

This is a group of women who are, therefore, in their child-care strategies, perhaps most likely to be affected by state provisions (for further details of the interviewees and interview schedule, see Windebank, 1999).

First, there is the question of who undertakes specific child-related tasks in dual-earner households. As Table 3.5 shows, the women in this study were much more likely than their partners to undertake each and every one of the child-care tasks in these dual-earner households in both Britain and France. Comparing the differences between the two countries, however, it is striking that British fathers rather than the French were more likely to conduct all of these daily child-care tasks.

Does such a finding not fly in the face of the expectation that in a country, such as France, with a more deep-seated tradition of women's employment, one would find greater equality in child-care work also? One possible explanation is that the greater flexibility in labour markets and lack of state support in Britain leads to a more equal gender division of child care in the British group than in the French because both partners needed to be involved in caring for children in order to liberate the labour power of the woman in which men have a financial or emotional interest. Indeed, in the French sample, there were numerous men who were available to look after the children during the week when the wife was employed (for example, teachers who did not work in the school holiday or on a Wednesday afternoon) but nevertheless, did not take responsibility for child care when they were free. This was not the case in any of the British sample where sequential scheduling of jobs was used by couples to minimize formal child-care provision. It is sometimes asserted that giving men the opportunity to partake in child care will facilitate their participation. This study suggests that where men are forced out of financial necessity or lack of alternatives to do so, a more equal gender division of child-care is perhaps more likely to result. This idea will be discussed further in subsequent chapters.

The second issue ignored by survey-type discussions of child care is that of responsibility. If British fathers spend marginally greater amounts of time doing a slightly increased range of tasks when their wives are employed than French fathers, this should not hide the fact that across both nations, fathers rarely take responsibility for the management of these tasks. This has been shown in other studies of both Britain (Brannen and Moss, 1991; Harris, 1987; Hill, 1987; Martin and Roberts, 1984; Morris, 1990) and France (Chabaud *et al.*, 1985; Daune-Richard, 1988; Haicault, 1984; Nicole-Drancourt, 1989). In France, for example, Daune-Richard (1988) concludes that fathers helped only in very limited ways and, in each case, everything was prepared by the mother for what the father was about to do. Nicole-Drancourt (1989) says that in the study of women with careers that she carried out, it was the women who took sole responsibility for managing the domestic work and child care. In Britain, meanwhile, Corti and Laurie (1993) find that women were still the 'responsible adult' in 98 per cent of cases of child care and in 92 per cent of cases they bore the financial responsibility of finding substitute care if paid care was required.

Indeed, in the above study of dual-earner couples, such findings on responsibility are again borne out. Whatever the child-care arrangements made for pre-school or school aged children in the group analysed, the vast majority of both the French and the British mothers perceived themselves, rather than their partners, to be ultimately responsible for managing these in the sense of gathering information on child-care alternatives, making practical arrangements and subsequently monitoring the quality of care received by their children (see Table 3.6). A typical example of this phenomenon is Jessica, a British woman with three children aged between three and nine, working half time as a bank clerk who reported:

Table 3.6 Responsibility for making and managing external child care

	France n=46*	%	Britain n=53*	%
Regular care				
Who assumed responsibility for gathering information on child care possibilities?				
– Mother	38	83	42	79
– Father	0	0	0	0
– Joint	8	17	11	21
Who made the initial arrangements?				
– Mother	38	83	45	85
– Father	0	0	1	2
– Joint	8	17	7	13
Who monitors the quality of the care received?				
– Mother	30	65	37	70
– Father	0	0	0	0
– Joint	16	35	16	30
Emergency care	n=53**		n=55**	
– Mother	47	89	45	82
– Father	0	0	0	0
– Joint	6	11	10	18

* This is not the full sample because some women have never used any external child care while others had the experience of family or friends offering to care for children and thus did not have to make external arrangements which they would feel they had to 'manage' or 'monitor'.
** This refers to the last incident where 'emergency' care (because of illness, etc) had to be arranged for a child rather than what 'usually' happens.

Source: Windebank survey

> When I was on maternity leave and we had to get somebody to look after Robert, he just waved his hand and told me to get on with it. And now, when he ever goes and picks the kids up, I ask him 'Was everything all right?' And he says 'How should I know?'

Similar patterns of continuities and differences between these two groups of mothers emerge if we examine responsibility for organizing irregular (rather than regular) child-care arrangements which constitute an important, although sometimes overlooked, facet of mothers' child-care strategies. Examining who ensures that children are looked after when they are too ill for their normal child care arrangements, the main difference between the two groups of women

Table 3.7 Arrangements for looking after sick children (last incident of illness occurring)

What arrangement was made to look after child in most recent bout of illness?	Britain n=49	%	France n=43	%
Mother took all necessary time off work	18	37	21	48
Father took all necessary time off work	3	6	3	7
Mother & father shared time off work	3	6	3	7
Mother took limited time off, then replaced by unpaid/paid carer	9	18	12	28
Unpaid carer came to house	9	18	2	5
Child sent to unpaid carer	3	6	2	5
Paid carer came to house	2	5	0	0
Child sent to paid carer	1	2	0	0
Child stayed at home	1	2	0	0

Source: Windebank survey

in this study is that the French mothers took more time off themselves to look after their own children and called less upon family and friends than did the British mothers (see Table 3.7). That said, however, overall the differences between the British and French mothers are less marked on this than on other issues with the main source of care for sick children in both groups being the mother herself with fathers playing only a minor role in providing this type of care. It could be suggested that the lesser differences between the British and French women on this question reflect the strong ideological influences which come into play on this emotive issue of looking after children when they are at their lowest ebb and is indicative of who is most 'responsible' for children in a general sense. It is perceived on the whole among the research participants that in such periods of difficulty for children, it is their mother, rather than their father or a third party, that children need and that in these instances, maternal feelings demand that the woman puts her child before her employment. Moreover, whatever the arrangements made, it was overwhelmingly the mothers in both groups who perceived that it was their responsibility to make them (see Table 3.6 above). In no cases did the French or the British women feel that their partners took sole responsibility for such arrangements, although a small minority in each country felt that responsibility was shared. Such findings are echoed in the single-nation study of France by de Singly (1993).

Interestingly, the respondents in the two countries justified the fact that it was they rather than their husbands who took responsibility for child-care arrangements in remarkably similar ways. The first is that fathers, rather than mothers, have to make their jobs their priority, whatever these may be. The second justification is that mothers have more of a natural instinct to worry about their children and cannot therefore leave responsibility to their partners who are more lax about the whole business. This echoes previous research into the question of responsibility for domestic work and child care, carried out mainly in the US (Darling-Fisher and Tiedje, 1990; Hill, 1987; Leslie *et al.*, 1989; Pleck, 1985).

In sum, this comparative study, echoing results from previous research, reveals fundamental similarities between these two groups of British and French mothers concerning responsibility for children. These women overwhelmingly perceive that it is they, rather than their partners, who are responsible for their children. In other words, the greater involvement of French women during this century in the labour market and the support that they have received from the state for this involvement, appears to have had little impact on the perceptions of responsibility for their children held by these women, nor on what it means to them to be a mother as opposed to a father when compared with the British case. Neither has it had much influence on fathers' perceptions of their role in child care. It could be suggested, therefore, that on this evidence, British and French women share a core ideology concerning the nature of the responsibilities of motherhood. This ideology perhaps does not advocate the need for mothers to spend 24 hours a day with their children, and differs between the two groups as concerns the extent to which it is acceptable for a third party to undertake care of children and the amount of time that mothers need to liberate for their children. Nonetheless, it does suggest that a mother should be above all devoted to the well-being of her children rather than to her employment and that she herself should strive to derive as much benefit as possible from having children by spending maximum time with them (the definition of maximum being different in the two countries). It could thus be proposed that the greater 'commitment' to paid work of the French mothers in terms of hours of work and the more extensive support which they receive from the state to facilitate this commitment has not lessened the normative burdens of motherhood for them compared with their British counterparts. Indeed, de Singly and Maunaye (1996) argue that although in France women are no longer expected to spend all their time with their children in order to be a 'good mother', this does not mean that their mothering burden has become lighter in comparison with the past since parents, or more properly, mothers, are expected to provide their children with more in terms of material and psychological well-being and educational assistance. This is partly due, in their view, to the increased competition in society for educational and material success and the increased expectations to provide children with the necessary skills with which to survive in this competitive world. This concurs with Gardiner's (1997) economistic view in the British context that the principal domestic burden on women is now the formation of the 'human capital' of their children.

However, it is clear that these similar perceptions of the fundamental duties of motherhood do not preclude there being a number of differences in the everyday experiences of British and French employed mothers, particularly at a practical level. First, there is a significant variation in the extent to which mothers in the two countries take time out of employment to care for their children themselves, both in a life-course and a weekly perspective (see Chapter 2). Second, there is a clear distinction in the ways in which British and French mothers have their children minded while they are at work, particularly when we are considering regular child-care. It can be seen, therefore, that the different state policies to be found in the two countries have had an impact on the degree to which it is possible and acceptable for women to delegate specified areas of their mothering duties to a third party – usually another woman – but much less on the extent of these duties, or indeed on the degree to which they are shared between the two parents. In other words, although state provision of child-care is much higher in France, this does not appear to have led to much renegotiation between men and women of the practical work of looking after children and much less the responsibility for child rearing. The sole output seems to be that some of women's responsibility has been commodified in the sense that women can now pay other women to look after their children rather than relying on informal arrangements usually with other women. It has done little to renegotiate the responsibilities between the genders. Caring for children in Britain and France can be seen as an example of what Leira (1994: 197) is talking about when she asserts: 'The institutional division of labor in care provision is in a process of change. The gendered division of caregiving work, however, remains remarkably stable'. This will be discussed further in the following chapter as the issues raised refer to all caring tasks and responsibilities, not just child care.

Indeed, the provision of formal child-care facilities in France appears to have done little to create a more equal gender division of child care than in Britain and why should we think that it would? It could be suggested that in cases where a woman's income in Britain has not been sufficient to warrant paying high costs for child care, but for whatever reason the woman remains in employment after the birth of her children, couples devise strategies to enable this to happen which oblige the husband to undertake child care, lending credence to the view that changes to the gender division of domestic work come about through force rather than state-provided opportunity. Women in Britain want to work or have to work for financial reasons. The state has not been there to step into the breach, so the burden more often falls on men's shoulders than in France.

In conclusion, this in-depth examination of child care thus reinforces the more general finding that despite women's increased participation in paid work, men's contribution to the domestic workload has not kept pace with these changes. Such a finding has been interpreted in various ways. Hochschild (1989) has described it as a 'stalled revolution' in the sense that although women have increasingly moved into the previously male-dominated sphere of employment, there has been no equivalent increase in the amount of unpaid work conducted by men. A slightly more optimistic slant is the view of Gershuny *et al.* (1994) who have referred to this as a process of 'lagged adaptation'. Examining the husband's proportion of the household's total work in various types of household distinguished by the length of the wife's experience of employment over the last ten years, they find that in British households where the wife has spent 20 months or less in employment, the total of the couple's work is divided in the ratio 46:54 between the husband and wife; over the range of 21 to 60 months the total of work is divided 48:52; and where the wife has more than five years' work experience, the total work is evenly divided. For them, therefore, change will come about, but slowly, and possibly over a number of generations.

However, the Anglo-French comparison set out here suggests that the picture is more complicated. The gender division of domestic labour and child care, on the basis of the available evidence, appears, if anything, to be more unequal in France than in Britain. In other words, if the 'lagged adaptation' thesis were correct, then France, with its longer history of women's participation in the formal labour market and thus more 'advanced' status, would by now be showing a more equal gender division of domestic labour. Here, we have shown that this is far from the truth and therefore suggest that a simple causal relationship between more paid work for women and more unpaid work for men, even if a time-lag in this change is built into the equation, is rather simplistic.

Domestic labour in single-person and single-parent households

Up until now, there has been little research on either the nature and extent of domestic labour nor the 'divisions' of domestic labour which affect single-person or single-parent households. Superficially, this can be explained quite simply. Given that the aim of much of the research on domestic labour is to identify gender divisions, it appears that research on such households has very little to offer the subject. If there is only one responsible adult in a household, it is s/he who will undertake the domestic work of that household. However, to accept such a proposition would be a mistake. Both single-person and single-parent households are the most rapidly expanding household types in Britain and France (see Chapter 2) and people are spending increasing amounts of time in such households at various points in their lives due to postponed marriages, higher divorce rates and a preference among adults in all age categories for independent living. As such, their domestic coping strategies are important to understand and explain in their own right. Neither should one assume, as we shall now show, that such domestic strategies are not heavily gendered and do not have an impact on the gender division of domestic work at the societal level. To display this, we first investigate single-person households and explore how they may be 'doing gender' in ways not so far well understood in the literature. Second, we examine single-parent households and the domestic labour associated with them.

Domestic work in single-person households

Despite the fact that single-person households are among the most rapidly growing household-type in both Britain and France, little is known about the domestic strategies of such households. As we have explained above, however, they are important to include in any general overview of gender divisions of labour.

On the one hand, there is the issue that individuals bring to couple-based households much baggage from their previous lives and that this will have a major impact on resulting gender divisions of domestic labour. For example, we do not know whether couples in which the man has been living alone for a significant number of years actually result in more equal gender divisions of domestic labour than those couple-based households in which the man has previously lived in households with other women. This has implications for cross-national comparison since, for example, graduate men in Britain are much more likely than graduate men in France to have lived independently through their college years. On the other hand, we do not know whether single-person households are in fact gendered in subtle ways which will provide help in understanding gender divisions of domestic labour more generally. For example, to what extent do such households rely on external sources of support and how is this gendered? How does this vary between single-man and single-woman households? Do men-only households do less domestic work than woman-only households? How does their domestic workload vary and why?

One of the few sources of empirical evidence uncovered on this subject is the time-budget data from France. As Table 3.8 reveals, men over the age of 65 years who are living alone spend less time engaged in domestic work than women of a similar age living alone. In 1975, they spent just 83.4 per cent of the time of a woman living alone and by 1985, this figure had increased slightly to 89.1 per cent. Consequently, single men appear to do less than single women, although significantly, this is reducing over time. Perhaps more important, however, is the fact that when living in single-person households, these data reveal that within this age-group, men conduct significantly more domestic work than men living in families, while single women conduct significantly less domestic work than women living in families. This displays that living in a couple results in women taking on more of the domestic workload and it should be remembered that this is at a time in people's lives when neither the man nor the woman are likely to be employed.

Table 3.8   Evolution of structure of time, 1974–75 and 1985–86, France

| | Man | | | | Woman | | | |
| | Alone | | In family | | Alone | | In Family | |
	1975	1985	1975	1985	1975	1985	1975	1985
Domestic work, of which	4h46	4h31	3h23	4h08	5h19	5h04	5h48	5h57
– housework	2h54	2h52	1h32	1h48	2h53	2h37	4h32	4h30
– DIY, Sewing	16	9	20	28	35	28	25	33
– Non-work, study travel	54	54	37	44	36	36	27	28
– Caring for others	5	4	8	10	3	5	6	10

Header spanning: **65 years old and over**

Source: INSEE (cited in European Foundation for Improvement of Living and Working Conditions, 1991: Annex 2).

Further evidence from the US displays that such inequalities are not unique to those over 65 years old. This shows that divorced and widowed men do substantially more housework than any other group of men and that they are especially more likely than their married counterparts to spend more time cooking and cleaning (South and Spitze, 1994). Women who are divorced or widowed, in contrast, do less housework than their married counterparts. For women, this difference is perhaps best explained by the reduction in the total amount of housework required which is brought about by the absence of a husband in the household. For men, inversely, divorce and widowhood means doing household tasks previously done by a wife. In empirical studies, nevertheless, widowed men reduce the time they spend doing housework as the years since widowhood pass, and they are more likely than widows to have help doing it (usually from a woman) as time goes on (Umberson *et al.*, 1992). Of course, today's widowers and widows came of age when the gendered division of labour in households was much more segregated than today and when living independently before or between marriages was much less common.

Such limited data, nevertheless, cannot take us very far in exploring cross-national differences in the exercise of domestic labour in single-person households in Britain and France, nor how these practices may impact on the gender division of domestic work at a societal level. Much more research is required before that can be more fully understood. Given the rising importance of these households in the populations of both Britain and France, this is of crucial importance. Questions which need to be asked include: whether the degree of externalization of domestic work and the amount of assistance given by others depend on whether the single-person household is composed of a man or a woman or whether other factors such as time and resource availability are more important; whether men deliberately do less domestic work than women in single-person households and how can this be explained; whether their past situation influences the extent and nature of their domestic work and if so, how; and whether single-person households composed of men really take full responsibility for their situation or whether they rely on other women such as daughters, sisters, female neighbours or paid help to undertake many of their domestic tasks. Until these issues are investigated, we cannot know the implications of the rise of this type of household for gender divisions of domestic labour and the associated variations across nations.

For the moment, therefore, any understanding of how non-couple households might still be 'doing gender' has to come from the more numerous studies that have been conducted on the divisions of domestic labour in single-parent households.

Single-parent households and domestic labour

Although more research has been conducted on the divisions of domestic labour in single-parent households than in single-person households, it is important at the outset to state that this is by no means of the same order of magnitude as the amount of research conducted on couple-based households. Hence, although this research can provide us with some further insights into the relationship between gender and domestic labour, it by no means provides a full picture and falls particularly short of perfection as far as our cross-national comparison is concerned. There remain significant gaps in our understanding of such households in terms of articulating the dynamics of domestic work.

In Britain, the proportion of all families with dependent children headed by a lone parent rose from 8.6 per cent in 1971 to 19.2 per cent in 1991. Indeed, by 1992, between one in five and one in six dependent children lived in a one-parent family (National Council for One Parent Families, 1994). Given custody arrangements in Britain, over 90 per cent of these lone parents are mothers (Haskey, 1994). In France, meanwhile, one family in eight is composed of a single parent, which is slightly less than Britain. So, while in Britain lone parents constituted 20 per cent of families with dependent children in 1992 and 8 per cent in 1971 (Burghes,

1993), they accounted for 13 per cent of families with children in France, compared with 9 per cent in 1968 (Lefaucheur and Martin, 1997). Similar to Britain, nevertheless, in France, 86 per cent of single parents are women (Lefaucheur and Martin, 1997) and the same trend is evidence of a shift away from widowhood and towards divorce as being the main reason which now explains single parenthood, divorce accounting for about half of all single-parent situations. The never-married, moreover, not very numerous twenty years ago, now constitute a fifth of single parents (Benveniste and Soleilhavoup, 1994; Duncan and Edwards, 1997b; Lefaucheur and Martin, 1997). As we have seen in Chapter 2, there are wide variations between the participation rates in employment of single mothers in Britain and France, more stark in fact than for mothers living in couples. We will examine here work in the domestic realm for single parents. First, we will consider the issue of the domestic workload itself and second, that of child care.

Domestic work in single-parent households

The first issue to address, therefore, concerns domestic work in single-parent households. Superficially, it might be assumed that this terrain is uninteresting for it is usually the single parent herself who will carry out the domestic work. However, this is untrue for two reasons. First, there is the issue that most single-parent households are the result of divorce and headed by a woman. On the one hand, it could be argued that living as a single parent means that a woman only has to look after herself and her children and not her husband, therefore improving her domestic lot. On the other hand, however, it could be argued that fathers, while being free and indeed encouraged to participate in chosen ways in their children's lives, are liberated completely from the day-to-day work which accompanies them. Whichever argument holds true, if single-parent households continue to rise in number and importance, this will have an impact on the gender division of domestic work at the societal and also at the individual level.

Second, there is the issue of whether single-parent households in Britain and France are in fact gendering the division of domestic labour in ways hitherto ignored. In the US, for example, children's contribution to housework has been examined. This has shown that the domestic contributions of boys and girls mirror that of adults, with girls doing stereotypically 'women's' chores and spending more time doing housework than boys (Benin and Edwards, 1990; Berk, 1985;

Blair, 1991; Goldscheider and Waite, 1991; Hilton and Haldeman, 1991; Timmer *et al.*, 1985). Examining single-parent households, Zick and Allen (1996) find that the gender division of domestic labour among children is more exaggerated in these than in couple households.

Based on this information about the division of domestic work in single-parent households, a key question that needs to be answered is whether single parenthood is a liberating phenomenon for women. From the available evidence, one can suggest that although it might be liberating for the individual mothers concerned, it is not 'progressive in gender relations' on a societal level. If the American research holds true for other societies, including Britain and France, then children in single-parent households may be more rigidly gendered in terms of the tasks that they undertake than in couple-based households thus arguably reproducing gender relations to a greater extent than couple households. It may also be the case that these households also rely on other women (rather than men) to a greater extent in their coping strategies than in couple households.

Child-care in single-parent households

The question of child care in single-parent households is obviously bound up with the question of custody. For those women having children without having had a cohabiting relationship with their father, the question of 'custody' rarely arises: if they decide to keep the child, its remains with them. For separated and divorced mothers, the vast majority want custody of their children and win it in both countries. However, even if on the whole, this is a 'victory' in personal terms for individual women, it means that the practical tasks and responsibilities of caring for and bringing up children rest more squarely on the shoulders of women with fathers opting in and out in terms of the time and effort they expend on their children as they so please (see above). This is the same in Britain and France.

In both nations, furthermore, the fact that women remain responsible for child care is reinforced by the ways in which custody arrangements work. In Britain, in most cases, custody goes to the mother while in France, although most children live with their mothers, the right to make decisions is often a joint affair. The result is that women have the responsibility for caring in France but not the legal right to take autonomous decisions. Instead, men have a joint right in decision-making but none of the practical responsibility for day-to-day care.

However, the difference between the two countries, as we have seen in our discussions of child care in general, is that in France, single mothers have been able to call upon formal sources of child-care support to a greater extent than in Britain due to both its greater availability and lower cost, as well as women's higher wages. In Britain, in contrast, single mothers have not only had relatively less access to appropriately-priced formal child care but also less access to jobs that will pay sufficient amounts to make entering the labour market a feasible option. Indeed, at the time of writing, the main thrust of child-care provision being developed by the Blair government is aimed at lone mothers as part of its 'welfare to work' strategy. The result is that French single mothers have greater opportunity to externalize to the formal sphere some of their child-care activities than British single mothers.

Conclusions

In sum, the above discussion of domestic work suggests that there is little difference between the two countries so far as the gender division of domestic labour is concerned but that where variation has been found to exist, it is in fact in Britain that men are participating in a larger share of the overall domestic workload, including more of the routine domestic work. As such, while cross-national comparisons of paid work alone usually suggest that the better institutional arrangements made for women to combine motherhood and employment mean that 'progress in gender relations' is greater in France than in Britain, this chapter finds that when the division of domestic work is given prominence in analysis, the situation is not so straightforward. As we have shown, women's more extensive entry into employment in France has not been matched by a comparatively greater renegotiation of the division of domestic labour relative to Britain. Quite the opposite if anything. French women suffer from the 'dual burden' of domestic work plus paid work to a greater extent than women in Britain. We must suggest, therefore, that change in the employment sphere is not closely or necessarily related to change in the household. Equally, it can be seen that we should not confuse a situation in which the state takes over some of women's caring functions, as in France and in the Britain of the new millennium, with a situation in which men and women undertake domestic work more equally.

However, any differences in this regard which do exist between

Britain and France should not be over-exaggerated. Common to both nations is the fact that women undertake the vast majority of the domestic work, especially the routine domestic work, and it is universally women who take overall responsibility for planning, managing and arranging the domestic workload as well as for the emotional aspects of such work. Indeed, we could suggest that even single-person and single-parent households in the two nations must also be considered as being manifestations of a gendered division of domestic work at a societal as well as at a personal level. In sum, we can find no evidence that the differences in men's domestic roles in these two countries match the clear differences in women's labour market participation, nor in state policy towards women's work and motherhood. This raises fundamental questions about what constitutes 'gender progress' and the role of policy in that process, issues which will be discussed in depth in later chapters.

4
Women's Community Work

This chapter evaluates the similarities and differences in women's community work in Britain and France. Here, we are referring to unpaid work undertaken by household members for members of households other than their own such as kin, friends and neighbours. This is a form of economic activity that up until now has been mostly ignored in mainstream discussions of women's work, both in cross-national and single-nation studies, but is important if we are to obtain a rounded picture of women's overall workload and their caring responsibilities. In order to examine this activity, we breakdown our analysis into two principal forms of community economic activity: kinship work and neighbourhood activity. This is because each is based on different principles of exchange. Kinship work is chiefly based on 'kinship obligation' while neighbourhood inter-household transfers are primarily based on 'reciprocal exchange' (Finch, 1989; Short, 1996; Warde, 1990).

Taking each form of community work in turn, we first examine the amount undertaken by men and women in Britain and France and second, the gender divisions in the character of this work. This reveals that similar to the situation with domestic work discussed in Chapter 3, community work, whether based on kinship obligation or reciprocity, is conducted by women more than men and displays deep gender divisions. In consequence, community work will be shown to act as an additional load on women, resulting in many having a 'triple burden' of paid work, domestic labour and community work. Furthermore, by revealing how the available evidence suggests that community work is also gendered to as great, if not a greater extent in France than Britain, we will display that full-time employment for women in France has made as little impact on their share of community work as it has on domestic labour. Obviously, this has important implications for comparing 'progress in gender relations' in the two nations.

To review the magnitude and character of community work in Britain and France, an immediate problem to be confronted is that there is limited evidence based on little more than scattered one-off studies conducted in the two countries. No Anglo-French comparative work, so far as is known, has been undertaken in this field. Here, therefore, we have to piece together and compare individual studies that frequently use different definitions of the phenomenon under investigation, widely contrasting methods and have often been conducted at very different times.

Exchanges of labour within the kinship network

There is a popular conception in both Britain and France that kinship groups have broken down as sources of support and constraint for individuals and nuclear families (see Crow and Allen, 1994; Dechaux, 1996; Enjolras, 1995; Finch, 1989; Martin, 1996; Parker, 1988; Pitrou, 1996). However, although fewer families now live together in inter-generational households and groupings, this does not mean that family solidarities have totally disintegrated. As Colvez (1989) finds in France, despite elderly people living independently of their descendants, they still receive assistance from them. Of the 589 individuals needing assistance with small housework tasks in this study, 21 per cent were most often assisted by family of the same generation, 29 per cent by younger family, 5 per cent by friends and neighbours, 41 per cent by professionals and 4 per cent by others. Of the 1009 individuals who needed assistance with their shopping, moreover, 27 per cent were assisted by family of the same age, 44 per cent by younger members of the family, 5 per cent by friends or neighbours, 11 per cent by professionals and 3 per cent by others. It appears from this evidence, therefore that 'kinship economies' (Short, 1996) are still prevalent and their breakdown is perhaps not so widespread as many have assumed. Indeed, it is often the case in both Britain and France that the exchanges and transfers of money, goods and services within kinship economies are crucial for the maintenance of a decent standard of living for many households. The issue throughout this section, however, is one of who provides this kinship support in the two countries. In other words, on whose shoulders does the work fall and are there variations between Britain and France in this regard? To answer this question, we examine first the amount of kinship support provided by men and women and second, the character of the work men and women undertake in the two nations.

Amount of kinship work undertaken by men and women in Britain and France

In France, the principal source of data on the magnitude and character of kinship support is provided by a statistical survey on 'Family Assistance and Relationships' undertaken by the INSEE (Chabaud-Rychter and Fougeyrollas-Schwebel, 1989; Fougeyrollas, 1994). The results highlight the position that kinship occupies in everyday exchanges as well as the disparities in the practices of men and women. So far as the volume of such work is concerned, this survey examines kinship support within the context of men and women's overall workload. This reveals that of all the activities that they undertake, men conduct 39 per cent for themselves (20 per cent in the case of women), 16 per cent for the household (25 per cent for women), 4 per cent for kin living outside the household (4 per cent for women) and 5 per cent for other people (4 per cent for women) and the remaining responses are either meaningless or received no response. Besides the fact that French women are less oriented towards doing activities for themselves and more oriented towards doing activities for the household, thus reinforcing our findings from Chapter 3, the important point here is that the proportion of all work which is undertaken for kin living outside the household is approximately equal for French men and women. That is, of all activities performed during the course of a week, 4 per cent of both men's and women's work is specifically aimed at benefiting relatives (or one activity in every 25 undertaken). Some activities, nevertheless, are more likely to be undertaken for kin than others. For example, 18 per cent of all the 'odd jobs' performed in France are conducted for relatives living in another household. Likewise, 10 per cent of sociable activities (especially conversations) are conducted for and with relatives, 9 per cent of all gardening activities, 8 per cent of shopping trips, 6 per cent of cooking activities, 5 per cent of sewing, 4 per cent of housework activities and 3 per cent of meals (Chabaud-Rychter and Fougeyrollas-Schwebel, 1989).

The fact that both women and men perform the same proportion of their total workload for kin living in another household, how-ever, does not mean that men and women perform the same amount of kinship work. Women perform, on average, many more activi-ties for kin in a normal week than men, simply because they conduct many more activities in total per week than men. As Chabaud-Rychter and Fougeyrollas-Schwebel (1989) find, women perform on average four activities per day for their parents and parents-in-law, four for their children living outside the household and one activity per week for their brothers and sisters. Men, in contrast, conduct just two activities per week for their ascendants, three for their descendants and one per fortnight for their brothers and sisters. The result, as Fougeyrollas (1994) shows in a later analysis of the same data set, is that of all services provided to kin, 42 per cent are conducted by women, 31 per cent by men and 25 per cent by the two together, while 2 per cent are realized by other people in the household such as children or older people.

In Britain, similar empirical evidence of the comparative extent of men's and women's kinship activity is provided by a study con-ducted in 1997 of informal economic activity in a deprived neighbourhood of Leicester (see Williams and Windebank, 1998b). This reveals both comparable levels of kinship support in the con-text of everyday workloads as well as similar disparities in the practices of men and women in this sphere. Of all activities undertaken, men conduct 82 per cent for their own household (90 per cent in the case of women), 5 per cent for kin living outside the house-hold (5 per cent for women) and 13 per cent for other people (5 per cent for women). Superficially, therefore, it appears that men are just as oriented to providing kinship support as women. How-ever, when this is translated into the number of tasks provided, it becomes immediately apparent that women again engage in a larger number of activities than men which are aimed at benefiting rela-tives, simply because they conduct many more activities in total than men. That is, women had conducted an average of 12 tasks for relatives for every 10 tasks conducted by men. These findings are further reinforced in a study of a working-class housing estate in West Belfast which finds that 32 per cent of the respondents regularly did odd jobs for relatives and that this kinship support is provided more by women with the mother–daughter nexus being by far the most important relationship so far as inter-household kinship exchange is concerned. Nevertheless, men perform a share of the kinship load which is approximately equal to that identified in the Leicester study (Leonard, 1994). In both the UK and the French studies reported here, therefore, women conduct a larger number of tasks for relatives than men. Furthermore, the relative share of kinship work undertaken by men is slightly higher in the British studies than the French. Nevertheless, it should be remembered that the French study covers a cross-section of the French population while the UK studies are focused on deprived communities.

The vast majority of the research on kinship economies, however, focuses upon two specific types of kinship activity: support given to the elderly and, to a lesser extent, assistance provided by relatives in the realm of child care. Here, therefore, and due to the lack of availability of alternative data, we focus upon these specific realms of kinship obligation. Starting with the main body of evidence on kinship economies which addresses the issue of kinship support to the elderly, Gabrielle David and Starzec (1996) find in France that the recently constructed image of the retired as young, sporty, travelling, participating in multiple activities and making use of their time masks the reality of old age which is associated with dependence and isolation. For those aged over 80 and living independently, for example, they find that 72 per cent require help with a certain number of domestic tasks, while 11 per cent never go out and have neither relations nor even contact on the phone with anybody else. Who, therefore, provides support for these elderly people? In both nations, the majority of elderly people live 'in the community' rather than in any form of residential care and the family remains the most important locus of care. However, to talk about 'care by the community' or even 'family' care is to disguise the reality. As we will now see, care by the community almost always means care by family members and care by family members usually means care by women (see Parker, 1988).

Starting with who provides care to the elderly in France, the INSEE (1995) comes to the conclusion after a long trawl through the wealth of statistical data available that it is women, usually daughters who undertake this work. For example, in cases where there is at least one main helper providing care for an elderly person, 62 per cent of these helpers are women. In cases where there are at least two main helpers, one woman at least is involved in 85 per cent of cases. Indeed, of all children who help their parents (whether in a primary or secondary capacity), women are always more numerous than men: daughters represent 63 per cent of helpers, daughters-in-law 9 per cent and sons 29 per cent. In France, therefore, the task of caring for elderly relatives is very much women's domain.

In Britain, similarly, the role of carer is disproportionately assumed by women, usually daughters (Abel and Nelson, 1990; Brannen *et al.*, 1994; Evandrou, 1990; Finch, 1989; Morris, 1990). Take, for example, the results of the 1985 and 1990 General Household Surveys (GHS). The 1990 GHS reveals that 13 per cent of men and 17 per cent of women aged over 16 years old provide care and that this had risen from 12 per cent of men and 15 per cent of women in 1985. This rise, moreover, was entirely due to an increase from 10 to 12 per cent in the proportion of people caring for someone not living with them. Indeed, while in 1985, 8 per cent of men and 11 per cent of women were caring for somebody in another household, by 1990, this had risen to 10 per cent and 13 per cent respectively. In the case of caring for a dependant in another household, 62 per cent of these carers are women and 63 per cent of the carers who devote at least 20 hours per week to caring are women. Women, therefore, are more likely to provide care and are also more likely to provide care to somebody living in another household than their own (OPCS, 1992: Table 1). Examining the relationship of the carer to the dependant, the finding is that in the vast majority of cases it is kin. For example, in 1990, when a carer was caring for somebody in another household, it was a parent in 39 per cent of cases, a parent-in-law in 15 per cent of cases, another relative in 20 per cent of cases, a child in 4 per cent of cases and only in 25 per cent of cases was it non-kin such as a friend or neighbour (OPCS, 1992: Table 11). Caring in the community, therefore, means caring for kin and this is undertaken most of the time by daughters and daughters-in-law. As Qureshi and Walker (1989) show in their study of support given to the elderly in Sheffield, the categories of most likely carer can be ordered as follows: spouse; relative in lifelong household; daughter; daughter-in-law; son; other relative; non-relative. Finch and Mason (1993) echo this finding.

The gendering of elder care is therefore very similar in the two nations. However, this evidence, at least, suggests that British men appear to take on more of the caring functions for the elderly than French men, differences in methodology notwithstanding. Nevertheless, in both nations, it is women who shoulder more than their share of elder care and this has a significant impact on not only their labour market participation but also their overall workloads. The OPCS (1992: Table 6) report that of married women, 17 per cent with full-time jobs were also carers, as were 22 per cent of part-time employed married women. The result, therefore, is that at any one time, around one in five married women in Britain suffer from a 'triple burden' of having a job, remaining responsible for the majority of the domestic work and caring for an elderly person. Of course, over the life-course, a much greater percentage of all women will at some time suffer such a triple burden. To put a figure on the amount of time that this third burden imposes on women's lives, the figures from the 1990 GHS reveals that 30 per cent of women spent up to four hours caring, 25 per cent spent between 5 and 9 hours, 21 per cent between 10 and 19 hours, 12 per cent spent 20 to 49 hours and 12 per cent over 50 hours. Men, in contrast, are much more likely to spend fewer hours caring than women, with 38 per cent of men who cared spending 0 to 4 hours (OPCS, 1992: Table 9). When the dependant lived in another household, the time spent caring tended to be slightly less than when they lived in the same household as the carer (OPCS, 1992: Table 10).

In total, therefore, in both Britain and France, women are involved in a greater proportion of the total workload for kin than men, although this difference appears to be slightly less in Britain than in France. When this finding is thus coupled with the fact that French women's insertion into full-time employment is greater and French men's contribution to the domestic workload is no more and perhaps less extensive than in Britain, the result is that the 'triple burden' will be both more widespread and intensely felt by French women than by British women. Nevertheless, it is not solely the amount of kinship support that is provided which is important if we are to understand the gendering of kinship economies. There is also a need to explore the gender variations in the nature of the work undertaken.

Gender variations in the nature of kinship exchange

In both Britain and France, as we shall see, the types of activities that men and women perform for relatives are gendered in much the same way as domestic work. That is, men tend to perform tasks that are viewed as 'masculine', that are non-routine and have closed-ended time frames. Women, on the other hand, conduct tasks that are viewed as 'feminine' in nature, that are often routine and are frequently open-ended in character. In France, for example, Fougeyrollas (1994) finds that 96 per cent of DIY tasks undertaken for kin are conducted by men, as is 77 per cent of household maintenance, while women conduct 97 per cent of the sewing and knitting carried out for kin, 81 per cent of the housework, 71 per cent of the caring activity, 54 per cent of the child care and 54 per cent of the shopping. In Britain, meanwhile, in the case study of Leicester cited above, a similar gender division of kinship work emerges. Men conduct all of the gardening work undertaken for kin, all of the car repairs and 90 per cent of the household maintenance, while women carry out all of the laundry and ironing undertaken for kin and 66 per cent of the housework. This is further reinforced in an earlier study by Pahl (1984) on the Isle of Sheppey, who finds that when the work that men and women conduct for relatives living outside their household is examined, men do all of the repairs and carpentry, 90 per cent of the decorating and 64 per cent of the gardening, while women conduct all of the dressmaking and laundry, 83 per cent of the housework, 80 per cent of the baby-sitting and 80 per cent of the hairdressing.

Nevertheless, to understand more fully gender divisions in the character of the kinship work undertaken, one has to examine the types of task being undertaken for different types of kin. Here, therefore, we distinguish between kinship work undertaken for ascendants, descendants and collaterals. As Chabaud-Rychter and Fougeyrollas-Schwebel (1989) find in France, when men engage in kinship work for ascendants (parents or parents-in-law), similar to domestic work, they perform household activities such as odd jobs (11 per cent of all activities conducted by men for ascendants) and gardening (13 per cent). However, they practically never cook and do very little housework. Some 20 per cent of the work that women provide for ascendants, in contrast, involves sociability and 15 per cent of the work involves cooking, 9 per cent shopping, 8 per cent care and 6 per cent housework. Indeed, men's work for their ascendants is frequently linked to a qualification or specialization they possess, often acquired in their employment and which is recognized in the framework of the family. Domestic chores, on the other hand, are performed by all daughters and daughters-in-law who provide assistance, usually in the form of tasks involving mobility or physical effort, such as heavy housework, shopping and general errands (see also Delbes, 1983).

Although directly comparable data does not exist for Britain, the OPCS survey (1992: Table 15) does reveal a similar gendered division of work by descendants for ascendants. When the dependant lives in another household to that of the carer, it is found that the most popular tasks are keeping them company (performed by 71 per cent of carers), keeping an eye on the dependant (70 per cent), taking them out (55 per cent), paperwork or financial matters (41 per cent), physical help such as with walking (12 per cent), personal care such as assistance with washing (11 per cent) and giving medicines (9 per cent). Who conducts such tasks, however, is heavily gendered. Personal bodily care of the elderly person was found to be entirely the woman's domain and it was discovered that where men were the only individuals available to provide such care, assistance was more likely to be forthcoming from outside professionals. In other words, when it is a woman who is responsible for care, it was found that outside services were less often sought, because these caring functions were seen to be part of the woman's 'natural' role, than when a man was responsible who saw himself, and was seen by others, as not competent to carry out these personal-caring functions.

Such statistics, however, distinguish only the gender divisions in the tasks undertaken. More qualitative surveys, such as that conducted by Favrot-Laurens (1996) in France, examine the question of responsibility. Favrot-Laurens (1996), for example, found that when couples took on the responsibility for looking after the husband's elderly parents, not only did the daughters-in-law conduct more tasks than the sons but they also took on the responsibility for their parents-in-law. The women respondents in this situation were more likely to own up to negative feelings about these responsibilities than were daughters whose own parents required assistance. Nevertheless, there was a clear impossibility for the daughters-in-law to refuse to undertake this work. The son had a responsibility for his parents, but he 'delegated' this to his wife. Despite husbands 'helping' their wives more when their own parents were being assisted than when it was their wife's parents who required help, it was the women as daughters-in-law who not only still conducted the vast majority of the caring functions, but also took responsibility for managing and organizing the care arrangements. As Favrot-Laurens (1996) found, this social construction that designates women as 'naturally' responsible for caring had an impact on their employment. Among the women surveyed, some had taken early retirement to look after elderly relatives while some who were unemployed had abandoned the search for work because of such caring responsibilities. Others, moreover, had moved from full-time to part-time employment in order to be more available to meet the needs of elderly relatives. Men's employment situation, in contrast, was little affected since the responsibility was delegated to a woman, whether it be his wife, sister, daughter or aunt.

When the types of work provided by descendants for ascendants is thus examined, a rigidly gendered division of activity and responsibility can be identified. However, it would be a mistake to end the analysis of kinship economies at this point. Ascendants are not purely passive recipients of care. The flow of assistance is not one-way. Aid also comes in the opposite direction. When examining the activities provided by ascendants for descendants, nevertheless, the majority of the literature has tended to focus upon the role of grandparents in providing child care (for example, Kornhaber, 1996), although kinship activity from ascendants to descendants involves a broader range of activities than simply child care, such as the provision of any good and/or service as well as financial aid.

In both Britain and France, nevertheless, the importance of child care by grandparents cannot be overlooked. As Marpsat (1991) finds in France, 40 per cent of grandparents have small children under 12 years old whom they look after during the holidays or at some other point during the year and 30 per cent of mothers who cannot look after their children aged under three leave them with the grandparents while they are in employment (see also Le Gall, 1996; Lefaucheur and Martin, 1997). A similar situation exists in Britain, although the figures are slightly lower so far as reliance on grandparents are concerned due to husbands taking greater responsibility for child care and fewer mothers being in employment (Brannen and Moss, 1991; Bridgwood and Savage, 1993; Dex *et al.*, 1995; Marsh and McKay, 1993; Martin and Roberts, 1984). Indeed, when grandparents are used, it is the case in both Britain and France that is most usually the woman's mother followed by the father's mother who is called upon (de Singly and Maunaye, 1996; Duriez, 1996; Gokalp and David, 1982; Hill, 1987). The issue, therefore, is that where women seek help from ascendants such as to release them to enter employment, this aid on the whole comes from other women. It does not come from ascendant men.

Besides caring for grandchildren, ascendants in both countries conduct a range of other work for their descendants and their descendants' spouses. Similar to the situation where descendants aid ascendants, moreover, the form of aid flowing from ascendants to descendants is heavily gendered. As Chabaud-Rychter and Fougeyrollas-Schwebel (1989) find in France, in addition to caring for grandchildren, mothers do sedentary kinds of work for their adult children such as ironing, sewing and knitting. Men's activities, however, are more oriented towards sociability and conviviality.

Some 17 per cent of the activities men participate in for their descendants are meals taken together and 19 per cent are other sociable and leisure-time activities. Among household activities, only cooking, which is associated with conviviality, plays a considerable role so far as men are concerned (13 per cent of all the activities they undertake). Odd jobs and gardening only constitute 4 per cent and 3 per cent respectively of the tasks that they undertake for descendants. Despite this, and as Dechaux (1990) finds, a large proportion of DIY is conducted by parents for children no longer living in their household. For example, 13 per cent of individuals called upon their parents for help with DIY activities such as painting or electrical work. Consequently, there is a distinct difference between what men do for parents and parents-in-law and what they do for their children and grandchildren. Women's activities for descendants and ascendants, however, are not so starkly differentiated. For women, cooking is always present and sociable activities also play a major role in both cases, whatever the kinship group under consideration. The only difference so far as women are concerned is that while women do housework (6 per cent of all activity) and shopping (9 per cent) for ascendants, they do not do these activities for descendants (3 per cent and 1 per cent respectively). On the contrary, they do the household linen for their children and grandchildren (6 per cent of all the activities they undertake) but not for their parents and parents-in-law (1 per cent).

In a further study in France, Pitrou (1990) comes to much the same conclusions about the gendering of this type of activity. She finds that help by ascendants for descendants is very heavily gendered with women preparing meals, doing general housework and washing and ironing clothes while men provide help in the realms of activities such as DIY and car maintenance. Delbes (1983), furthermore, in an analysis of the services provided to independent children living in another household, discovers that 24.3 per cent of the fathers' help is in the realm of DIY (but just 4.8 per cent of women's contribution), while 27.3 per cent of the mother's help is in the sphere of knitting and sewing (but just 4.0 per cent for fathers) and 11.3 per cent is in the realm of housework (just 4.2 per cent for fathers). The gender division of domestic work, therefore, is replicated in kinship exchanges from ascendants to descendants in France.

Unfortunately, however, such detailed information on help provided by ascendants for descendants in other households is not available in any similar form in recent research conducted in Britain so far as is known. As such, it is difficult to discern whether the gender divisions of ascendants' work for descendants is less or more rigidly structured in Britain than in France. The only comparable data that is available concerns the work conducted by children for parents who live in the same household. Morrow (1996) finds that there is a rigid gender division of domestic labour so far as the work which boys and girls undertake in their households for parents, which mirrors the gender divisions of domestic labour discussed in the previous chapter. Moreover, in a study of Leicester, Williams and Windebank (1998b) find that 25 per cent of the children in the households interviewed had been paid to engage in particular tasks and again the work for which they received payment was heavily gendered. Boys tended to be paid to do activities such as washing the car and doing the mowing while girls tended to receive money for doing the ironing, the housework and child care. It was not only young children, however, who were paid by ascendants to engage in domestic activities. Such activity is also subject to payments when adults are involved. In the Leicester study, it was found that although exchanges involving fathers and mothers were not based on payments, those involving sons, daughters, brothers, sisters, uncles and aunts did often involve the exchange of money for goods and services provided. In many of these cases, however, such payments were a way of providing financial aid to the kinship member in a manner that did not appear to be 'charity'. For example, it was a way of redistributing income to an unemployed member of the family in a way deemed acceptable to both parties. Such payments for kinship exchanges, moreover, are not unique to Britain. In France, Madinier and Mouillard (1984) find that when young people aged 18 to 25 years old engage in activity for their parents, 23 per cent have been paid for their work by their parents. Contrary to the view that all kinship work is unpaid and based upon 'kinship obligation' in the form of a 'labour of love' (Dechaux, 1996; Finch and Groves, 1983), these British and French studies find that such exchanges are sometimes monetized and based upon cash exchange. It is clear, however, that the motivations for such payments are redistributive and are not based on the same rationality as exchanges in the formal sphere.

In sum, so far as kinship economies are concerned, the evidence from both Britain and France displays that women not only undertake more kinship work than men but that there is a gender division of kinship activity which mirrors the gender divisions prevalent in domestic work. Comparatively speaking, moreover, it appears that if anything, women undertake a slightly greater proportion of all kinship work in France than in Britain. When this finding is thus coupled with the fact that French women's insertion into full-time paid work is greater and French men's contribution to the domestic workload is equal to or smaller than that of their British counterparts, the result is that the 'triple burden' will be both more widespread and intensely felt by French women than by those in Britain. Furthermore, by examining kinship activities, it becomes clear that in both countries, when women require help to carry out the routine domestic and caring work in their own household, they often rely on their women ascendants and descendants rather than on their male partners. Indeed, almost all women find themselves in an inter-dependent circuit of exchanges with other women with whom they have kinship ties whereby they fill in for them by doing a part of these other women's domestic and caring work. As such, there exists a relative interchangeability of women at the service of each matrimonial family, such as where the mother intervenes to permit the daughter to deliver her household responsibilities while also taking on employment (Chabaud-Rychter and Fougeyrollas-Schwebel, 1989; Dechaux, 1990). This inter-dependence of women, however, merely serves to perpetuate the cleavage in men's and women's roles since it reduces the need for a renegotiation of the gender division of domestic labour even when the woman in the household is unable or unwilling to carry out the traditional duties of the 'woman at home'.

Non-kinship exchanges of labour within the neighbourhood

Community work, however, does not only cover kinship economies. Besides engaging in activity for kin, there is also non-kinship exchange which is undertaken by household members for friends and acquaintances living in other households. On the whole, this activity occurs within the neighbourhood. The degree to which such material and non-material assistance is provided, nevertheless, is in major part dependent upon the nature and extent of the social networks in which individuals are embedded. Here, therefore, we examine both the magnitude and character of non-kin exchange undertaken by men and women in the two countries.

Amount of non-kin exchange undertaken by men and women

Examining the extent to which men and women in Britain and France engage in neighbourhood exchange with friends and neighbours, the primary issue is that there is very little research that directly focuses on this issue. The vast majority of the evidence available tends to be a by-product of investigations into either other forms of work or the way in which care is provided for specific social groups. As such, the evidence available on non-kinship exchange is the most limited of all the forms of work examined in this book. Nevertheless, some clear trends can be identified.

In Britain, indicative evidence that non-kinship community work is the province of women more than men is provided by the General Household Survey data on elder-care. This reveals that in 1990, 5 per cent of all women aged over 16 were providing care for a friend or neighbour compared with just 3 per cent of adult men. In 1985, similar gender inequalities existed with 4 per cent of all adult women and 2 per cent of all adult men providing such care (OPCS, 1992: Table 15). Comparing the relative magnitude of non-kinship care with kinship care, this survey reveals that of those who provide care to dependent people living in private households other than their own, 26 per cent of these carers were caring for a friend or neighbour in 1985 and 25 per cent in 1990 (OPCS, 1992: Table 11). It could be calculated, therefore, that about three-quarters of all community care is kinship-based and one-quarter non-kinship oriented. Indeed, for some households, this even involves taking friends into their own household in order to administer care. As the OPCS (1992) found, 2 per cent of carers who had a dependent living with them in their own household were caring for a friend rather than kin or a spouse. This was the same in 1990 as in 1985.

Although directly comparable statistics are not available for France, the same general tendency of women undertaking the majority of non-kinship work can still be identified. Chabaud-Rychter and Fougeyrollas-Schwebel (1989) find that some 4 per cent of all activities undertaken by men and women are conducted for non-kinship acquaintances living outside their household. Given that women conduct a larger number of activities on average than men, the result is that women undertake a greater volume of non-kinship based community work than men.

This is reinforced by a further study of support given by relatives and friends to single parents conducted in 1990 among 336 mothers living in Normandy who were divorced or separated for more than four years and received, or had previously received, benefits from the Family Allowance Fund (Martin, 1996). This identified that the vast majority of support from friends given to these single mothers came from women rather than men. Nevertheless, there were some distinct differences in the nature of assistance provided to different groups of these single parents. The less qualified and lower-income single mothers were much more likely to rely on kin than on non-kin for help and to state that they had few if any friends than the better qualified and higher-income households. Of the less qualified, who were more likely to be unemployed, one in two said that they had no close friends, and only one in six claimed more than five friends. In contrast, the more qualified single parents, who were more likely to be employed, relied less on kin and their social networks were highly friendship based: four out of ten claimed more than five close friends and only one said that she had no close friends. The result is that the more qualified were the most likely to say that they received their principal support from friends (60 per cent compared with 21 per cent). Overall, they were much less likely than the non-qualified single parents to feel that they were 'lonely' (20 per cent as against 50 per cent) and more likely to feel that their social network was 'rich, wide and complex' (60 per cent compared with 25 per cent).

This division of social networks and support for single mothers according to qualifications was also found in a French survey conducted in 1992 by Gautier among 158 single mothers living in a working-class district of Reims. Reported in Lefaucheur and Martin (1997), this reveals that many single mothers were very isolated (23 per cent never invited anybody to their house, 16 per cent were never invited to visit anybody besides their parents) and these tended to be much more likely to be unqualified and unemployed. In contrast, the higher qualified and employed single mothers felt well supported, meeting friends frequently and feeling that they provided support. Such polarization in non-kinship support among single mothers is reinforced by a broader study of the employed and unemployed by Lemel (1996) who finds in a study of 10 000 households that non-kinship assistance is much greater in higher educated, managerial and higher-income households. These findings are echoed elsewhere in France (CERC, 1994; Le Gall, 1996).

This has a resonance with the finding in Britain that social networks tend to rapidly deplete when people are made redundant, resulting in the long-term unemployed having few if any friends and those few friends that they do have tending to be in the same situation with the result that the unemployed have fewer people to call upon for help (McKee, 1987; Morris, 1990; White, 1983). Further evidence of this trend is identified in Britain in the study of a deprived neighbourhood in Leicester. Here, 1.9 per cent of all the work undertaken in the households investigated had been carried out by neighbours or friends. Such activity, however, was strongly correlated with employment status. Those households with one or more in employment were much more likely to give and receive help from friends or neighbours than those households in which all were unemployed. However, it was principally women in these households who were the major providers of activity to friends and neighbours rather than men, but only to a minor extent. Similarly, the earlier study of the Isle of Sheppey by Pahl (1984) finds that women conducted 58 per cent of all of the work households undertook for non-relatives who lived outside their household and that multiple-earner households were more likely to provide and receive help than no-earner households. This is replicated in the data collected under the Social Change and Economic Life Initiative that investigated the strength of people's 'support networks'. As Gallie (1985) reports, the availability of support seemed to be linked to employment status in that the unemployed received less help than those who were in employment and had smaller social networks. Morris (1995) finds much the same in her study of Hartlepool. She finds that a greater proportion of the long-term unemployed were unable to name any close friends (24 per cent) than were the securely employed (16 per cent) and were less likely to receive aid from friends and neighbours than were the employed. This is again echoed in a study of a former coal-mining village in central Scotland conducted by Turner *et al.* (1985) and a study of a working-class estate in West Belfast (Leonard, 1994). In all cases, moreover, it was women rather than men who tended to conduct a slightly higher proportion of such non-kinship exchange. Comparing kin and non-kin support, therefore, it appears as Morris (1995) has asserted elsewhere that women show a higher propensity to engage in kinship work while in the realm of non-kin support, the gender division of activity seems to be slightly more equal.

Gender variations in the character of non-kin exchange

The finding in both Britain and France is that when the character of non-kin exchange is examined, the gender divisions identified in domestic work and kinship economies are yet again mirrored. As Chabaud-Rychter and Fougeyrollas-Schwebel (1989) identify in France, the gender division of non-kin exchange is very similar to the gender divisions of kinship economies with women conducting much of the 'female'-oriented, routine and open-ended work such as housework, caring and emotional support, while men tend to engage in more 'masculine'-oriented, non-routine and closed-ended activities such as DIY projects and odd-jobs such as car repair and gardening, often working with the friend or acquaintance in order to complete the task.

The same results are discovered in Britain concerning this gendered division of non-kinship exchange. Pahl (1984) finds that men undertook 87 per cent of all of the gardening undertaken for non-relatives living in other households, 92 per cent of all repairs and carpentry and 78 per cent of the decorating while women undertook all of the baby-sitting, housework, laundry, dressmaking, as well as 86 per cent of the shopping. Williams and Windebank (1998b), in their study of a deprived neighbourhood of Leicester, find that the gender divisions of non-kinship exchange mirror those identified elsewhere in the economy. Furthermore, they find that where such exchanges take place, they often involve cash exchanges (and, to a lesser extent, gifts). In major part, this is perhaps a result of the type of neighbourhood being examined where the bestowing of cash is deemed the appropriate response to a greater extent than in more affluent populations where a gift is the more accepted form of recompense and money would be frowned upon. Nevertheless, some distinct gender divisions exist. Where such work is undertaken for friends or neighbours on a paid basis, it is mostly men who conduct such work while when it is undertaken on an unpaid basis, it is mostly women. This is because the vast majority of such work undertaken by women is composed of social and emotional support rather than providing particular goods and/or services. For example, when households were given a list of various common household services and goods which they commonly acquire, just 1.9 per cent of these came from friends and neighbours. Indeed, when interviewees were asked why they had not undertaken such a form of work for other households, most asserted that they were either too busy in their own household and lacked the time, or that they had never been asked or knew nobody requiring help, thus reinforcing the notion of a community characterized by anomie and few kinship ties.

Nevertheless, 61.5 per cent of the households surveyed asserted that they felt part of some community, group or network and 38.5 per cent stated that such a community had helped them recently. This does not contradict the evidence that little work had been undertaken on such a basis. Instead, it reveals that such a community, network or group, where it provides help, tends to do so in terms of social and/or emotional support rather than in terms of concrete activities. This was borne out by the responses on how such communities, networks or groups had helped the participants. Typical responses were that they helped by 'providing understanding', a 'social life' and 'emotional support'. In nearly every case, moreover, it was women who were the principal providers of such support to these households. Perhaps this is also the reason why in similar studies conducted in France, very little support from friends and neighbours was identified. Both Foudi *et al.* (1982) and Barthe (1988) examined whether friends and neighbours undertook a range of tasks but omitted to consider the issue of emotional support which many participants do not consider to be the provision of 'work' to households. Indeed, Leonard (1994) finds much the same in her study of West Belfast. She describes how the vast majority of the men in her study would keep score of the reciprocal favours given and returned and could immediately recall who owed them what and what they owed to others. Women, in contrast, when asked whether they ever did favours for others, mostly replied 'No'. Yet during the ensuing conversations, many mentioned casually activities such as cooking, shopping and caring for old or sick people or instances where they had provided emotional support. Their off-hand treatment of these activities indicates that no counter favour was expected or even considered and often favours were directed towards those least able to reciprocate them such as the sick and elderly. As Leonard (1994) notes, male favours tended to be focused upon producing something tangible. Hence, the receiver is always reminded of the labour of the giver. Women's non-kinship work, in contrast, tended to be more intangible centring on emotional support, thus reinforcing the findings identified in Leicester.

Moreover, it is not just social and material support that non-kinship networks provide. As Edwards and Duncan (1996: 121) argue in relation to lone mothers, they also provide 'systems of beliefs of moralities and shared social identities'. These, furthermore, are spatially variable. As they state, the degree to which material and social support can be utilized may well depend on socially created or re-created neighbourhood moral beliefs about mothers working and about lone motherhood. In turn, these beliefs may play a role in the ability of lone mothers to take up paid employment. Indeed, transgressing the local norms or moralities may result in any available friendship (or kinship-based) child-care support being withdrawn. Jordan *et al.* (1992) similarly find on a deprived council estate in Exeter the importance of the need to comply with local neighbourhood systems of values. Economic rationality was less important than moral ideas about roles and responsibilities in mothers' uptake of paid work. The lone mothers had a stronger desire for paid work than mothers in heterosexual couples but had to juggle this with the local morality that mothers should prioritize caring for their own children and only 'fit in' paid work where this did not conflict with their primary caring responsibilities. These beliefs acted as a major constraint on these women's ability to draw upon non-kinship support so that they could enter employment. The spatial variability of such moral beliefs will depend upon the history of women's insertion into the formal labour market, local cultural traditions concerning women's employment and a host of other social, institutional and environmental factors, all of which combine to produce specific local beliefs and practices (see Williams and Windebank, 1998a).

The result is that in some localities and regions in the two countries, women will assist one another, particularly with children, in order to facilitate their entry into the employment sphere while in others they may not, or may not help particular groups of women due to the local cultural mores concerning who should be employed and who should not, as well as what sort of employment they should be doing. What is certain, however, whatever the social mores, is that in France, the higher participation of women in full-time employment, longer working hours and more continuous employment will mean that there is a smaller pool of women available than in Britain in the community to help out as friends (or family). The result is that French women will have less access to informal support networks of other women upon whom to call.

Conclusions: women's triple burden

In sum, the above discussion suggests that there is little difference between the two countries so far as community work is concerned but that where evidence for variation exists, it is in fact in Britain that men are participating in a slightly larger share of the overall community workload. Consequently, while cross-national comparisons of paid work alone usually conclude that 'progress in gender relations' is greater in France due to women's higher participation in employment, especially full-time employment, this chapter in conjunction with Chapter 3 displays that when the gender division of domestic work is coupled with the gender division of community work, such a conclusion is perhaps rather hasty. Comparing the differences between Britain and France, women's increased entry into paid work in France has not been matched by a comparatively greater renegotiation of the division of domestic labour and neither is the extent of French women's community work by any means less than that of British women. Quite the opposite if anything. In the previous chapter, we showed that the renegotiation of the gender division of domestic labour is no greater in France than Britain, meaning that women's 'double burden' is heavier in France than Britain when French women's higher insertion into paid work combined with their domestic workload is taken into account. Here, by revealing that community work is no less gendered in France than Britain, we suggest that this 'triple burden' is more of a problem for French than British women. The meanings of such findings for theorizations of women's work and for the future of policy to improve women's work situation are developed in Part II of the book.

Part II

Women's Work in an Anglo-French Cross-national Perspective: Theory and Policy

5
Theorizing Women's Work

We have seen in Chapter 2 that women's position in paid work in Britain and France has been characterized by both similarities and differences. On the one hand, women's activity levels are very similar in the two countries: they occupy the majority of part-time jobs; they are more likely to have temporary jobs in both countries; their pay is less than that of men on average; and they experience similar levels of segregation in employment. On the other hand, there is less continuity in employment for British women, higher levels of part-time working and greater wage inequality than in France. In France, by contrast, women have higher unemployment rates and higher rates of temporary work, but have penetrated highly qualified occupations to a greater degree than British women. In Chapters 3 and 4 we have found that despite these significant differences in women's position in the labour market, women in both countries undertake the majority of the domestic and community work. However, where evidence of national variation does exist, it appears that it is British men who undertake more domestic and community work than their French counterparts.

In this chapter, we explore the theoretical arguments and explanations which may help to illuminate these similarities and differences in women's position in paid and unpaid work.[1] In doing so, we shall be attempting to answer two principal questions: on the one hand, to what extent can these theorizations/explanations simultaneously account for both the universal features of and the societal variations in women's work in Britain and France that we have identified. On the other hand, to what extent is it true, as has been suggested by much cross-national comparative research relating to women's paid work, that it is primarily the role of state policy, and in particular its social policy, which accounts for cross-national variation in women's work situations? Two sets of theorizations/explanations exist. The first we will call 'universalistic theorisations'. These seek to provide universal theoretical models for understanding the gender division of labour across societies based on over-arching analyses of social structures or economic behaviour. The second we will call 'particularistic explanations'. This approach does not involve an over-arching analysis of social structures, is based more often on empirical research and focuses on one or more explanatory variable.

Before examining these arguments, a brief overview of the development of theorizations relating to women's paid and unpaid work is necessary. Up until the early 1960s, much research made the assumption that women's role in paid work was unimportant and that gendered divisions in paid work were uninteresting and relied upon common stereotypes about women (Dex, 1985). These false assumptions in sociology and economics led to women being excluded from explicit analysis in empirical work and to the notion of the 'unisex' worker. However, growth in feminist debate about women's role in paid and unpaid work and rising women's activity rates caused women's work to be taken more seriously. Initially, interest related to women's paid work and empirical studies began to investigate their position in employment, asking first similar questions as had been asked for men or using gender as an explanatory variable (Dex, 1985) and then seeking to explain differences by comparison with men (key questions being: why do women work less than men? why are women paid less than men? and why do they do different jobs from men? (Walby, 1990)). A number of theorizations of both universalistic and particularistic types began to seek to account for the specificities of women's employment: Human Capital theories, Marxist-Feminist, Liberal-Feminist and Labour-Market Segmentation theories.

At the same time, major reconceptualizations were beginning to be made in relation to women's role within the family, including notably the assertion that the home was not merely a sphere of consumption, but remained a place of production. Until then, not only was the economic importance of domestic labour ignored, but the relationship between women and domestic labour was deemed natural within mainstream sociology. The Parsonian view of the family dominated in which women's role as homemaker was seen as functional, and thus indispensable, to the stability of society

(Parsons, 1955). The family existed as a social institution because it performed essential functions for society: those of socialization of children and the stabilization of adult personalities. The relationship between men and women was considered basically to be one of being different but equal. Parsons conceptualized gender relations in terms of sex roles: men in the family performed the instrumental role and were orientated to the external world while women performed the expressive role looking after the internal needs of the family members. These roles, according to Parsons, must be kept separate otherwise there would be conflict and tension between the occupational structure and the kinship system. He argued that sharing work was less efficient than dividing it according to natural ability and that progress towards maximization of efficiency could only occur by specialization. In this manner, he justified and encouraged the gender division of labour and the specialization of women in home and family activities.

However, from the 1970s onwards the validity of conceiving of the family in this way came under fire from various angles, particularly in feminist circles. The Parsonian functionalist view of role differentiation was assailed on the basis that gender is not an essential trait but is constructed actively within historical and social locations, including domestic work, where gender relations are produced and reproduced on a daily basis (Berk, 1985). Indeed, research on instrumental and expressive traits failed to establish these or other characteristics as gender-specific (Ferree, 1990; Hiller, 1984). Consequently, it became necessary to decide why women maintain the relationship which they do to domestic labour, this being seen as a key to understanding women's oppression and exclusion from the labour market. The ensuing debates surrounding domestic labour sought to explain why women are responsible for it, what role domestic labour plays in the functioning of society and how women's position in domestic labour relates to their position in paid work. As such, existing theories were further developed while new universalistic theorizations – Feminist Marxism and Radical Feminism – appeared.

While some of these universalistic and particularistic theorizations have explicitly sought to explain variations in the division of labour across space, only fairly recently (that is, since the early 1980s) has this been the subject of detailed empirical analysis. This has focused on women's position in the labour force in particular and has helped to isolate the variables which give rise to the different features of women's employment in different countries and regions (Anxo and Daune-Richard, 1991; Barrrère-Maurisson *et al.*, 1989; Bradshaw *et al.*, 1996; Crompton with Le feuvre, 1996; Dex *et al.*, 1993; Duncan, 1994; Gregory, 1989; Hantrais, 1990; Hantrais and Walters, 1994; Jenson, 1986; O'Reilly, 1994, 1995; O'Reilly and Fagan, 1998; Pfau-Effinger, 1993; Rubery *et al.*, 1995, 1996, 1996a). This body of work has given rise to a number of additional particularistic explanations for women's position in paid work, which we group together under the heading of 'societal' approaches.

Universalist theorizations

The universalistic theories concerning women's work presented here fall into two basic categories: the first consists of the Microeconomists and the second, the rest. These two categories of theories hold not merely different views on gender, but opposing philosophical and political ideas on how society operates, the former being based on the notions of individualism and the latter on those of structuralism. The extent to which theorists choose to tip the scales of interpretation towards individualism or structuralism is a matter of ideological and political choice, this choice being attributable to their general perception of society. The essential difference between individualist- (for example, Microeconomist) and structuralist-orientated theorists (for example, Marxist and/or Radical Feminist) is the extent to which they accept or reject the socio-economic and political order in general, and more specifically in this case, the situation of women. In other words, the difference lies between those who find this order tolerable, either in a positive sense or because they believe it to be the only possible option, and those who find it intolerable and insist on the need for change. The less tolerable a theorist perceives the inequalities and injustices in society, the less likely she/he is to accept that this situation can be the product of individuals' choices. Analysing society in terms of a social structure based on class (social or gender) is a method of explaining an intolerable situation in such a way that change remains possible. That is, change can be brought about by removing the mesh of power and hierarchy woven by a particular social structure in which individuals are caught up at present. To focus less on the nature and origin of the structural constraints under which individuals make personal choices is to shift the argument away from how to engender progress and to accept the *status quo*. Consequently, change appears far less likely (Windebank, 1991). In sum, there-fore, the perceived importance of structural constraints has much to do with whether a theorist wants change in women's situation to be brought about and the extent to which she/he thinks such a transformation possible.

In this section, we commence with the more individualist ac-counts and then move on to the structuralist explanations for women's position in paid and unpaid work. In each case, we first briefly review how the theory explains gender divisions in such work and following this, how it would explain the cross-national variations identified in Chapters 2, 3 and 4. At the outset, how-ever, it needs to be made explicit that the explanations of each theory for the cross-national similarities and differences are derived from an extrapolation of the respective theories by the authors. Up until now few of these theories have examined paid and unpaid work in cross-national perspective.

Microeconomic theorizations

Theoretical premises

Within this discussion of Microeconomic theorizations, we will look at three principal sets of arguments: first, Human Capital Theory, which explains women's position within the labour market; sec-ond, the New Home Economics, which looks at how the couple divides its combined labour between the home and the market; and third, Hakim's more recent and controversial arguments con-cerning the diversification of women's priorities regarding family and employment.

First, therefore, we discuss Human Capital Theory. G. S. Becker, an American of the Chicago School of Economics (Becker, 1965), and his followers (Johnson and Stafford, 1974; Lloyd and Niemi, 1979; Polacheck and Siebert, 1993) developed Human Capital Theory in an attempt primarily to understand workers' position in the workforce. It is based on the assumption that the choices and de-cisions of the actors from both demand- and supply-sides of the labour market determine the position of workers in the labour force. Workers are viewed as a stock of human capital and investments in human capital produce a certain degree of productive capacity. The general hypothesis is that the more productive workers are, the more senior their positions in the labour force will be and the more money they will earn. Hence, if women are paid less than men it is because they are less productive workers. According to this theory, women generally make different decisions from men regarding the time spent in education, the type of studies, on-the-job training, the acceptance of full or part-time work and the continuation of their careers after the arrival of children, resulting in different investment profiles for men and for women. The result of these differences is a lower productivity for 'female workers, . . . which is according to this approach, the main reason that their chance of achieving higher-level positions or higher earnings is smaller than that of men' (Van Doorne-Huiskes and Van Hoof, 1995: 107). According to the Human Capital School of thought, employers invest in the human capital of their employees and calculate the long-term benefits of their investments. Their expectation is that women are more likely than men to have discontinuous careers and to occupy part-time jobs when they have children. These expectations result in employers being less willing to invest in women's human capital.

Second, we will discuss the New Home Economics approach. As far as unpaid work is concerned, it was also G. S. Becker who first developed a conceptualization of the household as a production unit within a microeconomic or neo-classical perspective (Becker, 1965) dubbed the 'New Home Economics'. Until then, if the household featured at all in the calculations of individuals' behaviour in the market, it was as a place of consumption of market goods and services and the time spent within it was considered leisure. Becker's starting point was that, as a microeconomist, he had found himself obliged to modify his economic model in order to explain the growing number of married women remaining in the labour force. Previously, the microeconomic model of the determination of labour supply had been based on the idea that the individual chooses between more work or more leisure. Thus, women entering the labour market in increasing numbers could only be explained by microeconomists as a change in preference for work as opposed to leisure which appeared wholly incongruous with the social values of the time. To explain this phenomenon in more realistic terms, Becker introduced the factor of 'household production' to his analyses. This allowed married women's entry into the labour force to be explained in terms of a choice between two types of production: market or domestic.

For him, therefore, the family is not purely a unit of consumption, or a black box, into which commodities disappear and from which utility – that is, satisfaction of a need or desire – is produced. The household, according to this analysis, has a productive function, organization and division of labour of its own just like any business or firm. Market goods are not finalities in their own right but require the input of the time of household members to be rendered ready for consumption. This combination of market goods and household time is 'domestic production', the main function of which is the procreation and rearing of children (Becker, 1976). Employing this model, the way was open for him and other microeconomists to analyse how couples choose rationally (or intentionally) to divide their combined time between employment and domestic work according to the economic circumstances in which they find themselves and to their own abilities and preferences.

Becker (1976, 1981) suggested that couples arrange the division of labour in the household to maximize family economic well-being. Successful families, he maintained, must determine the combination of commodities that maximizes their utility and the division of labour that most efficiently creates these commodities. This formulation, similar to Parsons', justified gender divisions in terms of the service of family utility. While this and many other aspects of the theory were controversial, its identification of household production as an important phenomenon worthy of scholarly attention proved to be a major contribution to the study of women's unpaid work.

A number of French researchers have taken up Becker's approach to look at the division of labour within heterosexual couples, for example, Lemmenicier (1980, 1988, and Levy-Garboua 1981) and Sofer (1985, 1986). Applying the notion of the household as a production unit, Lemmenicier (1980) and Sofer (1986) assert that married women specialize in domestic labour rather than paid work when their opportunity costs of working in the market are too great: that is, when the cost of paying for market alternatives to their domestic production, such as prepared meals and especially the prohibitive cost of child care, is not adequately covered by what they could earn in a job. Sofer in particular insists that it is the number of children in a family that is the determining factor when women decide whether or not to take employment, reflecting the empirical reality of her societal context.

On the level of the couple, therefore, husbands and wives specialize in employment and domestic labour respectively when the husband can earn more on the market than his wife and when the wife cannot cover the costs of running the home with her potential salary. From this, Lemmenicier concludes that the more specialized the couple's division of labour, the higher are the benefits of marriage and the less the likelihood of divorce. However, on this question of specialization within the couple, Lemmenicier and Sofer diverge, each according to his or her own political sensibilities. Lemmenicier and Levy-Garboua (1981) argue that men and women share a common utility function. In other words, they have common interests to which end they specialize in different forms of activity and exchange their specialized skills. All the while, they attempt to maximize the satisfaction derived from their efforts by mobilizing their forces in market and domestic production in the most efficient way possible.

Sofer (1986), on the other hand, maintains that this assumption of a common utility function masks the conflicts that exist between husbands and wives and hides the disadvantaged and heavily con- strained position in which many women find themselves. Sofer argues that husbands and wives have different utility functions which must be taken into consideration when explaining the choices they make. In this way, therefore, Sofer attempts to express her feminist sensi- bilities through the medium of the microeconomic model which she insists is capable of supporting positions other than economi- cally liberal or socially conservative ones. However, her decision to work with this model, and the fact that it focuses on individuals as opposed to social groups separates her from the more structural 'feminist' theorists discussed below. The microeconomists, adopting an individualist stance, assert that whatever the constraints, women always have a choice in these matters. For example, Sofer (1986) insists that women choose to form a couple, motivated by the de- sire for children, but that they can ultimately decide against this. Moreover, from this assertion that women choose marriage, Lemmenicier (1988) argues that no *a priori* exploitation exists in the marriage contract since it is negotiated between two free and legally equal partners. Nevertheless, within this approach, it is taken for granted that it is women who always have an absolute advan- tage in going into the type of employment which is as a housewife, producing children (Lemmenicier, 1988). This is because they have – until a scientific breakthrough drastically alters the human repro- duction process – an absolute biological advantage in this sphere over men.

Third, and finally, we will explore Hakim's propositions. Most recently Hakim (1991, 1995, 1996) has adopted a Beckerian approach and sought to explain women's nature and pattern of labour force participation in terms of their individual choice, arguing that the heterogeneity of women's employment statuses can be explained in large part by the heterogeneity of their ambitions and life objectives (Crompton, 1997). She argues that individual tastes and preferences are more important than material or structural factors, factors which are considered to be highly significant by other universalist and particularist theorists as we show below. For Hakim there are two 'qualitatively different' types of working woman, the 'committed' and the 'uncommitted', the former giving priority to their employment careers, the latter to their domestic roles. Women belonging to the second group will have paid employment as a secondary activity and are in low-skilled, low-paid, part-time, casual and temporary jobs more often than in skilled, permanent full-time jobs. She argues that the size of each group will vary spatially and over time, and that some women will switch between groups over their lifetimes. Occupational segregation, which hitherto had been poorly explained by the microeconomic approach (see Dex, 1985), is explained by Hakim's theorization. She (1996: 180) asserts that 'occupational segregation . . . has been reconstructed in the late twentieth century to provide separate occupations and jobs for women following the marriage career, which allows only non-committed contingent work and non-career jobs which are always subordinate to non-market activities'. Criticized for attaching too much importance to individual choice and for ignoring structural constraints (see Ginn *et al.*, 1996; Crompton, 1997).[2] Hakim's theorization did succeed in raising the profile of agency in the determination of women's paid work situations.[3] Once again echoing the theorists of the New Home Economics school, Hakim (1991, 1995, 1996) also sees women's tastes and preferences as being in part biologically determined by their role in reproduction. She argues that the fact that women are divided into 'the committed' and 'the uncommitted' serves to amplify the effect of natural masculine characteristics of assertiveness, dominance, aggressiveness and competitiveness, with the result that men are disproportionately successful in paid work (Crompton, 1997).

Evaluation of cross-national similarities and differences in women's work
How, therefore, would these microeconomic approaches interpret the similarities and differences in women's work in Britain and France described in Part 1? Starting with the similarities in terms of women's

labour force participation, it would be argued that men and women in both countries are pursuing a rational strategy of maximizing household utility as described above. The growth in married women's paid work in recent years in both countries could be explained within the New Home Economics approach by the fact that married women have been increasingly able to recoup the opportunity costs of having a job (costs of meal preparation and other domestic tasks, costs of child care) from their salaries, hence rendering paid work attractive. The fact that women in both countries suffer, on average, from lower pay and greater segregation in employment than men would be explained by Human Capital Theory in terms of women's lower productivity compared with men based on their fewer educational qualifications, less work experience and less training. Their greater concentration in temporary and part-time work would be explained in terms of their individual preferences for this type of work. In Hakim's terms, an 'uncommitted' group of women, who have amassed less human capital in terms of education and training than 'committed' women (and men), are more likely to 'choose' part-time, temporary work in less-skilled jobs which attract lower pay.

For some Microeconomists, however, the fact that French women are more likely to enter full-time employment than British women, is due to the greater state support given them to do so. This means that when women calculate the opportunity costs of working in the market in Britain and France, the state support offered in France means that the cost of paying for market alternatives such as child care is more adequately covered than in Britain where the cost of market alternatives is more prohibitive when analysed in the context of what they could earn in a job. Furthermore, net income may be higher in France for women working full-time under the influence of the operation of the national tax and social security system as well as of the operation of national pay minima (see Dex *et al.*, 1993). Others may hypothesize that French women have a greater commitment to paid work over a domestic career than British women and that this difference in working patterns is a manifestation of this. Similarly the greater continuity in paid work over the family formation period in France could also be explained by the same range of factors. The greater penetration by French women into higher-level occupations would be explained by their greater human capital, while the lower levels of wage inequality between men and women could be accounted for by both their greater presence in higher-level occupations and in full-time work and the impact of wage minima on pay levels.

The microeconomic explanation does not give an explanation for either the higher unemployment rates for French women or their greater presence in temporary work. If it is hypothesized, as Hakim does, that temporary work and part-time work are carried out by 'uncommitted' workers, then it is anomalous for part-time levels among women to be relatively low in France, while rates of women's temporary work are high.

As far as the degree of participation by women in the labour market and the overall division of labour within the couple are concerned, we have seen above that the individualistic nature of the microeconomic approaches enables them to account for many of our empirical findings. However, it is harder within this perspective to account for the gender division of domestic and community work which, as we have shown, remains relatively impervious to change in the labour market. Within the 'rational behaviour' model of the Human Capital and New Home Economics theories, there is no economic explanation for why women with full-time continuous employment, as are found most often in France, should still shoulder the major burden of unpaid work. The only explanations that can offered within this perspective as to why French women still tend to take as great, if not a greater share of the domestic workload than British women, despite their greater presence in full-time employment, is that this is a product of the different personal preferences in the two nations or the greater gap between women and men in French couples, relative to those in British couples, in their abilities to undertake domestic work. For these Microeconomists, therefore, there is a tendency to fall-back on individualistic explanations based on the notion of preferences and abilities when no obvious rationalistic economic explanation of a particular situation presents itself.

Marxist-Feminist Theorizations

Theoretical premises

With the arrival of the feminist movement in the late 1960s and early 1970s, a number of Marxist-inspired feminist theories began to question the lack of concern within orthodox Marxism for women's oppression and its inability to explain women's relationship to domestic and wage labour. Marx had not discussed the employment of women to any great extent. He had instead identified differing forms of industrial labour reserve (floating, latent and stagnant) which were thought to be vital to the process of capital accumulation. The principal work on women in capitalism until that time was Engels' analysis of the family (originally published 1884; reprinted 1972). In this work, Engels contended that the family was an anachronism and marginal to the survival of capitalism since it was a part of the social superstructure and, as such, possessed no material justification. Marxist Feminists set out to explain that women's oppression within capitalism does indeed have a material, and not merely an ideological, basis. That material basis is domestic labour. Indeed, the study of domestic labour in the early 1970s was very much a part of feminism's struggle to find an identity apart from socialism and Marxist structuralist analysis that had sidelined women's particular concerns and problems.

Marxist Feminism (with the prime emphasis on the Marxist rather than the Feminist being reflected in the order of the words) tacitly or explicitly addressed the question of women and domestic labour in capitalist society in order to fuse women's liberation to the class struggle (Dalla Costa and James, 1972; Gardiner, 1975; Godchau, 1970; James, 1975; Meillassoux, 1981; Moynot, 1978). It argued that capital is dependent upon the unpaid work performed within the family by women for its survival since the role of women as reproducers of the workforce and as a 'reserve army of labour' are essential and not marginal to the extraction of surplus value. Thus, although agreeing with orthodox Marxism that capitalism is the major reason for the subjugation of womankind, Marxist Feminism put more emphasis upon women's secondary status in capitalist society through its focus upon women's position in the home, using a 'material' analysis of domestic labour. The study of capitalism thus 'no longer stopped at the garden gate' (Williams, 1988: 42).

From the common acknowledgement that women inhabit a different place in the production/reproduction process to men because of their role in domestic labour, separate, but related, debates were engaged within Marxist Feminism concerning women's position in paid work and unpaid work. Three main Marxist-Feminist accounts for gender relations in paid employment followed on from the basic premise that women's patterns of employment were determined by capitalist relations: the cyclical reserve army theory, Braverman's theory and Marxist segmentation theory (Walby, 1990).

Cyclical reserve army theory applies Marx's (1954) notion of industrial labour reserve, which he argued was vital to capital accumulation. The cyclical reserve army theory then holds that women are pulled into employment by capitalism when there is a boom in the economy and returned to the family when there is a recession (Beechey, 1977, 1978; Bruegel, 1979; Milkman, 1976). This theory has been widely criticized and has been disproved by events of the past 25 years (Walby, 1990, 1997).

Braverman's theory, by contrast, argued that women are integrated into the economy over a much longer period and not as a function of cyclical variations (see Braverman, 1974). He explained this in terms of two changes: first, a progressive deskilling of jobs in contemporary monopoly capitalism as a result of a Taylorist-inspired[4] managerial strategy, which led to women taking these newly deskilled jobs; second, by the progressive shift of household tasks (for example, clothes making, bread making) to the factory, hence reducing the amount of domestic labour required in the home and releasing women for paid work outside the home. Braverman's theory has generated considerable debate as to whether such a process is taking place in the UK, whether indeed women's employment has grown mostly in less-skilled areas of employment and whether the amount of time spent on housework by women has in fact decreased in recent years (see Chapter 3 and for a review of debates, Walby, 1990; 1997).[5]

Finally, Marxist Segmentation theory (Edwards, 1979; Edwards *et al.*, 1975; Gordon, 1972) has offered an approach which has sprung from Labour Segmentation theory (which is described in full below) and which seeks to understand divisions (by gender and ethnicity) within the labour market in terms of the outcome of the struggle between capital and labour. It argues that employers segment the labour market as part of a divide and rule strategy, hence preventing the proletariat from resisting the demands of capitalism. This strategy is seen as one of many used over time to attempt to control the proletariat. Pre-existing divisions based on gender and ethnicity are used as the basis for a segmented workforce.

The debate in relation to women's unpaid labour also took place in the 1970s. This concerned whether or not women's domestic labour was unproductive or productive labour in a Marxist sense. Known as the 'domestic labour debates', but perhaps more properly called the Marxist-Feminist domestic labour debates, some argued that domestic labour is unproductive labour and others that it is productive labour. For those who asserted it is unproductive labour, this is because, to be productive in the original Marxist sense, an activity must fulfil both of two criteria: first, it must be exchanged on the market against a wage, and second, it must work directly with capital's means of production to produce commodities which have a calculable exchange value from which surplus value is directly extracted. Domestic labour fulfils neither of these criteria. Such work only produces use-values for consumption in the home and not exchange-values nor surplus value. Since housewives are not employed by capital, their contribution to profit-making, although necessary, is not direct. Women's production of use-values is outside the exchange of labour for wages even though economically part of the creation of surplus value (Gardiner, 1976, 1997; Harris, 1983). It is thus unproductive labour.

Other Marxist Feminists realized, however, that labelling domestic labour 'unproductive' relegated it to a place of secondary importance behind wage labour and consequently rendered women's oppression a side-issue to the class struggle once again. These women set out to argue that domestic labour was indeed productive (Dalla Costa, 1972; Dalla Costa and James, 1972; Edmond and Fleming, 1975; Edmond and Ronay, 1975; Hirschmann, 1975; James, 1975). The initiators of the productive labour thesis were Dalla Costa and James (1972) who contended that the main product of domestic labour, the human being, is no different in nature to any other commodity. Women's domestic labour produces something which is sold to capitalists – namely, labour power – even if women have no legal ownership of it. Domestic labour is therefore productive. As Dalla Costa (1972: 52) argues: 'housework as work is productive in the Marxian sense, that is, producing surplus value', because through child-rearing and the maintenance of labour power, it reproduces and maintains the supply of wage labour. Viewing domestic labour as productive labour, it is argued, shows how women are oppressed in capitalist society. They remain unpaid for their production while men are paid.

As the only difference between wage labour and domestic labour is said to be that domestic labour is unpaid, the call from these feminists was for women to be paid 'Wages for Housework', which would show women's oppression to be a function of capitalism. 'Wages for Housework' would put the burden of reproduction on to the shoulders of the oppressors. The fight for 'Wages for Housework' was therefore intended to be a part of the class struggle because in paying such a wage, the state and capitalists would incur reproduction as a direct cost. However, the 'Wages for Housework' campaign never drew widespread support since it coincided in its practicalities with right-wing proposals to entice women back into the home. Indeed, no feminist theorist in France ever took up this argument (see Windebank, 1991).

In Marxist Feminism, in sum, capitalism is viewed as the primary source of women's oppression; the focus when studying women's subjugation is upon the oppressive capitalist relations under which they live as domestic labourers and the reason for studying domestic labour is to show how capitalism subjugates women as domestic labourers in the home so as to explain their secondary position in the labour market and in capitalist society. How, therefore, would this approach interpret the similarities and differences in France and Britain identified in earlier chapters?

Evaluation of cross-national similarities and differences in women's work

Here, we will first discuss how Marxist-Feminist theories explain the similarities in women's work situations in France and Britain, and then go on to address the issue of the explanation of difference. We will therefore begin with the cyclical reserve army theory. This theory is of limited application, as we have already stated, as it is unable to explain the increasing labour force participation of women which has been seen in both Britain and France through periods of recession (see Maruani, 1985; Rubery and Tarling, 1988).

The increasing role of women in paid work in Britain and France would be explained by Braverman's theory in terms of capitalism's increased use of women in the general process of the deskilling of jobs. Their growing employment in part-time work would also be seen as evidence of this process. There has, indeed, been considerable discussion in French literature of the role women play as a reserve labour source in enabling the French economy to undergo restructuring (Bouillaguet-Bernard *et al.*, 1986; Nicole-Drancourt, 1989).

The aspect of Braverman's theory related to the commodification of household tasks rests on less stable ground. While it is true that certain functions once carried out in the home have been 'commodified', others have been 'privatized' in the sense of being returned to the home while new demands on household work time have arisen. As we have shown in Chapter 3, time spent on domestic work relative to paid work actually increased between the 1970s and 1980s in both countries, while authors such as Gershuny (1978) and Murgatroyd and Neuberger (1997) have identified this trend as a move towards the 'self-service' economy.

Indeed, the relative imperviousness to change of the division of unpaid work between men and women displayed by our Anglo-French comparison is evidence of the general Marxist-Feminist stance that capital remains dependent upon the unpaid work performed within the family by women for its survival. Despite women's entry into the labour force in both countries, they remain responsible for reproducing the workforce through their domestic work. For these analysts, therefore, capitalism is the major reason for the subjugation of womankind and the examination of women's secondary status in capitalist society due to their continuing responsibility for domestic labour highlights that their entry into employment has done little to alter this 'material' basis of their oppression. Furthermore, the contrasting division of responsibility for children between the state and mothers in the two countries, as evidenced by the greater provision of state-sponsored child-care provisions in France, could be explained with reference to the differing needs of the two economies for 'reserve armies' of labour and for types of 'segmented' labour. In other words, the capitalist state in France required more women's labour power to be freed than in Britain.

A similar explanation could therefore be proffered for the differences in women's participation in the labour market in the two countries. Alternatively, the differences in levels of activity for mothers, in levels of part-time work, in degrees of wage inequality and in the occupational profile of women could be deemed to be due to the different speeds of application of the deskilling process in the two countries, Britain being ahead of France. This last theory, however, does not fit well with the different processes underway in France, for example the simultaneous increase of women into higher occupational categories and a reduction in wage differentials with men, while there are increasing levels of part-time work.

Finally, Marxist Segmentation theory explains women's position of inequality in the labour force in Britain and France in a similar way to general Labour Segmentation theories: women's concentration in part-time and temporary work, their lower pay by comparison with men and their greater segregation in low-skilled jobs would be explained by their being part of a disadvantaged secondary labour force. In the case of Marxist Segmentation theory, however, this segmentation of women would be explained by capital's attempt to subjugate labour. The better position which French women occupy in the labour force (higher participation rates, greater concentration in primary sector jobs and greater parity with men in terms of pay), would be imputed not only to capital's greater demand for women's labour but also to women's greater success in resisting capital's segmenting tendencies. Edwards (1979) did recognize that not all gender differences could be explained in terms of segment differences and that women workers required an analysis linked to the history of capitalism in a particular country. He therefore provides an additional explanation for differences in the labour market situation of women in Britain and France.

Feminist-Marxist theorizations (dual-systems approaches)

Theoretical premises

Other theoretical perspectives have questioned Marxism further by asking whether women's position in paid and domestic labour serves patriarchy or capitalism, or a combination of the two, and whether in fact gender relations are part of the capitalist mode of production, the 'patriarchal' mode of production, or both (Baxandell *et al.*, 1976; Brown, 1979; Dubinoff, 1979; Eisenstein, 1978; Hartmann and Bridges, 1981; Rothschild, 1983; Sachs, 1983; Sokoloff, 1980; Walby, 1990, 1997). Not all socialist women, that is, argue that gender relations are first and foremost functional to capital, nor that there is only one mode of production – the capitalist mode of production. In the mid- to late 1970s, a school of thought developed which could be described as 'Feminist-Marxist' which challenged Marxist-Feminist analyses to explain both how patriarchal relations in employment pre-dating capitalism could exist (see Walby, 1990) and how it is that women and not men undertake domestic work (see Williams, 1988; Windebank, 1991). Marxist-Feminist analysis does not explain how patriarchal relations in paid work (such as in the British Guilds) could have existed before the advent of capitalism and it only tells us that domestic labour is essential to capitalism, not why women should carry out that domestic labour. The Feminist-Marxists' answer to these questions is that women's oppression in paid work and domestic labour is situated at the point of interaction between patriarchy and capitalism.

For this brand of Feminism, therefore, the fact that patriarchal relations in employment existed in pre-capitalist times indicates that women's position in paid work has to be examined as part of a patriarchal system. Furthermore, the fact that domestic labour does not fit into the criteria set out to describe wage labour – and thus constitutes reproduction as opposed to production – is the indicator that women's domestic responsibilities too need to be examined as part of the patriarchal system. The benefits derived from women's unpaid work in the home by men as well as by capitalism are a proper cause for concern within this school of thought. In this analysis, women (and their domestic labour) belong to men first and capital second. Women's confinement to the domestic role puts them in their specifically disadvantaged position. Hartmann (1979) argues that this confinement derives from men excluding women from the best jobs (by means of their better labour organization) which results in men marrying women on favourable terms and ensuring that they have the primary responsibility for domestic tasks and child care. This domestic work, in turn, prevents women from acquiring the training they require to obtain better jobs in the labour market (Walby, 1990).

This theory also envisages tension between capitalism and patriarchy. Taken to its logical conclusion, capitalism would have freed women from the home in order to put men's and women's labour power into complete competition. This did not happen because capitalism had to accommodate the patriarchal social structure which pre-dated it, such as by paying a 'family wage' and by introducing child and female labour regulations and laws preventing wives from seeking employment without their husband's consent (see for example Hartmann, 1981; Kuhn and Wolpe, 1978; Elles Voient Rouge Collective, 1981). This theory, in consequence, does not describe patriarchy as ideological and limited to the family, as in Marxist Feminism. Rather, it contends that patriarchy, like capitalism, is firmly grounded in a material base.

As Walby (1997) argues, gender relations are neither a by-product of the capital or the capital-labour relation, nor are they contingent. Instead, she (1997: 118) views 'gender relations as autonomous or relatively autonomous relations from capital'. To explain why capital did not free women from the home, therefore, Walby (1990: 178) takes earlier dual-systems theories one step further and distinguishes between what she calls 'private' and 'public' patriarchy. Private patriarchy is based upon household production, with a patriarch controlling women individually and directly in the relatively private sphere of the home. Public patriarchy, in contrast, is based on structures other than the household, such as institutions conventionally regarded as part of the public domain. In private patriarchy, the beneficiaries are primarily the individual husbands and fathers of the women in the household, while in the public form there is a more collective appropriation. With capital's increased demand for women's labour, she asserts that there has been a shift from a more private to a more public patriarchy in countries like Britain and France (Walby, 1990). Nevertheless: 'The household does not cease to be a relevant structure in the public form, but is no longer the chief one' (Walby, 1997: 6). The consequence is that there has been a shift from excluding women from the public arena, as Hartmann (1979) describes, to segregating and subordinating women in the public sphere. Walby's theorization (1990) also seeks to explain differing degrees of gender inequality over time and space. She does so by arguing that: 'There are different forms of both patriarchy and capitalism. Further, there are complex historically specific ways in which the structures and practices which make up those systems intersect' (Walby, 1990: 45). She states, for example, that the British form of public patriarchy involves the market as well as the state, but that in Eastern Europe there is a different sub-type of public patriarchy by which the state plays a more central part in comparison with the market. In her more recent work, Walby (1997: 78) reasserts the importance of spatial variation in the constructs of capitalism and patriarchy: 'The form of gender regime and the relationship between gender, class and ethnic structures varies between nations, localities and industries'. Here, 'gender regime' is taken as another term for 'form of patriarchy'.

A final theorization which includes elements of Feminist Marxism is Connell's (1987) theorization of gender relations. Connell considers the existing theorizations such as Marxist Feminism and Feminist Marxism to be too categorical in that they draw all men and women together into distinct categories. He seeks to overcome this by concentrating on how such categories are established in the first place. He holds that structures are constituted by practice and that practice is constrained by the pre-existing structures. For him, structures are historically constructed, and as such can be reconstructed. Connell then links structural and cultural accounts into the notion of 'gender order'. This has three components: a division of labour; power, expressed in the connection of authority with masculinity; and cathexis, which refers to the emotionally charged relations with people, particularly sexual relations. In this way Connell draws on notions of both patriarchy and capitalism in his theorization. He suggests that these three components have independent effects and may come into conflict with one another. They are not totally independent of each other but interact to produce a unity which changes over time. Connell also uses a concept of 'gender regime' which he considers to be the interaction of the aforementioned categories at the level of institutions, such as labour market regulation, customs, workplace practices, family relations and behaviour in the street.

The usefulness of Connell's theorization is at a number of levels: first, that cultural specificity is located at the level of the individual (agency) and at societal level (structure) – in the form of prescriptive norms and gender stereotypes. Second, he also identifies the state as playing an important role in defining and maintaining the existing gender order. Finally, he sees the three components of the gender order as being capable of being reaffirmed through practice, or challenged and reconstructed.

In sum, the main features of mainstream Feminist-Marxism are that both capitalism and patriarchy are treated as sources of women's oppression; and the focus when studying women's oppression is upon the gender division of labour in both the home and the market.[6]

Evaluation of cross-national similarities and differences in women's work

How does mainstream Feminist-Marxist theory interpret the similarities and differences in the two countries identified in Part I? The similarities are easily explained as being due to the common ways in which patriarchy and capitalism exploit women in Britain and France. In both nations, the increased entry of women into the labour force is explained in terms of private patriarchy being replaced by public patriarchy resulting in a more collective appropriation of women's labour rather than its appropriation by individual men. Nevertheless, women's continued responsibility for domestic work is evidence of the continuing interplay of both capitalism and patriarchy which together form the source of women's subjugated position. The differences between Britain and France, meanwhile, are explained in this approach to be the result of how new forms of patriarchy build upon old forms and are differently interpreted in different spatial and temporal contexts (Walby 1997). Britain, therefore, is undergoing a slightly different experience to France due to the ways in which the dynamics of new forms of capitalism and patriarchy pass through the lens of different historical contexts to result in nationally specific outcomes. Connell's (1987) variation on Feminist-Marxist theory, by allowing that the three components of the gender order (division of labour, power and cathexis) can be challenged and reconstructed, accounts for variation in time and space and thus would also enable us to explain the Anglo-French specificity in women's work outlined in Chapters 2, 3 and 4.

Radical Feminist theorizations

Theoretical premises

For Radical Feminists, the Feminist-Marxist revision of the ortho-dox Marxist explanation of women's subjugation is still seen to be insufficient. These scholars argue that it is not some combination of patriarchy and capitalism but patriarchy *per se* (that is, the domi-nation of the social class 'women' by the social class 'men') that is the cause of women's oppression (Delphy 1984; Leonard 1984). As Delphy (1984: 69) puts it:

> there are two modes of production in society. Most goods are produced in the industrial mode. Domestic services, child-rearing and certain other goods are produced in the family mode. The first mode of production gives rise to capitalist exploitation. The second gives rise to familial, or more precisely, patriarchal exploitation.

Women as a class are viewed as oppressed by patriarchy alone, the roots of their subjugation being firmly embedded within this dom-estic mode of production in which women's unpaid labour for the family is exploited by men. For them, the domestic mode of pro-duction is embodied in the social institution of marriage because it is through marriage that the domestic labour of women is appro-priated by men. As such, Delphy maintains that the relationship between marriage partners is entirely different from that between employer and employee since the time of the wife is appropriated as a whole by her husband. In return, the wife is 'kept' according to the income and generosity of her spouse. She is not given a set sum per hour for the work which she accomplishes.

Radical Feminists have written relatively little on women's paid employment. In general, the focus of their work has been on sexu-ality and violence and in terms of women's work, on domestic labour (Walby, 1990: 38). However, later work which Delphy undertook in partnership with Leonard on women's relationship to marriage and the family (Delphy and Leonard, 1992) has addressed paid work, but in a different way to that of Feminist Marxists. They argue that it is women's position within marriage which influences their position in the labour market because as wives they are not treated as permanent features in this market which, in turn, explains their low wages and scant career prospects. Unmarried women are also affected because they are assumed to be about to take their position in the domestic mode of production at any minute. Delphy and Leonard (1992) also examine the extent to which full-time employment has influenced married women's position. They conclude that little has changed since even when married women have well-paid, full-time employment, they still do the bulk of child care and domestic work, which for them, is evidence of the intransigence of patriarchy (Delphy and Leonard, 1992). They nevertheless argue that a stronger public position for women is a route to emancipation from men by giving them the material means to be completely independent of them.

Consequently, although accepting the existence of a capitalist mode of production, this brand of Feminism does not believe that this mode can help explain women's subjugation. For Radical Feminists, therefore, domestic labour is not a mode of reproduction within the capitalist system, nor is patriarchy an a-historic concept which has influenced the structure of capitalism. Instead, patriarchy develops historically, having, like capitalism, a mode of production which is the root cause of women's oppression.

This is a theory of women's oppression based on the notion of gender-classes with men as a class benefiting from the oppression of women as a class. Delphy, for example, refuses to describe the situation of women as being based on their exclusion from the market and production as that would be to imply that women are something other than a socially-constructed category, that is, the product of a certain set of social relations. Just as the social class of the proletariat does not exist outside its relationship to the means of production, neither does the gender class of women exist outside its place in the patriarchal or domestic mode of production. In this light, it is interesting to note that Delphy refuses the dichotomy of production and reproduction with its biologistic overtones and instead favours conceptualizing society as being composed of two separate modes of production.

As Delphy and Leonard (1992) point out, the other side of the coin to the supposition that women are dependent on men's paid labour, is that men are dependent on women's unpaid labour. For them, this has been an under-recognized fact. They thus assert that not only is women's labour, both paid and unpaid, differently regarded and rewarded but it is also routinely depended on by men. Men have historically not questioned their right to a housewife to expropriate their unpaid labour, and this has contributed to their careers, wealth and comfort. As Delphy and Leonard (1992: 97) posit:

> If full-time employed men and women want to get domestic labour done for them they typically get it done under quite different sets of social relations. Employed men get it done as unpaid family labour, by a wife. Women get it as paid labour by a servant . . . Men's need to support a wife is a culturally acceptable reason for seeking high pay and being ambitious; women's need (even single mothers' need) for nannies is not.

In sum, Radical Feminism views women's oppression as due to patriarchy that is located in the domestic mode of production and which determines their position of inequality in the labour force.

Evaluation of cross-national similarities and differences in women's work

How does this theory interpret the similarities and differences in Britain and France? For Radical Feminists, the common position of inequality of women in the labour force in Britain and France can be explained by their ongoing subordination in the family. The common responsibility of women for domestic and community work in the two countries, despite their increasing and differing entry into the capitalist mode of production, is a sign that patriarchy continues to manifest itself through the domestic mode of production. Indeed, given that it is the 'double' and 'triple' burden of responsibility for domestic and community work which continues to stop women performing on an equal level with men in employment, the only conclusion that can be reached for them is that patriarchy is manifested solely in the domestic mode of production. Consequently, the fact that women remain responsible for the domestic labour and community work in the two nations serves merely to reinforce the premises of this theory for its adherents.

So far as the differences between Britain and France are concerned, the stronger position of French women overall in the labour force would be taken as a sign that French women are setting themselves more rapidly on a course for independence from men than their British counterparts. As far as the differences regarding the responsibilities of the state for child care in the two countries are concerned, the important fact for these analysts is not whether some of the domestic work has been commodified to a greater extent in one country than another, but the fact that is still women who undertake such work and that it is women's inter-dependence that liberates some women to engage in employment at the expense of other women, leaving the lives of men little altered. The telling issue for these scholars is that in neither country have men taken responsibility for domestic and community work, displaying the intransigence of patriarchy in the domestic mode of production.

Particularistic explanations

In contrast with many of the universalistic explanations discussed above, the majority of the particularistic explanations to be analysed here have derived from empirical research and could be termed 'middle theory', as opposed to the 'high theory' of the universalistic explanations. Indeed, some of this research has directly compared some aspect of women's paid work in Britain and France (Dex *et al.*, 1993; Gregory, 1989; Hantrais, 1990; Jenson, 1986; O'Reilly, 1994). We have classified these theorizations/explanations into three types: 'Liberal-Feminist explanations', Segmented Labour Market theories and Societal approaches. The discord between the approaches in this case arises from the degree of importance which is attached to structural factors and notably to the role of the state compared with other factors such as individual behaviour and the operation of the labour market.

Liberal-Feminist explanations

Theoretical premises

This approach conceives of women's subordination as being the summation of numerous small-scale deprivations and the sexist attitudes which act to sustain the situation. It takes for granted the pre-existing notions of cultural differences between men and women and does not seek to explain them. Furthermore, it often seeks to provide practical solutions for the problems exposed. Similar to the

Microeconomics approach in that it leans towards individual-orientated explanations of women's work patterns, this form of Feminism, therefore, does not have an over-arching analysis of social structure, in contrast to the universalist feminist theories detailed above.

A key Liberal Feminist text, as Walby (1990) points out, is Myrdal and Klein's (1970) analysis of the problems encountered by women playing the dual roles of workers and mothers. They draw on a Parsonian framework in order to help to understand how these roles were generated, but do not provide a material analysis of the observed divisions of labour. From the mid-1970s onwards, as far as paid work is concerned, this approach has been most prevalent in management literature as well as in popular journalism (Green and Cassell, 1996). As Green and Cassell (1996) point out, women's behaviour in management and their under-representation in senior positions has often been attributed to their individual characteristics such as personality traits, way of thinking and attitudes. A second approach has been the 'organization structure perspective', developed first by Kanter (Green and Cassell, 1996). Kanter's (1977) pathbreaking *Men and Women of the Corporation* famously described the obstacles to career progression facing women in US corporations. In so doing, it drew attention for the first time to the impact of the masculine ethic, how jobs are sex-typed, how women are excluded from informal support networks which contribute towards career progression and how they suffer from a lack of women role models. In the 1980s and 1990s, these two approaches have been taken forward in the Women in Management and Women in Organizations literature, as well as in many 'how to' manuals for working women seeking to pass through the 'glass ceiling' (see for example the large body of work on women in management by Cooper and Davidson, both independently and jointly (Davidson, 1985; Davidson and Cooper, 1992, 1993)). This literature points to the problems for women in getting management jobs in the first place and then being blocked in their careers, the problems of reconciling work and family and the persistent difficulties derived from prejudice and lack of role models, which Kanter (1977) identified. Proposed solutions have included providing women with more training, career planning and counselling, improving their ability to reconcile paid work and family responsibilities (through flexible working hours and the provision of crèches) and changing corporate and societal attitudes.[7]

Attempts to explain the division of domestic labour between men and women in the couple within Liberal Feminism mostly emanate from North America rather than from Britain or France. Indeed, journals such as the *Journal of Marriage and the Family* tend to be heavily dominated by such accounts, as is the US literature in general. Liberal-Feminist attempts to explain the imbalance in the domestic division of labour tend to adopt one of three approaches: the time-availability explanation, the resource-theory approach or the sex-role attitudes approach (see reviews in Coverman, 1985; Ferree, 1991; Godwin, 1991; Shelton, 1992; Spitze, 1988). The time-availability hypothesis assumes that within a household, the person having more time available, in other words, free of labour market commitments and employment-related travelling time, will do a larger share of the housework. This is said to explain why women do more domestic and care work than men. The second approach is the relative resource hypothesis which assumes that the more resources (that is, education, earnings and occupational position) a husband has both in absolute terms and relative to his wife, the less domestic labour he does because he exchanges these resources against domestic labour (see, for example, Baruch and Barnett, 1981; Biernat and Wortman, 1991; Blood and Wolfe, 1960; Coverman, 1985; Cowan and Cowan, 1987; Glaude and de Singly, 1986). Third, and finally, there is the gender-role ideology hypothesis. This asserts that beliefs about and attitudes toward gender roles are responsible for the division of domestic work (Baruch and Barnett, 1981; Deutsch *et al.*, 1993; Greenstein, 1996; Huber and Spitze, 1981). Consequently, this hypothesis can explain why gender roles in domestic labour survive which appear to fly in the face of practical changes in men and women's employment lives. Furthermore, it assumes that women's and men's relative contributions to housework become more balanced as their gender roles become less traditional (for example, Presser, 1994).

Therefore, Liberal Feminism can be termed 'shallow feminism'. With respect to paid work, it fails to take cognisance of the structures that have led to women being in the minority in paid work and which explains why there are differing work cultures for men and women. As regards unpaid work, it fails to take into account the structures that led to women having more time available for housework and possessing fewer resources than men, or indeed, the prevailing gender-role ideology. This approach does not ask *why* it is the case that men are in employment, that resources are unequal or sex-role ideology exists. Indeed, as Ferree (1991) and Thompson and Walker (1991) point out, much more variance between men and women is explained by gender than by any of the other factors in these models. For these analysts, therefore, the solution for improving the division of labour is simple. There is a need to seek equal rights in the formal labour market (reduce discrimination against women, improve access to training and promotion), since this will supposedly lead to more egalitarian gender divisions of domestic labour, and to attack single dimensions of the formal labour market such as spousal incomes, the assumption being that change can come about by altering one of these variables.

Evaluation of cross-national similarities and differences in women's work

To explain the similarities in women's paid work situation in Britain and France (notably, vertical segregation and wage inequality) the Liberal-Feminist Women in Management literature would in particular focus on the sex-typing of occupations deriving from a male-dominated (paid) work environment and the barriers raised by men to women's progression in employment. The greater penetration of French women in higher occupational categories, the lower levels of pay inequality, as well as the lower levels of part-time working compared with Britain, would be explained by this approach in terms of French women's greater ability to break through the 'glass ceiling' and challenge male discrimination as a result of better training, a more positive institutional framework and a wider range of measures to allow women to reconcile paid work and family responsibilities.[8]

To explain the Anglo-French similarities in domestic and community work identified in the previous chapters, we will take each of the three hypotheses of Liberal Feminism in turn. First, there is the relative resources notion. In France, with its more egalitarian distribution of relative resources due to greater numbers of women being in full-time employment for instance, there should be a more egalitarian division of domestic work than in Britain. This is not the case. Liberal Feminists would thus perhaps turn towards explaining this fact in terms of sex-role ideology. That is, France, with its more traditional sex-role ideology, as displayed by Kiernan (1992), results in women doing as much, if not more of the domestic labour than in Britain, despite French women being more likely to hold full-time jobs. However, this in itself does not explain why France has a more traditional sex-role ideology than Britain. Other

Liberal Feminists, therefore, might turn towards the time-availability hypothesis, asserting that although French women work longer hours than British women, both French men and British men work longer hours than their wives/partners. In both countries, it is indeed men who have the higher-paying occupations and better education, the greatest investment made in employment and the greater time commitments to employment which in sum means that women end up doing the vast majority of the domestic work.

Segmented labour market theorizations

Theoretical premises

As Dex (1985) explains, theories of segmented labour markets originated in the US in the 1960s. Their roots can, however, be traced back to institutional economists like Kerr (1954) and prior to that, to classical economists like Cairnes and J. S. Mill. These theorizations were offered as a distinct alternative to the neo-classical labour market models of the 1960s.

The initial and most simple labour-market model described how there were two segments (often called dualistic models) although this was followed by models based on a larger number of segments. The basic premises of this dualistic approach can be gleaned from Piore's segmented labour-market model. This model has two major segments with a subdivision within the first segment. The first segment is called the primary sector. It offers jobs with relatively high wages, good working conditions, chances of advancement, fairness and established procedures for the administration of work rules (Piore, 1975), and above all employment stability. The second sector is called the secondary sector and, by contrast, tends to be low-paying with poor working conditions, little chance of advancement, considerable job instability and high labour turnover. Piore makes a further division of the primary sector into upper or 'primary independent' jobs, composed of professional and managerial jobs and 'subordinate primary jobs', which might be lower-level non-manual jobs or craft-based manual jobs. These lower-tier jobs would have much less work variety and little opportunity for individual creativity. The former were characterized by higher pay, higher mobility and turnover patterns, resembling somewhat those of the secondary sector. Formal education was a requirement of jobs in the upper primary sector and thus represented an absolute barrier to entry. The theory states that workers compete within each market for jobs, wages and employment conditions in general, with mobility barriers prohibiting the movement from one sector to another.

Doeringer and Piore (1971) also added the concept of 'internal' labour markets to labour segmentation theory. The internal labour market was thought to be a feature of the primary market. It is one in which candidates for a job are restricted mainly to those already working for the firm, with recruitment from the outside confined to a small number of entry points. An internal labour market (ILM) therefore provides a career ladder within the firm. Doeringer and Piore (1971) argued that it was in the interests of management and unions to promote the development of ILMs; 'for unions, they provide better conditions of work, promotion prospects and great security of employment; for management, they offer a stable workforce which, if training or recruitment costs are high, minimise these costs and reduce the cost of labour turnover' (Dex, 1985: 133). From this concept has derived that of the 'external' labour market by which firms recruit primarily from candidates outside the firm. Use of the external labour market is thought to characterize secondary sector jobs. It has tended to be assumed that ILMs and the primary sector develop in oligopolistic markets which are unionized and have capital-intensive production processes while secondary jobs develop in unconcentrated industries and competitive firms (Dex, 1985).

One of the most recent dualistic models of note has been Atkinson's model of the flexible firm (NEDO, 1986). He identifies four types of flexibility: numerical flexibility by which employers can vary the amount of labour they employ at short notice; functional flexibility by which workers can take on a wider range of tasks (multiskilling), distancing (especially sub-contracting) and pay flexibility. The first two are considered the most important. In Atkinson's model, a division is made between core and peripheral workers. Peripheral workers are semi-skilled or unskilled and numerically flexible (as a result of working on short-term contracts, agency hiring/ sub-contract work, part-time work or job sharing). Core workers are likely to be skilled and have permanent jobs and be employed by a firm for a long period. Atkinson states that the distinction between the two has grown since 1980 and that the UK labour market has become more segmented over the period (Walby, 1997). The reasons Atkinson gives for this growth in the flexible firm are: recessionary conditions (causing a weakening in union power and greater labour supply), technical change, legislative change (although this is considered to have had only a minor effect), and changing business objectives (faster responses required in the business environment, decentralization and headcount reduction) (Walby, 1990).

In recent years, the concept of dualistic labour-segmentation models has been challenged in a number of ways (see review by Michon, 1994). It has been argued that while labour-market segmentation is affected by industrial structures and employer strategies, the latter are far more complex than a dualist structure would allow (Rosenberg, 1989) and can vary under changing conditions (Wilkinson, 1987). Trade union organization and collective strategies by workers are seen as playing a key role in the determination of pay and employment systems (Rubery, 1978). Finally, differentiated- or segmented-labour supply influences payment structures, job characteristics and employment conditions (Armstrong, 1982; Crompton and Jones, 1984; Craig *et al.*, 1985).

Very few early segmented labour-market theories specifically examined the position of women, which has been one of the major criticisms levelled against them (see Beechey, 1978). Piore (1975) stated that the majority of women were part of the secondary sector workforce, hence explaining their lower levels of pay. The reason given for their location in these jobs is that women have fewer opportunities to invest in their professional life as they shoulder a larger burden of unpaid labour than men (Doeringer and Piore, 1971). In another labour-segmentation theory advanced by Thurow (1975), women's position in external labour market jobs is explained by the fact that employers deciding the choice of candidates for internal and external labour market jobs will take into account whether employees are likely to stay with the company or not. Internal labour market jobs are relatively costly for the firm because people are hired for starting positions and then offered on-the-job training and career guidance. Employers therefore judge that women as a group are less reliable than men because there is a greater risk that they will interrupt their careers or work part-time and consequently reserve internal labour-market jobs for men. Barron and Norris (1976) looked specifically at the role of women in a dualistic framework. They suggested that women workers 'fitted the description of a secondary workforce since they had lower pay, that they were concentrated in unskilled and insecure jobs, that they were more likely to be made redundant then men and less likely to upwardly mobile' (Dex, 1985: 134). Barron and Norris (1976) suggested that women's 'attributes' suited them to jobs in the secondary sector: easily dispensable, attaching little importance to economic rewards, easily identifiable as a group, not very ambitious to acquire training or work experience, relatively ununionized and unlikely to develop 'solidaristic links with their fellow workers' (Dex, 1985: 134). Atkinson (NEDO, 1986) does not specifically offer a gendered account of the move he saw over the early 1980s towards the flexible firm. However, he does note that part-time workers and 'distanced homeworkers', who constitute the majority of the numerically flexible workforce, are usually women. Horrell and Rubery (1991) in the UK and Nicole-Drancourt (1989) in France also bear witness to the existence of gendered flexibility. Perhaps the most convincing recent labour-market segmentation theories, in terms of their consideration of women, have been advanced by Craig *et al.* (1985) and Burchell and Rubery (1994). Their theories move away from privileging the demand side of the labour market and highlight the importance of segmentation of labour supply in firms' employment policy. Both emphasize the impact of the firm's actions and policies as well as institutional and social factors, and notably the social reproduction of labour in the family, in shaping women's labour-market experiences.[9]

Evaluation of cross-national similarities and differences in women's work

Segmented Labour Market theorizations do not attempt to explain women's domestic situation, depending more often on a Parsonian view of women's role in the home to explain the operation of the labour market. We shall therefore concentrate here on employment, turning first to how such theories might explain the similarities outlined in Chapter 2 in women's situation in paid work. Women's concentration in part-time and temporary work, their lower pay and greater segregation in low-skilled jobs compared with men is explained by their secondary labour-market characteristics, notably their greater devotion to the home than men (Doeringer and Piore, 1971) and by their lower overall continuity in employment compared with men (Thurow, 1975). Barron and Norris (1976) would attribute their location in secondary jobs to women's 'attributes'. The growth in part-time work in recent years in both Britain and France would be explained by the development of the flexible firm, by which women have become concentrated predominantly in numerically flexible employment. According to Craig *et al.* (1985) and Burchell and Rubery (1994), women's disadvantaged position in the labour force in both countries would be explained primarily by the interaction between companies' actions and policies and the system of social organization, in particular the social reproduction of labour in the family.

How, then, would Anglo-French dissimilarities be explained by such models? The greater concentration of French women in primary sector jobs (more full-time than part-time work and greater penetration of higher occupational categories) would be imputed to higher levels of training and investment made by French women in their careers (Doeringer and Piore, 1971) and to their greater continuity in employment (Thurow, 1975), hence making them more 'reliable' employees in the eyes of their employers. Their greater concentration in primary-sector jobs would explain French women's greater parity with men in terms of wage levels. For Craig *et al.* (1985) and Burchell and Rubery (1994) the different configuration of women's employment in France would reflect, in part, the impact of a different system of social organization for the reproduction of labour (notably, less expectation of women interrupting their careers due to the public system of child care, more opportunities for women to take advantage of promotions) as well as the impact of differing company actions and policies. Atkinson's explanation for the trend towards the flexible firm in the UK in terms of the impact of recessionary conditions, differences in the spread of technical change, legislative change and changing business objectives, might help explain Anglo-French differences in the use of women in part-time and temporary work but would require detailed testing.

Finally, a persuasive partial explanation for women's greater continuity in employment in France derives from the evidence of Eyraud *et al.* (1990) and Marsden (1989), which uses labour market segmentation theory to explore labour markets in the UK and France. They find that an Occupational Labour Market (OLM)/external model predominates in the UK, while an Internal Labour Market model (ILM) predominates in France. The first of these models relates to persons holding a particular qualification sanctioned either by a diploma or by the judgement of their peer group and on labour mobility between firms across OLMs. The second conforms with the description given above by which: 'an employer regularly fills certain vacancies by upgrading or transferring existing staff, confining recruitment from outside to a limited number of entry points' (Eyraud *et al.*, 1990: 502). The implication of the existence of different labour market models in the two countries is that women (and men) have more to lose by leaving employment in France than they do in Britain because they stand less chance of finding another job for which they are qualified and because recruitment from the external labour market is limited. This difference may explain in part the greater employment continuity of French women (Dex *et al.*, 1993). Indeed, Dex *et al.* (1993) find, on the basis of their comparison of mothers' employment in Britain and France, that mothers' continuous employment in France was often for the same employer, while mothers' discontinuous employment in Britain was for different employers.

Societal approaches

Explanatory framework

A growing literature comparing working practices in different countries (see Gallie, 1978, Maurice *et al.*, 1982, Sorge and Warner, 1986) has spurned debates over globalization, convergence, economic integration and political harmonization. Countering the argument that industrial and technological imperatives will lead to a convergence in industrial organization at a social, political and economic level, is a school of thought, based on cross-national comparative empirical work, which holds that despite universal pressures to conform to a simple model, in practice there seems to be more of a trend towards particularity in economic life than towards similarity and convergence (see review of debates in Gregory and O'Reilly, 1996). This particularistic view is commonly called a 'societal' approach because there is an attempt to seek to explain differences between nations by reference to the societal factors in each country which structure economic and social organization. The 'societal approach', as Gregory and O'Reilly (1996: 209) point out, encompasses both approaches which attach greater importance to: 'the structural role of social institutions and those who emphasise the importance of actors in creating and re-creating specific social relations'. Similarly in cross-national studies of women's work which adopt a 'societal' explanatory approach, there is a division between those authors (the majority) who give particular credence to the effect of state policy and those who seek to explain cross-national differences in terms of both the impact of national (and international) institutional frameworks and of other factors at a national, sectoral, local and individual level. We will now examine this literature.

Let us then first examine the considerable body of cross-national comparative studies of women and work that we term 'structuralist' and which places the emphasis on the role of state policies in shaping gender relations (Beechey, 1989; Borchorst, 1990; Dex *et al.*, 1993; Dominelli, 1991; Eisenstein, 1983; Hantrais, 1990; Hantrais and Letablier, 1996; Lane, 1993; Leira, 1992; Lewis, 1992a; Siim, 1990; Willemsen *et al.*, 1995). The state's influence has been highlighted particularly in relation to policies which help women to reconcile paid with unpaid work. On the basis of her comparison of women's employment patterns in Britain, France, the Czech Republic and Norway, Crompton (1997) provides further clarification of the state's role: she explains that it is the history and nature of the welfare state and the nature (or absence) of the state's role in supporting women's unpaid work, in particular that of mothers, that is important in structuring women's patterns of employment. However, the extent of the state's influence in gender relations has not been limited to social policy, it has also been shown to relate to its equal opportunities policy (Crompton, 1997; Dex and Shaw, 1986), education policies (Hantrais, 1990) and its regulation of the labour market (Rubery, 1988). Both policies which are explicitly intended to be 'gendered' and those which are not intended to be so, have been found to impact on women's work situation (Crompton, 1997; Dex *et al.*, 1993).

The role which states play in regulating gender relations in production and reproduction have been classified in a number of ways (see overviews by Crompton, 1997; Duncan, 1996; Mósesdóttir, 1995). These are Esping-Andersen's (1990) welfare-state regimes which are based on the concepts of decommodification, stratification and state–market relations; those based on a woman's ability to live independently of a male breadwinner (see Hobson, 1994; Lewis, 1992a; Orloff, 1993; Sainsbury, 1994); Schmid's paradigms (1991, 1992, and 1994) based on analysis of variations in wage formation and employment in order to locate their impact on the gender division of work; and Mósesdóttir's (1995: 633) egalitarian, ecclesiastical and liberal regimes, which are based on 'the consolidation of the mode of regulation as well as the norms and institutional arrangements concerning paid and unpaid work'.

It has been argued that state policies which influence women's position in paid and unpaid work derive from the pre-existing gender contract between men and women, which is understood to set up a particular gender coding '... of what people of different genders should do, think and be' (Duncan, 1996: 271). Hence, the pre-existing norm of women as full-time workers in Finland was supported by a policy of extensive state-supported child-care, whereas in Germany, part-time work was allowed to develop, so supporting the dependent motherhood role for women (Pfau-Effinger, 1993). State policies are, however, subject to competing interests,[10] resulting sometimes in contradictory outcomes (Connell, 1987; Walby, 1990). Pfau-Effinger's analysis of the use of part-time work in Finland and Germany (Pfau-Effinger, 1993) showed that the gender contract in itself is historically determined: deriving from 'the particular historical route from agrarian into industrial society, and the role various social groups played in this transition' (Duncan, 1996: 272).

In sum, these 'structuralist' societal approaches attach particular importance to the role of the state in explaining women's work situation. There is, however, a small but growing literature which pays attention to the importance of understanding the impact of both the state and of other factors at a national, sectoral, local and individual level in explaining women's work, and particularly their paid work situation. In the UK, Rubery's (1988) extension of labour-segmentation theory revealed the need to understand women's position in paid work in terms of both production under the influence of organized labour and social reproduction. More recent cross-national comparative work (Rubery *et al.*, 1995) has detailed a number of factors which impact on women's patterns of participation in employment. These include state policies for social reproduction, labour-market organization and regulation, wage levels, and social values. Gregory and O'Reilly's (1996) model of labour-market practices offers a framework for understanding employers' use of part-time labour cross-nationally which not only takes into account the role of the state in the supply of labour (via training, child care and tax and benefits) and its influence on employment regulation via national employment legislation and industrial relations frameworks, but also gives attention to the effect of business concerns (competition, service and personnel policy) and collective bargaining practices, which they assert can vary nationally, sectorally and locally. Gregory and O'Reilly (1996) also highlight the potentially important role of supra-national employment regulation where a country's national labour-market regulation is limited, as it is in the UK. However, this framework makes no explicit reference to the operation of the family economy and the division of labour in paid and unpaid work. O'Reilly (1995), however, has proposed a dynamic societal model drawing on Connell's (1987) theorization of gender relations, based on her analysis of part-time work in East and West Germany, which goes some way to filling this gap and which ties together the roles of the economy, the family and the state. She sees the state, the economy and the family as independent structures but all acting on each other. The state, through its ideology, its social protection and its different forms of regulation influences both the economy and the family. The economy is affected by the division of work, the impact of organized labour and education and training and, in turn, interacts with the state and the family. The family, through the division of domestic work between men and women, family income and emotional ties, interacts with both the economy and the state.

Explanation of similarities and differences in women's work

How, then, do societal approaches provide an explanation of the similarities and differences found in women's work situations in Britain and France? We will begin by looking at the more structuralist explanations which highlight the role of the state and then examine those deriving from other societal approaches.

Similarities in women's paid work situation in Britain and France (that is, increasing activity levels in the postwar period, concentration of women in part-time and temporary, work, pay inequality with respect to men and vertical and horizontal segregation in employment) are features which cannot be imputed to common policies of the state in *both* countries since these policies have little in common. However, it could be argued that the similarities derive from certain areas of gender inequality surviving in France despite more 'advanced' labour market and family policies. Nevertheless, within this body of theory, much more emphasis has been placed on the explanation of difference in the two countries so it is this issue on which we will concentrate here.

Social policy, notably policy which has mediated between work and family for women in Britain and France, has played a crucial role in women's paid work situation. It is now well documented that the French state has intervened in the development of family policy and extensive publicly provided child-care,[11] while the British state has, until 1997 at least, adopted a position of non-intervention.[12] At the same time, the French state has also developed more extensive employment rights for mothers than the British state (Hantrais,

1990). Jenson (1986) has shown how the position of the state in Britain and France has been determined by the different historical place of women's paid work in the two countries[13] and by the impact of a coalition of interests (capital, trades unions, feminists' and women's organizations, politicians, and other politically motivated groups such as pro-natalists), which has been differently configured in the two countries. Together, these social and employment policies have provided a more positive institutional framework in France for the continuation of full-time paid work by women once they have children.

It has been suggested that education policy, too, may have had a differential effect on women's paid work situation in the two countries (Hantrais, 1990; Hantrais and Walters, 1994). Women's presence in higher education in France has been greater in absolute and relative terms in the postwar period, and they have made more progress than British women in some of the traditionally male-dominated science and engineering-based subjects (Hantrais, 1990). The reasons for this difference may include the respective requirements for the French *baccalauréat* and the British 'A' levels, and the greater respect in which science subjects are held, in particular engineering, in France. Hantrais (1990) suggests that the relative improvement by French women in the education system may be one of a number of factors which have contributed to the greater progress of French women into high status employment.

Hantrais and Walters (1994) also provide evidence of greater state control of professions in France from an earlier date than in Britain, leading to an earlier standardization of entry around academic credentials (this occurred in the 1940s in France compared with the 1970s/1980s in Britain). This, they suggest, has helped to produce a more substantial feminization of law and accountancy in France.

Finally, the state has been found to differentially segment the labour market in the two countries (Rubery, 1988), with concomitant effects on women's employment. Rubery (1988) points to two components of this process: the institutional regulation of the employment contract and the institutions of collective bargaining. She argues that in France the employment contract has been given greater protection through judicial decisions than in Britain. As a result, the distinction between temporary and permanent contracts developed as the major segmenting distinction between standard and non-standard forms of employment (Crompton *et al.*, 1990).

Our own research shows that while the French state has increasingly given support to the growth of part-time work – since the mid-1980s in particular – its protection in law has been on equal terms with full-time employment and there has been a preoccupation with associating its development with guarantees for employees.[14] In Britain, by contrast, the distinction between standard and non-standard employment has been organized around full and part-time hours, and state policy has deliberately supported this development (Crompton *et al.*, 1990).[15] This differing regulation of the employment contract in the two countries can provide a partial explanation for both the higher rates of part-time working among women in the UK and the higher rates of temporary working among women in France.

Rubery (1988) also argues that the nature and organization of unionism in the two countries has impacted on the labour market in the two countries. In France, trade unions are drawn into a corporatist relationship with large employers and a *dirigiste* state whereby the workforce is regulated and protected by institutional mechanisms, rather than from the organized protection of unionism. This has included the effective control of low pay within the formal labour market through the National Minimum Wage (the SMIC). In Britain, by contrast, unions have followed a policy of protecting their workers through differentiation and have not followed general policies to equalize wage rates. Furthermore, in France, 'Industry agreements structure the system of differentials and methods of payment whereas in Britain there is more emphasis on plant and company-based payment structures' (Rubery, 1988: 271). The outcome, she argues, is that broad industrial or occupational categories have more homogeneity of pay, status and career prospects within them compared with Britain, with knock-on effects for women. Hence, Rubery's argument can, in particular, help explain less pay inequality among women in France compared with Britain.

Research undertaken by one of the authors also suggests that the different operation of the collective-bargaining systems in the two countries has also impacted on the diffusion of working-time practices. Relative homogeneity in working conditions, including working time provisions, which derived from the French collective bargaining system began to be challenged in the 1980s when the French state, in the name of increasing companies' flexibility in working time, both stimulated more collective bargaining over working time generally and encouraged a shift in levels of bargaining to company/plant levels for working-time issues. It has also permitted derogation over working time arrangements at this level (Caire, 1985).[16] Hence, the French state through its intervention has given an additional stimulus to the growing diversity of working-time practices seen in recent years in France,[17] which has in turn impacted on women through, for example, the growth in part-time work. In Britain, by contrast, where there is a strong tradition of plant/company level bargaining, working conditions, including working time arrangements, have been able to develop freely, only subject to the organized protection of unionism. This has been challenged recently, however, when in October 1998, European working-time regulations came into force.

In sum, the state has played an important role in influencing women's position in paid work in the two countries, by means not only of its social policy, but also by its education policy, organization of occupations and regulation of the labour market. However, the fact that we have noted a pattern of convergence in a number of features of women's employment situation in the two countries (integration, differentiation and polarization) despite very different institutional frameworks, would lead us to conclude that state policy alone cannot determine women's position in paid work and that other factors must be considered. We shall therefore now examine the cross-national comparative literature for France and Britain which indicates that women's paid work situation in the two countries cannot be understood without reference to other societal factors in addition to state policies.

The main evidence to support his view derives from Gregory and O'Reilly's (1996) Franco-British comparison of the use of part-time work in banking and large-scale grocery retailing. They found that the levels and use of part-time work in a specific sector could not be attributed to the nature of the regulatory framework alone (national legal frameworks and industrial relations systems as well as supranational regulation), but could also be determined by the influence of business concerns and collective bargaining on the demand for labour. These factors did not necessarily only have national characteristics but also an important sectoral and local dimension.

With regard to business concerns it was found that the use of part-time work in the two sectors could be determined in part by the differing basis on which firms competed, and in part by dissimilar competitive pressures in the two countries. With respect to the basis on which firms competed, for example, in French banking, greater emphasis was given to offering a high quality service and detailed product knowledge, albeit with less complex products than those offered by British banks. This decision resulted in the onus being placed on developing polyvalence rather than part-time work, the application of till technology (decentralized clearing) and work design being used to this end. In British banking, by contrast, where there was less onus on providing a high quality service, the centralization of clearing and till technology allowed companies to make greater use of part-time work (O'Reilly, 1994). With respect to the impact of dissimilar competitive conditions, for example, it was found that in large-scale grocery retailing recessionary pressures appeared earlier in Britain than in France, contributing to an earlier recourse to part-time work.

With regard to the role of collective bargaining, Gregory and O'Reilly (1996) found that the use of part-time work could be affected by the strength of the unions not only nationally but also sectorally and locally, as well as by tensions between different levels of negotiations and by the importance attached nationally to specific issues: British unions in both sectors, for example, have been more accepting of moves towards greater flexibility in working time (shift work, part-time work etc.) than have French unions, perhaps reflecting the differing contexts for working time (Gregory, 1989). Marsden (1989) has also found that French unions have pressed for greater protection from redundancy than British unions, providing an additional strand of explanation for women's greater employment continuity in France. Finally, evidence from the previous section (Segmented Labour Market theorizations) revealed the explanatory power of company actions and policies in segmenting the labour market (see Burchell and Rubery, 1994; Craig *et al.*, 1985) and, in particular how the existence of an ILM (in France) or an external/OLM (in Britain) could contribute to an understanding of women's continuity of employment in the two countries.

In short, while state policy can clearly explain to a large extent women's situation in paid work in Britain and France, its explanatory power is limited and consideration must also be given to the impact of other factors such as how business concerns relate to the functioning of the labour market and the influence of collective bargaining traditions and practice. Just as state policy is inappropriate for fully explaining the similarities and differences to be found in paid work between French and British women, so too are they wholly inadequate for explaining the similarities and differences in the division of unpaid work between men and women. State policy has not sought to explicitly redistribute unpaid work between men and women in Britain and France, probably because the underlying assumption has been for so many years that more equality in the home will flow inevitably from more equality in the employment place. Rather, it has been the extent to which the countries have or have not intervened to provide state child-care facilities, or state-regulated child care, which has been one of the key state influences on the private domain. As we have already seen in Chapter 3, France has seen a policy which has sought principally to commodify child care to enable women to combine parenting and full-time employment while Britain, by contrast, has been characterized by non-intervention into the private domain: if women have chosen to enter paid employment then they have been expected to bear the child-care costs themselves. In spite of these differing institutional frameworks for child care, the responsibility for children continues to be that of mothers and a core ideology concerning the responsibilities of motherhood prevails in both countries. Indeed, the widespread availability of state child-care facilities in France seems to have done little to create a more equal gender division of child care, or indeed of domestic or community work. Ironically, it has been in Britain, where the state's policies have not made it possible or acceptable to delegate specified areas of their mothering duties to a third party, that the division of labour in child-care has shifted the greatest with more men being obliged to participate in child care because of lack of state support. The in-depth comparison of women's unpaid work situations carried out in Chapter 3 suggests that state policies to facilitate the reconciliation of paid work and parenting may, in fact, relieve men of their responsibilities in this area rather than help bring about more equality in domestic and care work between men and women.

In sum, there is a large body of evidence derived from Anglo-French comparisons of women's work to suggest that state policy can explain to a large degree differences in women's position in paid work, but that due attention must also be given to other factors. State policies would, however, seem to have limited explanatory power when similarities and differences in women's unpaid work situations are considered.

Conclusions

In this chapter, we have reviewed the contrasting theories and explanations for explaining cross-national similarities and differences
in women's relationship to paid and unpaid work. On the one hand,
we have examined 'universalistic' interpretations which, as we have
explained, attempt to provide universal theoretical models for understanding the gender division of labour across societies based on an
over-arching analysis of social structures. On the other hand, we
have examined 'particularistic' explanations, which are not based
on over-arching analyses of social structures but are based more
often on empirical work and focus on one or more explanatory
variable for the phenomenon under study.

As with all such projects, the choice of theorization/explanation
is ultimately that of the reader. As we stated earlier, the choice
among *universalistic* theorizations depends upon the degree of choice
which one perceives women as exercising and/or the nature of the
structure one perceives as shaping that choice. Analysing society in
terms of a social structure based on class (social or gender) is a
method of explaining an intolerable situation in such a way that
change remains possible. That is, change can be brought about by
removing the mesh of power and hierarchy woven by a particular
social structure in which individuals are caught up at present. To
focus less on the nature and origin of the structural constraints
under which individuals make personal choices is to shift the argument away from how to engender progress and to accept the *status
quo*. Consequently, change appears far less likely. In sum, therefore, the perceived importance of structural constraints has much
to do with whether a theorist wants change in women's situation
to be brought about and the extent to which she/he thinks such a
transformation possible. For the reader, in consequence, the decision
about which universalistic theory appears more or less correct will
be bound up with their own interpretations of these issues.

Among *particularistic* explanations the choice depends in part on
the degree to which the reader considers the state to be a key force
in shaping women's lives. We have shown that comparative research
reveals that while the state's actions (in terms of its social policy
framework, education policy, organization of professions and regulation of the labour market) play an important role in determining
women's position in paid employment, the state is by no means
the only force at work and due attention must be given to other

factors which are often societally specific, but which may also show variation at a sectoral, local and individual level: the impact of business concerns, organized labour, and the operation of the family economy, which give rise to women's degree of availability for paid work. The potential impact of the supra-national regulatory framework should also be taken into account. We have also shown that state support for and encouragement of full-time employment for women by means of a range of social policies is in no way linked to a change in domestic and community work.

Although we have set out these arguments in two opposing groups, we do not think it is necessary to choose one sort of explanation or another but rather to combine elements of the two, linking together both agency and structure in order to understand women's work situations. This is an approach which may well fall into the category of 'postmodern complexity of interpretation' described by Walby (1997: 5) because it brings together a number of individual strands of explanation. In calling for this approach we are following in the wake of economists and sociologists in recent years (see, for example, Blackwell, 1998; Crompton *et al.*, 1990; Dex *et al.*, 1993; Lane, 1993; O'Reilly, 1994; Rubery, 1988; Van Doorne-Huiskes and Van Hoof, 1995). Crompton (1997: 23) also highlights the importance of a 'multi-stranded' approach: 'another point which has been stressed . . . is an emphasis upon the multi-strandedness of any explanation of gender relations, the gender division of labour, and "women's work". We should therefore anticipate that both capitalism and patriarchal processes, structural factors and individual choices, rather than any single theory of "patriarchy", will contribute to an explanation of the complex totality of women's employment'.

We, therefore, join Crompton in arguing for the use of more than one explanatory framework. We consider both Walby's (1990) Feminist-Marxist theorization and Connell's (1987) theorization of gender relations to be useful because they can explain both similarities and differences in paid and unpaid work in Britain and France and changes over time. The mechanics by which patriarchy and capitalism are operationalized in paid and unpaid work can be understood by drawing on societal explanatory frameworks, such as those proposed by O'Reilly (1995) and Gregory and O'Reilly (1996) and which link together the roles of the family, the economy (including organized labour), the state and supranational regulation in explaining women's work situations.

6
Gender Relations: Progress and Policy

Having completed both a comparative analysis of women's work in Britain and France and a discussion of the various competing theoretical explanations for the similarities and differences to be found in the two countries, the aim of this chapter is to draw out the policy implications of these findings so far as encouraging progress in gender relations is concerned. Conventionally, and as we asserted in Chapter 1, it has been assumed that if progress in gender relations is to occur, one needs primarily to allow more and more women access to full-time employment and continuous career paths. Indeed, this was a key strategy underlying the Third Equal Opportunities Programme 1991–1995 of the European Commission and is also clearly visible in the EU's current gender equality strategy, as we show below. So too is this the case in much national-level social and labour market policy in this area.

The main lesson to be learned from the Anglo-French comparison of women's work in Part I of this book, however, is that more paid work for women does not naturally or inevitably lead to greater equality in the distribution of unpaid domestic and community work. Nor does it lead to a lessening of their caring responsibilities. Although those cross-national studies which confine themselves to comparisons of paid work suggest that the better institutional arrangements made for women to combine motherhood and employment mean that 'progress in gender relations' is greater in France than in Britain, when we give equal prominence to the informal sphere of domestic and community work, this is not the case. There is no evidence to suggest that women in France, despite having more full-time and continuous careers than British women and having greater social policy support, witness a lesser degree of inequality in their unpaid work in the domestic and community sphere. Indeed, available evidence suggests that if anything, the division of unpaid work is more unequal in France than in Britain, resulting in French women suffering a greater double/triple burden than their British counterparts. This finding thus throws doubt on the assumption that progress in gender relations in a wide sense can come through women's insertion into full-time employment alone. There are thus lessons to be learned from this comparative study for both the present British Labour government which is enthusiastically pursuing a gender strategy centred on access to full-time employment as well as for the French government, which has invested heavily in such a strategy over a considerable time period.

To commence, this chapter explains why it is misguided to continue to focus upon encouraging women's ever greater insertion into employment as the principal strategy for achieving progress in gender relations. We argue that although women's insertion into paid work has indeed resulted in significant progress in some realms of gender relations, giving women more financial independence and access to action in the public sphere than they have had before, without a significant evolution within the private sphere which would see men taking on more domestic and caring responsibilities, further steps towards gender equality in the world of work are unlikely. We thus suggest that policies giving women access to the formal labour market need to be coupled with attempts to bring about a renegotiation of the gender division of labour in the domestic and community spheres and that for this to occur, it is not women but men who need to change. Indeed, with women's increasing insertion into employment and their continuing responsibility for domestic and community work, it could be said that men are becoming the 'redundant sex' and action is required to start to provide men with a more balanced and active role in both paid and unpaid work. In a second section, therefore, this chapter explores some of the ways in which such an objective may be achieved, focusing on the need to re-value unpaid work and shift men's work patterns towards those conventionally associated with women, rather than call on women to adapt to structures created for and by men.

The 'employment equals liberation' thesis: a critical evaluation

The assumption that providing full-time employment for as many women as possible is the key to gender progress lies at the heart of much of the current discourse on women and work, both at a national and cross-national level. Indeed, full-time employment for women is frequently taken as a principal barometer of progress in gender relations. The result, for example, is that France is nearly always placed above Britain in any 'league tables' of comparative gender equality. Here, however, our aim is to contest both the relevance and validity of taking full-time employment as the main indicator of gender equality and of making access to paid work the chief policy-tool for achieving social and economic justice for women.

The first reason for questioning the notion that gender progress will flow from the extension of full-time employment for women is practical in the sense that there is a general demise of employment in many developed countries (see, for example, Royal Society of the Arts, 1996). When a greater proportion of people are becoming excluded from the realm of employment, it is swimming against the tide to expect greater employment opportunities for any social group, including women. Examining the direction of the advanced economies such as Britain and France over the past 25 years, it is clear that the efforts of such nations to re-create the supposedly 'golden age' of full-employment which characterized the 30 years following World War II have failed. However, this is hardly surprising given that it was in fact only an era of full-employment for men, based on a cultural, rather than economic, exclusion of women from the employment-place. Indeed, as we have shown in Chapter 2, this was perhaps the era when French women were most excluded from formal employment. Furthermore, not only are there rising numbers of people completely excluded from employment, but also a steady increase in under-employment as permanent full-time jobs are gradually being replaced with temporary and part-time employment (see Chapter 2). The result is that conventional definitions of unemployment underplay the true extent of inactivity, non-employment and under-employment among both men and women. Indeed, it is perhaps the willingness and ability of women to accept part-time and flexible jobs in the UK which has resulted in it being the only European country where unemployment for women is lower than that for men (see Chapter 2). In sum, if the pattern of full-time continuous employment is becoming less of a prospect for men, how can we base our hopes of achieving gender equality on replicating this pattern for women?

Coupled with this demise in formal employment has been a growth, both practically and perceptually, of the informal sphere as a site of production (see Williams and Windebank, 1999). An examination of the results of UK time-budget studies reveals that while work outside employment already occupied 48.1 per cent of individuals' total time in 1985–86 (Gershuny and Jones, 1986), by 1995, this had risen to 58.2 per cent (Murgatroyd and Neuberger, 1997). In France, meanwhile, two time-budget studies conducted by the INSEE find that in 1975, unpaid domestic work alone was a more time-consuming activity than professional work (including time spent in employment as well as time travelling to and from work), occupying 52 per cent of total work time (professional + domestic work time) for that year (Chadeau and Fouquet, 1981). A decade later in 1986, however, unpaid domestic work had risen to occupy 55 per cent of total working time (Roy, 1991). Consequently, these time-budget studies identify a shift in the economic structure of both Britain and France towards informal means of getting work done.

This is an important trend because the perception has been that formal employment is the dominant mode of production, while informal provision, centring largely on women's unpaid domestic work, is a marginal or residual activity. The fact that informal modes of work now represent the principal method by which productive tasks are undertaken, at least in terms of time commitment, means that any policy approach that places its primary emphasis on employment creation as a route to women's liberation is ignoring these wider social and economic trends.

However, it is not only the fact that these trends are undermining the possibility of women enjoying the same employment opportunities as those currently, or perhaps formerly, enjoyed by men. We must also consider, even if full-time jobs within continuous career structures were to become the norm for both genders, how the currently unpaid domestic and community work carried out by women would be done, particularly the caring responsibilities for the young, infirm and elderly which cannot be 'contracted' into the time left over from full-time employment. We must also ask whether the possible alternatives would enhance or undermine gender equality. In order to do this, it is fruitful to look at how women have combined full-time employment with their unpaid work responsibilities to date.

In the past, when married women and mothers were on the whole housewives, financially dependent on their husbands and with little choice other than to stay at home with the children, the key to women's liberation was perhaps correctly seen to be access to employment, aided by the state. The problem is that it was tacitly assumed that a more egalitarian division of domestic work and child care between men and women would flow from this process and in turn, further facilitate women's integration into the workplace. Indeed, this is what Gershuny *et al.* (1994: 151) have described as the 'adaptive partnership' view of the domestic division of labour according to which the division of domestic labour reflects the changes in the pattern of participation of household members in employment. Numerous studies over the past 25 years (see Chapter 3) have shown that the 'adaptive partnership' model was wildly optimistic. For example, Nicole-Drancourt (1989: 69) argues in the context of France that projections which associate the insertion of women into the labour force with an increase in men's participation in domestic tasks have been proved wrong and that therefore it is hard to talk about 'new family models'. The idea that women's employment would lead to a new family form which was not based on gender-role differentiation has rapidly come up against its limits. She contends: 'If the development of women's economic activity has shaken up family structures [today couples with both partners employed are the most common family form in France], it has not revolutionized family models [which remain based on a classical gender division of labour]' (Nicole-Drancourt, 1989: 75). As a consequence, a series of more nuanced models have developed which attempt to explain the relationship between women's role in paid work and their role in domestic and community work.

The most optimistic of these models is that propounded by Gershuny *et al.* (1994) who have referred to the relationship between women's employment and the division of labour in the home as a process of 'lagged adaptation'. For them, change will come about, but slowly, and possibly over a number of generations. It is not surprising, therefore, that we have not yet reached a situation of complete equality. However, if the lagged adaptation thesis were correct then, in our comparison of Britain and France, we would expect to have found that France, with its longer history of women's participation in the formal labour market and thus more 'advanced' status, would by now be showing a comparatively more equal gender division of domestic labour. However, the findings presented in Part I show this not to be the case. In both countries, it is women who not only continue to undertake the vast majority of the domestic and community work, especially routine tasks and emotional work, but also retain responsibility for organizing and managing such activity. Indeed, available evidence suggests that the division of domestic and community work is perhaps more unequal in France than in Britain.

This state of affairs can be explained within Delphy and Leonard's (1992) thesis that patriarchy has an enduring nature that adapts to change, rather than capitulates to it. The fact that the need of capitalism for women in the labour force has not undermined patriarchal relations in the home can be seen as evidence of this. However, such an argument leaves women without hope and encourages inaction. Other theorizations of the relationship between employment and the domestic division of labour leave more room for the possibility of change in the future. The first of these is that of Hochschild (1989) who has described the current state of affairs as a 'stalled revolution' in the sense that progress in gender relations has come up against the obstacle of men's refusal to participate more in the home. However, a 'revolution' has still been underway and the implication is that it could once again be 'kick-started'.

Furthermore, on this issue, and drawing upon Chapter 5, dual-systems theory is useful. Walby (1989), for example, argues that patriarchy is composed of various structures which are to a certain extent independent of one another. At an economic level, she asserts that there are several patriarchal structures. The first of these is the patriarchal mode of production by which women's labour is expropriated by their husbands within the marriage and household relationship. The second is patriarchal relations in paid work, the key feature of which is the closure of access for women by men (for example, in occupational segregation). The third structure of patriarchy is the 'patriarchal state' that operates so that women are excluded from access to state resources and power. Walby argues that patriarchy can take on different forms and can be present to different degrees. The different forms are dependent upon the interaction of these patriarchal structures. In different times and places, some of the structures are more important than others. The elimination of any one patriarchal structure does not lead to the demise of the system as a whole. Walby (1990) differentiates between public and private patriarchy. Private patriarchy is based upon the relative exclusion of women from arenas of social life apart from the household, with a patriarch appropriating women's services individually and directly in the apparently private sphere of the home. Public patriarchy does not exclude women from certain sites, but rather subordinates women in all of them. In this form, the appropriation of women takes place more collectively than individually. This echoes Calasanti and Bailey (1994: 39) who assert that:

> the socialist-feminist approach points to the need to take care in making unconditional assertions about the relations between private and public spheres. That is, changes in the society at large do not necessarily presage changes in the household: family relations have their own dynamic and relative autonomy. The growing participation of women in the labor force or state policies which aim at levelling structural differentiation between women and men in the public sphere may result in greater equality in the domestic division of labor . . . but this connection is by no means necessary.

In other words, change can come about in one sphere of life, or indeed, work, without bringing about change in another. So far as our analysis of Britain and France is concerned, this appears to ring true. In both nations, there has been progress in gender relations in the dwindling public sphere but the growing private sphere of informality appears to have stayed just as much gendered as was ever the case. More employment for women alone, therefore, is unlikely in and of itself to lead to more equality elsewhere.

Consequently, it is clear that in France, and to a large extent in Britain as well, women's entry into paid employment has been facilitated not by men taking on more of women's domestic, community and particularly caring responsibilities, but rather by a new division of this work *among women*. This redistribution has come about in France primarily through a formalization of care work under the auspices of the state while in Britain, until 1998 at least, it has come about either informally within the extended family or formally through the market. In both cases, however, the result has been that those women with the greatest labour market potential have realized it by delegating some of their caring responsibilities to other women who are unable and/or unwilling to find either less 'traditional' women's employment or indeed any employment at all. For some, although it is imperfect, this is nevertheless a solution to problems of gender equality because it is giving employment to an ever-greater number of women. Indeed, the Labour government in Britain is quite explicit in this view suggesting that the tax credit to be paid to mothers for child care to allow them to take up paid work outside the home will 'trickle down' to assist those women who undertake paid caring work. However, the stumbling block of such a view is the status accorded to caring, whether it be formal or informal, paid or unpaid. This status is rooted in a gendered ideology of caring work, which has its roots in ideologies of motherhood as being a labour of love and self-sacrifice, and which is inherently 'feminine', rather than an activity which requires skill and confers social status. Indeed, for some women to be employed and to free themselves from total identification with their caring role, in present circumstances, there must be a pool of women carers whose lives are more heavily influenced and structured by this dominant gendered ideology of caring.

Take, for example, the case of childminders who are vital for providing care for the under three's in both countries, particularly for those whose mothers work full-time (see Chapter 3). For childminders, although caring is their employment, there is a certain ambiguity regarding their status as employees, in terms both of their own identity and the perception of them by society. When care is provided by childminders for example, children continue to be cared for within a 'home' environment, and also often within a 'family' environment, where they can relate on a one-to-one basis with an adult. The relationship between child carer and child in this instance can become very close which can mean that the child carer of her own volition provides a better service than her remuneration demands because of her feelings for the child. The child-care provider is also at risk from her employers treating her as a 'member of the family', and all that entails as regards self-sacrifice and the wish to 'help out'. Furthermore, for childminders with young children of their own, the distinction between their employment and their 'labour of love' for their own children can become blurred. As Nelson (1994: 181) argues, childminders, along with all those who provide care services to individuals, for example, home helps for the elderly, 'straddle the public-private boundaries'. Indeed, childminding is usually provided by women who cannot (for material reasons) or will not (for ideological reasons) undertake employment which conflicts with their own caring responsibilities.

Equally, it can be the case that older women are available to provide such care because in the past they have subjugated their labour market activity to the needs of their own families.

It could be argued, however, that if more care functions were provided collectively, the status of caring work would be enhanced and perhaps less gendered. This is because carers in collectivized facilities are more a part of the 'public' world than other types of carer. Indeed, it is acceptable for them to have a more distanced relationship both from the person whom they look after and from their families. As Nelson (1994: 182) states, 'in the public world, relationships may remain impersonal, competitive, contractual and temporary. Although in institutional settings, paid caregivers may engage in many of the same activities as relatives, they do so with different prerogatives and they must accomplish their tasks without becoming overly attached to, or identified with, their clients'. Such carers can achieve a physical, if not emotional, separation between their private lives and their paid employment. Moreover, institutional arrangements exist to protect such care workers from being expected to provide flexibility (for example, extra hours for no extra pay) or to take on extra responsibilities. That said, it should not be forgotten that those providing care in collective or institutional arrangements still find themselves near the bottom of the professional ladder with little respect, low pay and few chances to progress to different types of work.

Nevertheless, it is probably impractical to imagine that a considerable extension of collectivized care will take place in the foreseeable future. First, this is because of the perceived lack of quality of collective care facilities and cultural dislike in both countries of institutionalized care for the most dependent in society. When looking at the question of child care, various surveys, even in France (Hatchuel, 1989; Windebank, 1999) have found a clear preference for individualized and home-based care, particularly for the youngest children. Similarly, Favrot-Laurens (1996) notes that even though there was a substantial development of residential homes in France, particularly in the 1970s, there was never a social consensus in favour of the value of life inside these institutions. The norm of quality of life and quality of death remain attached to the ideal of remaining in one's own home. Social consensus still judges badly those who 'abandon' their relatives in homes. Social pressure thus comes to bear on the family, or more properly women, to undertake these caring duties within the home environment. In Britain, moreover, the notion of 'care in the community' has been a driving force behind care strategies for the elderly and disabled for nearly two decades. Second, a considerable extension of state-subsidized collectivized care is unlikely because it would go against the grain of developments in the welfare state in both countries which are attempting to reduce social costs to the taxpayer by returning more responsibilities to the 'community'. We could conclude, therefore, that the commodification of caring work, particularly on an individualized service-provision basis, will not challenge the present-day gendered ideology of caring and will serve to polarize the position of different groups of women rather than bring about more equality between men and women.

Indeed, we will argue here that for further progress in gender equality in the field of work to take place, the only answer is for men to take greater responsibility for caring and to provide more of the flexibility necessary to reconcile care and employment. As the comparison of Britain and France in Chapters 3 and 4 suggested, the higher levels of formal care provision in France could be allowing men to abdicate their responsibility to third parties while in Britain, where formal provision such as in the realm of child care has been notable by its absence, or very expensive, men have been obliged to take on a greater share of the caring workload.

This raises an important issue. It appears that men's participation in domestic and community work has been greater where they have been forced through a lack of alternatives to engage in such work. Given that the alternative of formal modes of care provision are almost entirely delivered by women workers, as discussed above, the result has been little or no transfer of such activity to men. An argument can be put, therefore, that social and labour market policy targeted at women's insertion into the formal labour market needs to be coupled with policy that targets a renegotiation of domestic and community work and recognizes that the opportunity for men to participate more in this work alone is not sufficient. So far, policy based on this two-pronged approach has not been developed in either Britain or France. However, it must also be stressed that even where men are obliged to undertake a greater number of caring tasks, it is an almost universal phenomenon in both countries that they take little responsibility for such work.

In sum, social policy in neither Britain nor France appears to have had much effect on men's role. Not only do employed women retain overall responsibility for organizing care when they themselves are employed but, as importantly, women as a group remain the principal providers of care, whether this be in the state, private or voluntary or community sector on a paid or unpaid basis. Consequently, whether or not this work is carried out in the family or within the market or state sector, has less impact on women as a group than might be thought at first. This comparison of Britain and France shows that whether care provision is informal or formal, it is still women who conduct the vast majority of such work. There is no renegotiation of the gender division of caring tasks when state services are provided and neither is there much evidence of any renegotiation even when informal modes of care are the main thrust of provision. Therefore, analysts are perhaps wrong to assume that state provision is the panacea that they imagine. In other words, women's entry into paid work over the past 30 years has come about through a redistribution of care tasks and responsibilities among women. In that sense, women's entry into employment has not led to a fundamental deconstruction of the relationship between gender and caring. This is broadly true in both Britain and France and across all social groups. Therefore, in both countries, the ability of some women even partially to deconstruct their 'caring' role and enter employment on the same footing as men relies on the existence of other women who are not in such an advantageous position. Although social policy that has the objective of giving women access to employment can make some difference to the proportion of women who can engage in paid work, in neither country has it done more than redistribute traditionally defined caring roles among women. Further creation of full-time employment for some women, without more change on the part of men, can only lead to a situation of greater inequality between women. State policy, if it continues in its present form, can do little to alter this situation.

Policy to assist progress in gender relations

In the preceding section, we have shown that if current employment trends continue and traditional state policies of 'relieving' women of their unpaid domestic and community work by formalizing it as low-status, low-paid women's employment persist, it is unlikely that there will be a significant improvement in gender equality as concerns the societal distribution of work taken as a whole. For any further progress in gender relations to be made, there will need to be a focus upon encouraging men to participate in the private sphere of domestic and community work. In other words, given both the informalization of advanced economies such as Britain and France and the way in which gender inequalities in the private sphere appear greater than in the public sphere, there is a need for policy-making to shift its attention away from changing patriarchal structures in the public sphere to those in the private sphere. However, how can this be achieved? Before answering this question with particular proposals, it is necessary to consider perspectives on the usefulness of the state at all in these areas. First, we will look at theorizations of the role of the state in conditioning women's lives in general and then move on to discuss the question of the influence of the state on women's caring duties more specifically.

There have been four main positions on the general role of the state in gender relations. The first is that the state has served to perpetuate patriarchal structures. Lewis (1992a: 70), for example, asserts that:

> Many feminists have remained at best ambivalent as to their expectations as to what state policy can deliver. While recognising that the outcomes of social policies have changed familial and other structures in society such that male power has been challenged, they have argued that the state has also served to perpetuate patriarchal structures.

The main proponent of a this view is Eisenstein (1978). The role of the state is, she argues, to institutionalize patriarchy and create social cohesion between capitalism and patriarchy. In order to keep women's role as mothers primary and to control their potential power as reproducers of the species, the state is continually involved in questions of reproductive control and motherhood. However, some have found the attitude of Eisenstein to be too dogmatic. For example, Borchorst (1990) contends that Eisenstein over-emphasizes the state as an oppressor of women and suggests that this derives from her experience of the conservative/liberal American context.

An opposite position to that of Eisenstein (1978) has been taken by some Scandinavian feminists who have argued that patriarchal relations have been modified in some states which have been dubbed 'woman friendly'. Kolberg (1991: 144) has dismissed any idea that the Scandinavian welfare state might be patriarchal, insisting that it has increased women's 'independence, empowerment and emancipation'. However these positions do not enable us to explain the lack of change in men's domestic and child-care roles. One explanation could be that in fact things are changing, but very slowly. For example, Segal (1990: 54) states that 'while it is true that the "new man" has not yet arrived, it may well be true that "men can and do change"'. Barrère-Maurisson *et al.* (1992) also imply that some welfare states and labour markets are better for women than others and that on the basis of such indicators as women's integration into the labour market and child-care policy, some countries are further along a spectrum leading from 'tradition' to 'modernity' than others.

A middle ground approach has been taken by others researchers. Borchorst (1990), for example, thinks that only some states act as oppressors of women. However, she does not go all the way to saying that some welfare regimes are 'woman friendly'. Borchorst (1990) is of the opinion that although state policies for gender equality, even in Scandinavia, fail to take seriously the problem of combining paid and unpaid work, increasing public responsibility for pre-school children has undoubtedly relieved mothers of some of the burden of responsibility and it has contributed to the empowering of women through employment and education in the sense that they have obtained a higher degree of autonomy and independence from husbands and marriage. This concurs with Lewis' (1992a: 170) assertion that:

> The position of women within different welfare regimes revolves around two related issues, the valuing of unpaid work and the sharing of it. Nowhere have these issues been addressed directly. In moving from the male breadwinner to a dual-breadwinner model, Sweden may be judged to have gone a long way towards solving the first issue but not to have touched the second.

The same could be said about France and the new approach of the present British Labour government.

Finally, there is Walby's (1997) view of the state as both patriarchal and capitalist but capable of changing the degree of patriarchy so that the fact that under some welfare regimes women have better access to the labour market and more welfare benefits is entirely possible. Walby's theory also allows us to understand how state actions can often be contradictory, and hence help, us to explain the recent actions of the French and British states. She argues that the actions of the state cannot be simply read off from its patriarchal and capitalist impetuses but are influenced by political struggle including feminist struggles. A similar explanation for understanding the role of the state is that of Connell (1987) who maintains that the state is an important element in the gender order by which politicians (who are mostly male) can be expected to produce legislation, policy and measures which reflect the gender politics of the time, but which will not always necessarily be consistent or coherent with the subordination of women. He explains this in terms of the room left for collective resistance and bargaining as well as incompetence (Dex *et al.*, 1993).

In sum, what emerges from all these general perspectives on the state is that even under the most optimistic scenario of a 'women friendly' state, the state still has a relative inability to act in the private sphere, with change coming about incrementally and not apparently in line with government polices. The question then becomes one of the relationship between the state and the private sphere and of how the state can act to improve the gender division of labour in unpaid as well as paid work.

Turning now to the question of how the state should deal with the caring responsibilities that remain at the core of much of women's domestic and community work, it must first be noted that feminist scholars are divided on this issue. On the one hand, one group regards motherhood as the source of women's oppression, not only because of mothering duties themselves, but also because of the values related to motherhood and imputed to all women, particularly those of caring and women's relationships to the private sphere. Corresponding with this conception is the old argument that women must slough off all their previous roles and follow an androgynous pattern of life, based for a large part on the model of men's lives. On the other hand, there are those who view motherhood and the values of caring in a far more positive light, regarding motherhood as a source of all women's identity, culture and power. Corresponding with this conception is the argument that it is the social ideology that ascribes status to different activities which is erroneous, being a product of patriarchy, and that values associated with women's lives (such as caregiving) should be promoted in society.

These different positions have given rise to broadly two equity models which reflect different forms of support for women's carework. Fraser (1994), for example, has proposed the Universal Caregiving

Parity Model and the Universal Breadwinner Employment Model. The former would promote equity through support for women's informal work of caring. The latter would provide day-care and services that permit women to become equal participants with men in the labour market. Lewis (1997a, 1997b) has recently modified them in the context of a study of lone mothers to propose a framework of care regimes: the Caregiver Social Wage Model and the Parent-Worker model. The caregiver social wage model assumes that all mothers will be carers and are entitled to care benefits equivalent to an adequate wage for the duration of the childrearing years. Unlike social benefits that require recipients of state benefits to seek employment, the caregiver benefit assumes that mothers will not be in paid work. The parent-worker model assumes all mothers will be active labour force participants and that care services are available and affordable for working parents. It also provides recognition of care in the form of parental leave benefits and benefits to care for sick children that are dependent upon employment status.

These models effectively encapsulate the feminist dilemma over equality versus difference, that is, whether to treat women like men or to recognize gender differences. They have given rise to considerable debate over the best way to progress gender relations. For example, Lister (1990: 464) opts for a Parent-Worker model arguing that 'If women are to be fully integrated into full democratic citizenship, radical changes in personal and domestic life are required'. She demands both the entry of women into the public arena, as the only way that their second-class status can be ended, and that women's presence in the private realm of caring be accommodated. However, as Walby (1997: 175) asserts 'the suggestion that women should become more like men in order to obtain economic and social rights is contentious within the debate on gender and citizenship'.

There are, however, a number of arguments against both of these positions, the main one being that these models and conceptions do not explore the role of men: they are men-blind. Clearly, adopting the Universal Breadwinner Employment/Parent-Worker model will not on its own promote progress in gender relations, and where it does so by removing childcare responsibility from men may positively act against women's interests: 'Organizational and public policies that merely enable women to combine the two domains leave men's roles untouched, perpetuating women's double burden and the lack of fit between family and work life' (Lewis, 1992a: 221). In addition, adopting this model has led to some women sloughing off their responsibilities to other women further down the social hierarchy (whether or not this is sanctioned and financed by the state) so that the mothering role is simply redistributed among women and does not impinge on men. Furthermore, as we argue above, unless a collectivized system is set-up which offers such carers rights, status and adequate pecuniary reward, then women as a group will lose out from the process (Windebank, 1996). But, according to this model, women will not be put on an equal footing with men unless complete collectivization of childcare is achieved and this, as Windebank (1996:160) points out, is unlikely because it would imply 'a total change in our social construction of child rearing as being a function of the nuclear family'. Not only is this an option women do not favour, but also it runs against the current social trend away from collectivization and towards individualization seen in both Britain and France.

The Universal Caregiving Parity Model, meanwhile, reinforces the view that caring work is women's work, thus leaving the dominance of the formal sphere untouched and facilitating the reinforcement of the informal sphere as a realm for women. This view, based on gender difference, can easily serve as a rationale for women's inferior position in society. Furthermore, there are a number of well-rehearsed reasons for women engaging in paid work. These include, first, women's ability to accumulate wealth. Given the centrality of money for access to life chances, the impediment that women's contribution to unpaid work represents to their opportunities to accumulate wealth must be taken seriously (Joshi *et al.*, 1996). A second reason is in terms of women's power and status: in addition to the immediate financial rewards and occupational welfare benefits (such as superannuation and a range of fringe benefits), the public domain of work offers very significant rewards by way of power and status. A third is the issue of citizenship. At present, citizenship rights can only be sought through paid work, not unpaid work. Until the late 1980s EC legislation was concerned exclusively with workers' rights, and although it is now paying more attention to citizenship rights (Hantrais, 1995) this situation is unlikely to be changed significantly without a major rethink about the role and value of caring in society.[1]

In sum, these models for carework which focus on women's roles are flawed primarily because they do not address men's role in caring. However, a consensus is increasingly being arrived at among policy makers, as witnessed by the meeting of the EU Ministers for Women in 1998 (Freely, 1998: 5) and the OECD document *Women and Structural Change: New Approaches* (OECD, 1994), politicians (Hewitt, 1993), and sociologists (Briar, 1997; Lewis 1992c; Lister, 1997; Windebank, 1996), that men should be more heavily involved in caring activities in order for any real progress in the division of work to take place. For example, numerous European Commission policy documents (Commission of the European Communities, 1993, 1994, 1997), and indeed the Fourth Medium Term Equal Opportunities Programme (1996–2000) includes specific reference to the need for men and women to share both paid and unpaid work. Such a change would chime with the trend towards the favouring of private rather than collective approaches to social issues associated with the swing towards neo-liberal conservatism in recent years (Bryson, 1996).

Indeed, the evidence from this Anglo-French comparison displays that the greater attempt by the state in France compared with Britain to shoulder some of women's domestic and community burden has merely resulted in taking away much of men's responsibility to conduct such unpaid work. In Britain, as shown in Chapter 3, where the level of support provided by the state has historically been much less, men have been forced to take on a greater share, particularly of child-care work. One interpretation of our findings, therefore, is that men will participate more in unpaid work when forced to do so. If such an argument were accepted, then it would appear that men will participate more in domestic and community work when they are obliged to undertake some of this work. Here, two options are available. First, the state could adopt a *laissez-faire* approach whereby a lack of direct state support and indirect support in the form of helping to maintain and develop kinship and non-kinship networks, coupled with a lack of financial means to pay their way out of domestic responsibilities, would force men to take greater responsibility. This approach might be asserted to have been applied in Britain in recent history. The result, however, as the evidence displayed in Part I, is far from gender equality. Alternatively, therefore, men might be obliged to participate more fully in domestic and community work if a more pro-active and constructive policy response were to be adopted.

Much of the writing on progress in gender relations focuses upon changing women's position and most of the theorizations about the relationship between gender and the state concern the relationship between women and the state. Here, we argue that this is missing the point. For further progress in gender relations to be made, it is not women but men who need to change. As such, policy needs to shift its attention not only away from the public sphere and towards the private realm, as discussed above, but also away from women and towards men when discussing progress in gender relations.

Just as many typologies employed to describe the cross-national variations in social policy have been rightly criticized as being gender-blind (for example, Esping-Andersen 1990), it is perhaps the case that many of the gendered typologies that have been put in their place (for example Lewis 1992a, 1997; Orloff, 1993; Sainsbury, 1994) suffer from being either 'men-blind' in the sense of not analysing the changes required in men's work patterns and/or from assuming a strategy of change out of keeping with the macroeconomic changes taking place in society.

Measures seeking to improve gender relations at nation-state level in Western industrialized countries and at supranational level have tended to focus mostly on women, attempting to change their role (Acker, 1992). On the one hand, they have sought to improve women's access to the labour market by removing impediments to entry in terms of qualification levels, training and child-care constraints and, on the other hand, they have sought to improve their position and rights within the labour market. Hence, in Britain and France, policies over the postwar period have sought to open up education to women (Hantrais, 1990) and training opportunities for women were also prioritized by both governments from the mid-1970s (Comité d'information féminin, 1977; Junter-Loiseau and Guilloux, 1979; Ruggie, 1984). The French have also consistently sought to address the issues of women's entry into the labour market through their education policy[2] and have supported women's paid work when they have children through their extensive network of public child-care facilities, subsidies for family workers to look after children, and the introduction of measures such as parental leave, which have been taken almost exclusively by women. The French, in particular, have also sought to improve women's position in the labour force through a whole barrage of measures, for example, its *plans d'égalité professionelle* introduced by the 1983 *Loi Roudy* and the *Contrats pour la mixité des emplois* introduced in 1989.[3] Recent policies by the new Labour government in the UK also seem focused on improving women's ability to enter paid work, through the development of nursery schooling for three and four year olds and out-of-school child-care facilities (DfEE, 1998), and through such measures as the tax deductions for working families (Jay, 1998; *The Times*, 1998).

At EU level, too, successive measures have made little or no attempt to delve into the private domain. On the one hand, they have addressed conditions at work via Article 119 of the Treaty of Rome, the directives of 10 February 1975 (Council Directive 75/117/EEC instituting equality of pay or work of equal value) and of 9 February 1976 (Council Directive 76/207/EEC instituting equality of treatment for men and women in terms of access to jobs, training, promotion and working conditions) and the more recent framework agreement on part-time work (emanating from the draft directive on atypical working) due for application in December 1999 (Council Directive 97/81 of 15 December 1997). On the *other hand*, they have sought to facilitate the reconciliation of work with family, although without fundamentally challenging the status quo: notably by means of the Council Directive 92/85/EEC of 19 October 1992 on the introduction of measures to encourage improvements in safety and health at work of pregnant workers and workers who have recently given birth or are breastfeeding, the Directive instituting Parental leave (Council Directive 96/34 EC of 3 June 1996 amended by Council Directive 97/75/EEC of 15 December 1997) applicable from December 1999 and the Commission's recommendation of 31 March 1992 concerning child care (92/241/EEC). Although both the OECD (1993) and the Commission of the European Communities (1993, 1994, 1997) have called for the creation of a more balanced society with employment and family responsibilities more equally shared between men and women, few practical proposals have materialized to support this general proposition. The Fourth Medium Term Community Action Programme on Equal Opportunities for Women and Men (1996–2000) is a case in point: 'It supports innovative approaches to equal opportunities in general policies related to education, training, employment and the labour-market and the promotion of women into decision-making positions' (*Equal Opportunities Magazine*, 1997a: 6). Similarly the European Commission's Green Paper, *Partnership for a new organization of work* does not focus explicitly on the requirement to base new patterns of work on a new partnership between men and women in the division of paid and unpaid work, although the response to it by the European Commission's Equal Opportunities Committee revealed that this was recognized as a key issue (*Equal Opportunities*

Magazine, 1997b: 6). Again, within the context of the Fourth Equal Opportunities Programme 'mainstreaming' programme – which includes the objective of encouraging the equal sharing of work and family responsibilities between women and men – Member States' National Action Plans for employment also focus on women's employment in order to promote gender equality (*Equal Opportunities Magazine*, 1998: 6). Finally, projects to derive from the Equal Opportunities Action Programme (*Equal Opportunities Magazine*, 1998: 19), which have explicitly sought to target the redistribution of unpaid work in families, are innovative and pioneering, but remain small-scale and of limited influence.[4]

In other words, despite more attention to the issue of gender equality in paid and unpaid work, national and supra-national measures have tended to help women to adopt a male life model and, as Duncan and Edwards (1997c: 273) contend, to become 'second rate men'. However, these emancipatory measures, while helping women to improve their position in the labour force and increase their continuity in employment, have not, as we have seen in this book, challenged fundamental inequalities in the division of paid and unpaid work for the majority of women. As Briar (1997: 139) aptly summarizes: 'Instead, women have been expected to do all the women's work in the home, act like a man in employment and provide all the support required to others. Women remain "the domestic sex"'. Policies to enable women to reconcile work and family, to encourage employers to develop more flexibility in working hours or to reduce paid employment hours do not seem to lead to a greater division of labour in the growing informal sphere as we have seen from both British and French evidence in previous chapters. Rather, gendered flexibility is the result with jobs constructed as if individuals are primarily responsible for one domain or the other and men and women occupying different forms of flexibility (women in part-time work, men working overtime) and working hours remain divergent.

The different premises on which men and women continue to be employed are seen in men's and women's expectations over preferred reductions of working hours: men look for longer holidays whereas women prefer shorter days (Lewis, 1992b: 220). Measures taken to enable men more equally to share unpaid work (such as through access to parental leave as is the case in France) have met with little success (see above). As Burgess (1997) asserts, while there is now some flexibility in employment practices for women who wish to reconcile work and family, there is little or no such flexibility so far as men are concerned and such a demand from a man would probably mark the end of his career aspirations. In sum, efforts made to encourage men to participate more fully in unpaid work are being thwarted by the continuing definition of men's success being made in terms of the public economic realm rather than in private familial terms. At present, a man is judged more by what he does outside the home and how much money he generates for himself and his family than by what he does inside the home and how much attention and love he invests in his family (Hawkins and Roberts, 1992). Nor is there evidence that the late twentieth-century 'reflexive project of self' identified by Giddens (1991) and Beck (1991) by which individuals are reconstructing masculinities and femininities and their place in the universe of social activity through the daily question 'how shall I live?', is leading to fundamental changes in gender roles and identities. As far as women are concerned, although attitudes towards paid employment have changed considerably over the postwar period, those relating to their role in caring for children have not shifted substantially (Proctor and Ratcliffe, 1992; Windebank, 1999).

However, there is plentiful evidence that men in both Britain and France want to spend more time with their families. In a recent MORI survey in Britain, 88 per cent of working fathers aged between 18 and 34 said that they wanted to spend more time with their families and would welcome more flexibility over their working hours (Wilkinson, 1995). In Britain too, where fathers already do a substantial amount of child care, there are signs that policies allowing men to take a greater share of caregiving may be acceptable. As Pahl (1995) shows, many successful people are now re-evaluating their achievements and seeking fulfilment beyond employment. So too apparently are the younger generation in Britain who appear to be in favour of a major reconstruction of gender roles, even if this is more by force than by choice (Wilkinson, 1994).[5] In France, meanwhile, although men would appear to contribute less to housework and child care, there seems to be an eagerness among younger men to spend more time with their families. In 1994, an IFOP survey found that 58 per cent of men aged 25 to 34 gave priority to their role as father over their success at work and 40 per cent of them stated that the most important quality of a father was to be available for their children (Baumier and Remy, 1995: 34). However, despite this fairly positive context, few politicians have passed legislation encouraging men to participate more fully in care giving. Measures have been limited in remit and, although they have been referred to as applicable to parents, have implicitly assumed that mothers would be involved. In France, for example, as Pitrou (1996) has pointed out, discussions about the introduction of part-time work have been framed differently for men and for women: for women: part-time work is always formulated in terms of the 'conciliation of professional and family life' while for men the formulation is normally in terms of participation in associations, training, leisure and the like.

There are, nevertheless, very good reasons for encouraging men to engage more fully in unpaid work and notably in child care. Fathers who are highly involved in child care report increased closeness with their children (Hood and Golden, 1979; Russell, 1982), greater feelings of competence as fathers (Baruch and Barnett, 1981), more positive attitudes toward child rearing and greater satisfaction with parenting. Children with highly involved fathers, meanwhile, adopt fewer gender-role stereotypes, demonstrate more productive problem-solving behaviour, display greater development of internal control and show enhanced self-confidence and self-esteem (Radin, 1982; Russel and Radin, 1983; Servis and Deutsch, 1992). Fathers' involvement also benefits mothers by enhancing their professional identities, alleviating concerns about day-care (Ferri and Smith, 1996; Radin, 1982), reducing stress levels (Ferri and Smith, 1996) which may be particularly high for women employed full-time (Ginn and Sandel, 1997) and providing them with more leisure time (Hochschild, 1989). In dual-earner couples, when husbands take more responsibility for child care, wives also experience less depressive symptoms (Ferri and Smith, 1996; Steil and Turetsky, 1987). Furthermore, an approach that achieved a significant change in the role of men, including as a parent, would – theoretically at least – enable a recognition of differences between men and women, such as differences between motherhood and fatherhood – without necessarily reproducing inequality. This could have significant material benefits for single-parent families because presumably there would be as many single fathers as there are single mothers, with both having equal labour-market and domestic work participation rates. As single fathers usually have higher incomes than single mothers, the material results for the latter could be dramatic in many countries (Duncan and Edwards, 1997c). In sum, these numerous benefits of paternal involvement in childcare display clearly the importance of men taking on greater responsibility in this area.

If the benefits of a significant change in men's roles, and notably a greater participation in caregiving, appear convincing, how then could such a change be achieved? Although the state has been slow to recognize the link between the market activity of men and the non-market activity of women and to intervene in the private realm of individuals' lives (Bock and Van Doorne-Huiskes, 1995), as Briar (1997) states, men must change but they must also be given the opportunity to change and social policy is the obvious vehicle. This could be conceived at EU level, although there are reasons for believing that this is not a promising way forward: first, by the application of the principle of subsidiarity, the EU is showing more caution over the development of Directives in general and second, the greater role given to the social partners in formulating social policy after Maastricht (Gregory, 1995) is perhaps unlikely to give rise to proposals in the area of unpaid work.[6]

In the first instance, therefore, changes in the division of unpaid labour may be led by social policy at nation-state level. There are indications that a state can have a limited effect in this sphere, without undergoing complete social engineering as has been the case in China (Stockman *et al.*, 1995). Some success has been achieved in Denmark where the government is seeking to achieve a better division of labour (Liff and Cameron, 1997), in Italy where an innovative scheme was set up in 1991 to help increase men's involvement in child-care (O'Brian, 1995), and in Holland, where a working party was set up to consider 'the redistribution of unpaid work and in that connection an increase in the responsibility of men for care tasks' (Van der Uppe and Roelofs, 1995: 102–3), and where working hours and school hours have been made more flexible by legislation in order to encourage an improved reconciliation of work and family for both men and women. It appears, furthermore, that where the state intervenes, employers take more action to the same end (Van der Uppe and Roelofs, 1995).

How then could the state help to engender progress in gender relations? It is clear that calling for 'family friendly' policies, as the British government is doing at the time of writing (*The Times*, 1998a), is not adequate if a significant change in women's and men's roles is sought, a change which would seem to be implied in the government's strategic objectives for women (Jay, 1998). This is because it does not address the fundamental problem of the valuing of unpaid work (in all its forms) by men and society at large, and it often simply results in the reinforcement of women's role as lone carer. While there is no doubt that there has been some shift in employment practices over recent years (Hogg and Harker, 1992; Working Mothers Association, 1994), with measures introduced frequently in the self-interest of firms seeking to hold on to scarce labour in competitive markets (Esden, 1998; Holtermann, 1995; Matthews, 1998) in order to ease the reconciliation of paid work and family responsibilities, these have tended to focus on women and have not explicitly targeted men. The key challenge is to revalue caring activities in society and to encourage men to engage more in them. McMahon (1995) concludes that the fundamental values of society need to be changed. For her, the meanings of motherhood have the potential to transform society by offering alternatives to the dominant social relationships of commodification, inequality and exploitation. In such a society, caring roles would be centre stage and no longer subordinated to the demands of competition. It is, however, hard to imagine the realization of this objective in a context of growing international competition and the firm anchoring of the paid work ethos in Western industrialized society.

Even if the basis on which society is run is not overthrown to place caring at its core, it should still be possible to revalue caring functions and to make it socially preferable for men to take their place in caring activities as well as in paid work. There are number of approaches which we could advance in order to achieve this. In the first place, if the theory of gender role ideology is given credence, the state could influence debate over the appropriate roles for men and women in modern industrial society, although it will be but one influence, with other ones deriving from the cultural and religious heritage of a country, its family values and its work ethos as well as from academic research and intellectual thought and the impact of lobbying groups including feminists (Stockman *et al.*, 1995). As Lewis (1992a: 221) points out, in order to engender change in both paid and unpaid work 'the discourse on balancing work and family [must] be framed as an issue for men and women'.

More effective perhaps may be policies which seek to socialize men into caring functions and to set these in the context of the wider objective of equal opportunities for men and women in both paid and unpaid work, through for example, the removal of traditional gender stereotyping in schooling, the teaching of caring skills in schools and, as the EU Ministers for Women suggested in 1998 (Freely, 1998), more courses for fathers. There is also a need, as the

Ministers stated, for finding out more about why men seem to steer clear of caring activities.[7] Legitimating men's family roles may also derive from demonstrating the long-term advantages of taking parental leave, such as in terms of its impact on satisfaction with family life, which will translate into enhanced productivity in employment and in terms of greater flexibility through the learning of new skills and ways of working (Lewis, S., 1997).

If it is believed that a family's division of labour is affected by economic considerations such as the operation of the tax and benefit system (a microeconomic approach), then practical support for the sharing of care responsibilities could come in the form of financial incentives for change. One proposal is the introduction of a social wage scheme. As Briar (1997: 183) puts it, 'Arguably the most humanitarian and effective way to promote genuine freedom for all women and men would be to provide universal benefits, paid to individuals not households, irrespective of employment or family circumstances and geared to the cost of living, This would have the additional advantage of attracting the support of both women and men.' A basic income scheme was advocated by Juliet Rhys Williams, at the same time as Beveridge was introducing his Welfare reforms.[8] Such a scheme would arguably abolish poverty traps and would not stereotype women as carers as did the 'wages for housework' proposals, since it would also be paid to men, making it easier for them to accept caring responsibilities. However, in view of the trend towards neo-liberal conservatism referred to above, the development of such a policy seems rather unlikely at present. Other incentives for revaluing the caring role, such as the award of tax advantages to families where a partner stops work to care for a child are unlikely to encourage a redistribution of labour and may instead encourage a reinforcement of gender roles, as has been the case in France (Fagnani, 1995). Here, both men and women are legally entitled to take parental leave on the condition that the employee concerned has been with an employer for at least a year. In 1991, 99 per cent of the recipients were women (Fagnani, 1996). Men, therefore, even when state provision is available, do not take advantage of this facility.

State policies would also need to address the issue of employment-hours norms, shifting them away from the excessively long hours worked by men, particularly in the UK. Policy is moving in this direction in France with the recent introduction of legislation to reduce the working week to 35 hours. In the UK, however, there is little working-time legislation and the European working-time directive (Council Directive 93/104/EC of 23 November 1993) currently only restricts time spent in employment to 48 hours per week and allows for the law to be abrogated where there is an agreement between social partners (Gregory, 1995). There is a case now for men working more like women rather than women adopting men's working patterns, with both men and women working less than normal full-time hours and sharing unpaid work. The opportunity for such a change could derive in part from the processes of globalization[9] and automation, which are redefining employment, leading to a greater flexibility in forms of employment and to a greater proportion of the total workload to be undertaken by society on an unpaid basis.[10] As Austria's former Minister for Women's Affairs said:

> When labour is newly and differently defined, described and organised, politics of recognition must be combined and substituted by politics of redistribution. All social tasks must be shared equally by women and men. Newly and differently evaluated paid and unpaid work must be redistributed and shared equally by women and men. (*Equal Opportunities Magazine*, 1997b: 23).

But for a greater sharing of work to be achieved between men and women, for a change in the Total Social Organization of Labour (Glucksmann, 1995), a number of other changes would need to take place. First, there would need to be a reconceptualization of men's and women's roles in society as discussed above. Second, there would have to be significant changes in the employment-place. There would need to be a recognition in employment of men's enhanced role in unpaid work. Ideologies about employment practices would also need to change. A shift would be required in the notion of commitment to employment, away from the view that commitments outside employment inevitably reduce commitment to employment (Lewis, S., 1997). Also, it would be necessary to challenge the view that long hours are a sign of commitment and are expected from managers and professionals. Employees would need to be assessed on the basis of their output rather than their input (measured in hours of attendance). New measures would need to be built into appraisal systems and associated pay assessments to reflect this changed outlook (Liff and Cameron, 1997). Finally, it would be necessary to convince business that its own goals can be compatible with those of workers, families and the wider society. Recent research suggests that constructing a truly family friendly culture may represent a path to the enhancement of business goals (as described by Lewis, S., 1997).

In addition, the status of less than full-time employment would need to be enhanced so that it is not stigmatized for either men or women[11] and its availability extended to all sectors of the economy and to all hierarchical levels. This would require a fundamental rethink of the organization of employment in most enterprises. The state's role would be vital. It would need to play a key role in such developments by reinforcing the legislative framework and ensuring that the right to be employed less than full-time at any time in their working lives is available to all employees. It could also serve to promote the reorganization of employment on a less than full-time model through practical measures such as promotional campaigns, working with employers' organizations and giving financial incentives for organizations to change their *modus operandi*. A lack of state action, as Lewis, S. (1997) points out, would impede the transformation to a 'family-friendly' society.

Finally, if the maximization of family well-being is the basis for decisions by men and women about the division of labour in the family, as microeconomic theory advances, then inequalities between men and women in pay and in their opportunity to access more highly-qualified jobs, also need to be removed, as Lewis (1992a) suggests, so that men and women can make decisions about their contribution to paid and unpaid labour from a basis of equal opportunities and the possibility of both men and women working less than normal full-time working hours can become a reality. A number of current changes may be conducive to these developments: the introduction of a minimum wage by the current Labour government, and a reinforcement of the Equal Opportunities framework in the UK, particularly as it relates to pay, may stimulate greater wage equality in Britain; and rising qualification rates for women in both Britain and France are likely to add pressure for change in the years to come.

In sum, we have shown that there are a number of ways in which the state could intervene in order to promote a society in which a fairer distribution of all work between men and women could be achieved. However, while we would argue that intervention by the state is vital, it is our view that change must also take place through interpersonal processes. We join Gershuny *et al.* (1994) in the view that adjustment in work roles takes place through an extended process of household negotiation, extending over a period of years and indeed across generations, but disagree that within present circumstances this will lead to equality of unpaid and caring work. The implication of this view is that change will not come about if women (and men) comply with the *status quo* or indeed with changes that are to their disadvantage (such as the taking on of the triple burden of work, domestic work and work in the community). Instead, progress in gender relations will only occur if there is an effort on the part of women (and men) themselves to cause gender renegotiation in the private sphere. In other words, a degree of conflict and force is inevitable at the personal level for such change to come about.

Interpersonal interaction is how gender roles are produced and maintained in everyday life (Potucheck, 1992; Thompson and Walker, 1995; West and Zimmerman, 1987). Changes in gender roles go hand in hand with interpersonal conflict over appropriate role expectations. Thus, interpersonal processes constitute, maintain and enhance the gendered division of labour (Deutsch *et al.*, 1993; Kluwer *et al.*, 1997; Pittman and Blanchard, 1996; Scanzoni and Fox, 1980; Zvonkovic *et al.*, 1996). Conflicts thus play a crucial role in the construction and reconstruction of gender roles. Indeed, and to adopt a radical feminist stance, just as conflict is necessary in employment if the capitalist mode of production is to be tackled, so it is the same with domestic labour. Unless there is conflict in the home over the domestic mode of production, little will change and the powerful (men) will do little to release their power. Indeed, research has shown that men's participation in domestic work is positively related to marital conflict (Deutsch *et al.*, 1993, Kluwer *et al.*, 1996, 1997, Volling and Belsky, 1991). Deutsch *et al.* (1993) suggest that wives may pressure husbands to participate in housework and that, in families in which husbands do a lot of housework, a struggle has been won by the wives. This renegotiation need not necessarily be a negative process. Kluwer *et al.* (1997) find in the Netherlands that although egalitarian couples experience more conflict and negotiation, this also gives them the opportunity to work out their differences, provided that this is done in mutually integrative ways. Rosenfeld *et al.* (1995) also identify several studies showing that egalitarian couples are responsive to each others' self-disclosures and are willing to reciprocate them and employ decision-making strategies. The synthesis of both partners' positions, or the integrative agreement, that emerges benefits both parties (Rubin *et al.*, 1994).

In consequence, although marital interaction may be the means by which traditional gender roles are reinforced in everyday life (Ferree, 1990; Thompson and Walker, 1995; West and Zimmerman, 1987), marital interaction also may provide a way for women to break through traditional gender roles. Women's ability to enforce their position, so that they can not only have a right to participate in the formal workforce but also achieve a fairer distribution of unpaid work, will clearly be improved if they are both materially and ideologically empowered in the ways outlined above.

To conclude our consideration of practical approaches to change in gender relations, we must end by discussing men's role in progressing gender relations. Beck (1994) and Giddens (1994) both argue that agency is increasingly being freed from structure and that individuals are increasingly engaging in the reflexive construction of their own life narratives, less hindered by tradition and structure than at previous junctures in history. As Beck and Beck-Gernsheim (1995) assert, this is reflected in a number of ways in women's lives today in Western industrialized societies – such as the new type of unmarried mother where a traditional partnership with a man is unnecessary, and women's decisions to rear children or to take employment – and is resulting in diversity of beliefs about the way forward for woman. While, of course, it is not possible for women to escape structure, we do believe that it is possible for women to exercise agency, such that women consciously decide to have children without depending upon a man and that women choose to rear a child rather than go back to employment. In this sense, they are reflexively constructing their own 'life narratives' and are not merely passive victims of their social circumstances. What is now required, however, is for men to do the same. They are constrained by structures such as increased working times, societal ideologies about how to achieve status and meaning in their working lives, and legislative constraints relating to child care and have, perhaps, engaged in the 'reflexive' project of developing new 'life narratives' to a lesser extent than women. For further progress in gender relations to be achieved, it is also this reflexive project by men which is required in the twenty-first century.

7
Conclusions

Much research on women's working lives has been founded on the assumption that more paid work for women is the key to women's liberation and gender equality. A large body of cross-national comparative work, including studies comparing Britain and France, has concluded that policy environments play a key role in the nature and extent of women's participation in the labour market, and hence are influential in engendering progress in gender relations. In this book, however, we have argued that equating progress in gender relations with women's position in the labour force alone is to only look at part of the story: it ignores women's position in unpaid work and the impact of policy environments, or their absence, on this area of women's working lives.

This Anglo-French comparison of women's contemporary work situation has, therefore, provided one of the first accounts in the cross-national comparative literature on women's work which examines in equal depth all forms of women's work, both paid and unpaid. In doing so, we have, as the title of the book suggests, sought to address a number of questions. First, practice: whether progress in gender relations is being made in Britain and France? Second, theory: how can theorizations of women's work take into account the similarities and differences in women's work situations in the two countries? Finally policy: how can progress in gender relations be achieved, and what is the role of policy in this process? We will now examine the arguments made in relation to each of these areas in turn.

Practice: women's work in Britain and France

The comparison of women's contemporary paid work situation in isolation would suggest that greater progress in gender relations had been achieved in France than in Britain. A key indicator of this is that French women's employment continuity and employment status is not affected so significantly by the presence of children as are those of British women. French women's activity patterns over their life-cycles are increasingly resembling those of French men. In France, full-time participation rates are considerably higher than in Britain and, as a consequence, there is less disparity between men's and women's working hours. Also part-time work does not have such a negative correlation with occupational status as it does in Britain. Finally, although French women suffer from higher rates of unemployment than British women, French women have had greater success in penetrating higher occupational groups and also suffer from a lower degree of pay inequality than do their British counterparts, the latter attributable in part to the high incidence of part-time working among women in Britain.

However, women's situation in paid work is only part of the story. When women's situation in unpaid work is considered, we are led to conclude that women are not necessarily liberated if they have a stronger position in the labour force. We have shown in Chapters 3 and 4 that French women remain, like British women, confronted by a double/triple burden of work. There is, in fact, little difference between the two countries as far as the gender division of domestic labour and work in the community is concerned: in Britain and France both are rigidly gendered and it is women rather than men who carry out the majority of domestic and (both kinship and non-kinship based) community work. Women tend to undertake the tasks considered 'feminine' and those which are routine and open-ended while men conduct tasks that are perceived as 'masculine' and that are non-routine and closed-ended in character. Contrary to expectations, therefore, French women's increased entry in the labour force has not been matched by a comparatively greater renegotiation of domestic and community work. Quite the opposite. French women suffer from a greater burden of paid and unpaid work than British women. In major part, this is because their higher participation in full-time continuous employment means that they have less access than British women to informal support networks of non-employed women upon whom to call. It is tempting to seek to explain this difference in French and British women's unpaid work situation in terms of the reputedly more 'macho' French culture. However, such a situation persists even in less macho, more egalitarian, cultures, such as those of the Scandinavian countries.

Nor can we assume that the rise of single-parenthood is the precursor of a revolution in gender relations in either Britain or France. While single-parenthood may be liberating for the woman concerned, it does not appear to be progressive for gender relations at a societal level. In Britain, single-motherhood reduces women's employment opportunities considerably, while in both countries, custody and residency arrangements for children, although sought by women, mean that more of the work of child-rearing falls on mothers' than fathers' shoulders than is often the case in dual-parent households.

This comparison of women's work situation in Britain and France therefore raises fundamental questions about what constitutes progress in gender relations. If women are not present in the formal labour force, then there are major implications for women's citizenship rights, as these entitlements are increasingly linked to employment. However, the adoption of a 'male' employment model (full-time continuous employment) for women is likely to represent a backward step for gender relations in general while prevailing cultural, and arguably out-dated, mores regarding men's and women's roles persist. A third implication is for women's quality of life (and indeed health): the popular press and sociological literature in both countries is replete with examples of harassed women trying to combine full-time employment with all their domestic and community responsibilities, whether or not they actually feel guilty in attempting to do so (as they often do in Britain).

Our comparison of women's work situation in Britain and France also leads us to question the role of state policy, and notably state social policy, in engendering progress in gender relations. We have shown in Chapters 2, 3 and 5 how a number of state policies, both those which are explicitly gendered (such as family and child-care policies and equal opportunity legislation) and those which are not (labour market policies such as the minimum wage and working time regulation) have been conducive to French women being able to hold a position in the labour force which is more equal to that of men. In Britain, by contrast, a non-interventionist position regarding the organization of family life and the reconciliation of work and family, combined with a whole gamut of 'ungendered' policies (liberal labour market policies relating to pay, working time and organized labour), have acted against women's interests in employment terms. If the aim is to improve gender relations in employment then, clearly, state policies count.

However, explicit policies to redistribute unpaid work between men and women have been absent in the two countries. Rather, it is the extent to which the countries have or have not intervened to provide state child-care facilities, or state-regulated child care such as childminders, which has been one of the key influences within the private domain. France has pursued a policy which has sought principally to commodify child care to enable women to combine parenting and full-time work, although a parental leave system, notionally directed at both men and women, has undermined this principle somewhat in recent years. Britain, by contrast, has been characterized by non-intervention in the private domain. If women have chosen to enter paid employment, then they have been expected to bear the child-care costs themselves. The growth in child care seen recently in Britain has come from the private sector. Indeed, the use of paid formal child care is usually reserved for women in higher occupational groups in Britain. Whether interventionist or *laissez-faire* policies have been pursued, nevertheless, in both countries, the responsibility for children continues to be that of mothers and a core ideology concerning the responsibilities of motherhood prevails.

Indeed, and as we saw in Chapters 3 and 4, the greater prevalence of full-time continuous employment for women in France, facilitated by French family policy and the more extensive availability of state child-care services, has done little to create a more equal gender division of child-care, domestic or community work. Take, for example, child care. The French state's policies have made it possible and acceptable for women to delegate specified areas of their mothering duties to a third party – usually to another woman – but have not led to a renegotiation between men and women of the responsibility for child care. Ironically, it has been in Britain, where the male breadwinner model is more dominant, where the division of labour in child care and unpaid work has shifted the furthest.

Our in-depth comparison of women's work situations in Britain and France therefore leads us to the conclusion that state intervention which only seeks to facilitate the combination of paid work and parenting through, for example, the development of child-care facilities, leads to little renegotiation of the gendered responsibilities for such work. Our study also suggests that, in the absence of policies to promote an improved distribution of paid and unpaid work between men and women, 'progress' in gender relations may derive more from the imposition of responsibility for unpaid work, and notably child care, on men, rather than from their actively choosing to undertake this work. Hence, the new Labour government's policies to develop child-care facilities, to promote 'family-friendly' policies in the workplace and to promote paid work for mothers may in fact, like the long-standing French policies to enable women to reconcile paid work and family responsibilities, not result in a general move towards equality in all aspects of men's and women's work.

Theory: explaining similarities and differences in women's work

How then can we explain the similarities and differences in women's work situations in Britain and France? On the one hand, there are 'universalistic' theorizations, which seek to provide universal theoretical models for understanding the gender division of labour across societies based on overarching analysis of social structures or human behaviour. Under this heading we examined the Microeconomic approach, Marxist-Feminist theorizations, Feminist-Marxist or Dual Systems theorizations and Radical Feminist approaches. The reader was, in Chapter 5, urged to draw his/her own conclusions as to the appropriate universalistic theorization to choose based on his/her own view of the degree of choice they perceive women to exercise in their lives and/or the nature of the social structure they perceive as shaping that choice. However, we opted for Walby's dual-system theory (1990) and Connell's (1987) theorization of gender relations as providing the most convincing universalistic theoretical explanations for the Anglo-French similarities and differences outlined above and in Chapters 2, 3 and 4.

Walby (1990) argues that patriarchy is composed of various structures that are to a certain extent independent of one another. At an economic level, she asserts that there are several patriarchal structures: the patriarchal mode of production by which men appropriate women's labour within marriage and the household relationship; patriarchal relations in paid work and the patriarchal state. Walby's argument is particularly powerful because it states that patriarchy can take on different forms and be present to varying degrees. The

different forms are dependent on the interaction of these patriarchal structures. Hence, in various times and places, some of the
structures are more important than others. The elimination of any
one patriarchal structure does not lead to the demise of the system
as a whole. Walby (1997) also differentiates between public and
private patriarchy. Private patriarchy is based on the relative exclusion of women from arenas of social life apart from the household,
with a patriarch appropriating women's services individually and
directly in the relatively private sphere of the home. Public patriarchy, in contrast, is based on structures other than the household,
such as institutions conventionally regarded as part of the public
domain. With capital's increased demand for women's labour, Walby
asserts that there has been a shift from a more private to a more
public patriarchy in countries like Britain and France.

In short, Walby's theorization allows us to explain how change
can come about in one sphere of life, or indeed, work, without
automatically bringing about change in another. The explanatory
power of her theorization for the similarities seen in women's work
situations in Britain and France is clear. In both nations, there has
been progress in gender relations in the public sphere but the private sphere has stayed just as gendered as ever was the case. Hence,
more employment alone for women is unlikely in and of itself to
lead to greater equality elsewhere. Her theorization also enables us
to explain the cross-national differences in women's work situations. For Walby, these are the result of how new forms of patriarchy
build upon old forms and are differently interpreted in different
spatial and temporal contexts. Britain, therefore, is witnessing a
slightly different experience to France due to the ways in which
the dynamics of new forms of capitalism and patriarchy pass through
the lens of different historical contexts to result in nationally specific
outcomes.

Connell's (1987) theorization of gender relations, although offering a less explicit framework for understanding how progress in
gender relations can vary so significantly between the public and
private spheres, is nevertheless useful in three main ways. First,
because according to his theorization, cultural specificity is located
at the level of the individual and at the societal level – in the form
of prescriptive norms and gender stereotypes. Second, because he
identifies the state as playing an important role in defining and
maintaining the existing gender order. Finally, because he sees his
three components of the gender order, which draw on the notions

of both capitalism and patriarchy (a division of labour, power expressed in the connection of authority with masculinity, and cathexis, which refers to the emotionally charged relations with people), as being capable of being reaffirmed through practice, or challenged and reconstructed. Hence, Connell also provides an explanation for the variation in time and place of gender relations.

On the other hand, there are 'particularistic explanations' which do not involve an overarching analysis of social structures, are based more often on empirical research and tend to focus on one or more explanatory variables. Under this heading, we examined theorizations or approaches which we termed Liberal Feminist, Segmented Labour Market and Societal. The choice of particularistic explanations for the Anglo-French similarities and differences in women's work situations is dependent in part on the degree to which the reader believes the state to be a key force in shaping women's lives. Much cross-national comparative research to date has attributed cross-national variations in women's employment situations to the impact of differing welfare regimes. Our review of particularistic explanations showed that the state influences women's paid employment in Britain and France through its social policy, education policy and regulation of the labour market and that due attention must also be given to the impact of business concerns, organized labour, the operation of the family economy – which gives rise to women's degree of availability for paid work – and the supra-national regulatory framework. However, as we stated above, state social policy alone provides a poor understanding of the similarities and differences in women's unpaid work situations in the two countries. In the absence of these other influences on women's paid work situations, it is hard to explain the emerging strong similarities in women's employment characteristics in the two countries which we describe in Chapter 2: integration (rising participation rates of women and gradual desegregation of occupations), differentiation (the continued gap between men's and women's pay), and polarization (between women in more highly qualified professions working full-time or who can negotiate part-time work with good working conditions, and less well-qualified women, or younger women in particular in France, who find themselves more often in part-time work with poor conditions of employment).

Although we set out these arguments – universalistic and particularistic – in two opposing groups, we advocate a multistranded approach which embraces the two and also draws together agency and structure. We therefore argue for the use of Walby's (1997) Feminist-Marxist theory and Connell's (1987) theorization of gender relations to provide a theoretical framework capable of explaining changes in women's work situations over time and space, combined with a Societal particularistic approach of the types proposed by O'Reilly (1995) and Gregory and O'Reilly (1996), which allow the mechanics of patriarchy and capitalism to be operationalized by linking together the roles of the family, the economy (including organized labour), the state and supranational legislation in explaining women's work situations.

Policy: how can we engender progress in gender relations?

Some authors see little prospect for change in gender relations. For Delphy and Leonard (1992), patriarchy has an enduring nature that adapts to change, rather than capitulates to it, and the fact that the need by capitalism for women in the labour force has not undermined patriarchal relations in the home is considered to constitute evidence for this. We, however, hold a more positive vision of the future of gender relations (as espoused by Walby, 1990 and Calasanti and Bailey, 1994), believing that progress can occur in the public or private sphere without it necessarily impinging on the other.

How, then, can progress be made in the private sphere? The state's ability to influence the private sphere, even under the most optimistic scenarios (such as in Sweden) would seem to be limited. However, state policies over the postwar period have, even in the Scandinavian countries, focused predominantly on women: promoting women's employment and their ability to reconcile paid work with caring responsibilities. There are, as we have shown in Chapter 6, strong arguments against relying solely on a similar strategy in order to progress gender relations into the millennium. First, although it may be partially true that women's greater participation in the labour market has been liberating by comparison with a position where women had little choice but to stay at home with children, our evidence in Part I of this book suggests that this is no longer the case. Second, in a context in which full-time continuous employment is less a prospect for men and in which more time is now spent in informal than in formal production, we cannot base our hopes on obtaining gender equality by seeking to replicate this model for women in the dwindling formal sector. Finally, 'progress' in gender relations in the postwar period has been achieved by the redistribution of work among women, whether this has come about through a formalization of care work as it has in France or informally within the extended family and formally within the market, as it has in Britain. Although some may argue that this process is positive because it has created jobs for women, such jobs nevertheless carry the status accorded to caring work (that is, a labour of love and self-sacrifice, rather than an activity which requires skill and confers social status) and its associated employment conditions. Moreover, this process in no way implicates men in caring and does not engender a fundamental deconstruction of the relationship between gender and caring. In sum, more full-time employment for some women, without change on the part of men, can only lead to a situation of greater inequality between women (the carers and those disengaged from caring), and state policy in its present form can do little to alter this situation.

We therefore argue that there is a need to develop policies which explicitly couple women's insertion into the labour market with a renegotiation between men and women of domestic and community work and of the responsibility for this work. Both state and supranational policies to improve women's position in the labour force can be effective as we have seen in the case of Britain and France. However, this is only part of the story. Our evidence in Part I of this book suggests, however, that policies which simply give men the opportunity to engage in unpaid work do not bear fruit and that fundamental changes in men's perceptions of their roles and responsibilities must be engendered if progress in gender relations is to be achieved. This is not least because while women only remain the 'domestic sex', the operation of the labour market reflects this situation by constructing jobs as if individuals are responsible for one domain or another and thereby thwarting attempts to achieve equality in the public sphere.

Hence, we argue that to achieve progress in gender relations, the state should adopt a pro-active and constructive policy which aims to both revalue caring in society and increase men's involvement in this realm. The benefits of such a change in men's role for their well-being and that of their children, are now well-documented. A number of approaches could be advanced to achieve this end, which we describe in detail in Chapter 6. These include adopting policies, set in the context of the wider objective of equal opportunities for men and women in both paid and unpaid work, to seek to socialize men into caring functions through such measures as the teaching of caring skills in schools and the availability of more courses for fathers and by demonstrating the economic advantages of developing new skills and ways of working. Changing working hours norms would need to be a key feature of state policy to engender a greater sharing of unpaid work between men and women. We argue the case for men adopting working patterns which are more like women rather than the reverse, with both men and women working fewer than full-time hours and sharing paid and unpaid work. The opportunity for such a change could derive in part from the processes of globalization and automation, which are redefining employment and increasing the proportion of overall workload undertaken on a unpaid basis. The state, however, could give practical incentives for such a change in working hours by reinforcing the protective legislation for employees working less than full-time, by ensuring that the right to work less than full-time hours is available to all employees at any time in their lives, and by offering practical advice and even financial incentives for organizations to change their *modus operandi*. Hence, organizations could be encouraged to alter conventional notions of commitment to employment (by which commitments outside employment are seen as reducing commitment to employment), and to challenge the view that long hours are a sign of commitment. Employees would thus need to be assessed on the basis of their output and not input. For thorough-going change in business attitudes to be achieved, it would be necessary to convince businesses that their own goals can be compatible with those of employees, families and the wider society. A less feasible, but nonetheless potentially effective measure, might be to introduce a social wage scheme, thereby promoting genuine freedom for men and women in their activities, and making it easier for men to accept caring responsibilities.

However, for all such policies to be effective there would need to be a fundamental reconceptualization of the roles of women and men in society in both the public and private spheres. The state could clearly promote such a reconceptualization through debate and practical measures such as promotional campaigns, and notably help change ideologies in employment so that men's enhanced role in caring work could be recognized. That said, freedom of choice in terms of the division of work between women and men will not be achieved, particularly if no social wage scheme exists, until inequalities in access to highly qualified jobs and in pay are reduced and ultimately removed. State policies would also urgently need to address these areas.

While the state's role would be important in engendering progress in gender relations, in our view change must also take place through interpersonal processes. We believe that progress in gender relations will only occur if there is an effort on the part of women (and men) themselves to cause gender renegotiation in the private sphere. Interpersonal interaction is how gender roles are produced and maintained in everyday life and changes in gender roles go hand in hand with interpersonal conflict over appropriate role expectations. Women may therefore be able to break through traditional gender roles through personal interaction. Their ability to do so will clearly be improved if they are both materially and ideologically empowered in the ways outlined above.

Finally, we call on men to undertake the 'reflexive project of self' and to begin, as women have in recent decades, to disengage themselves from tradition and structure in order to construct their own life narratives. If men are, as surveys suggest, really serious about involving themselves in their children's lives then they too must 'kick start' the 'stalled revolution' and grasp the mantle of change.

Notes

Chapter 2 Women's Paid Work

1 A significant dissimilarity between the countries, of course, has been the rate of economic growth over the postwar period. It is generally accepted, by economists at least, that the postwar period in France has been exceptional for its economic growth, taking the economy from a predominantly agricultural one to a highly modernized one competitive on the world stage. Over the postwar period growth (measured as average annual growth of GDP) in France has consistently outperformed the UK. For example, from 1960 to 1973, average annual growth in GDP was 5.5 per cent in France and only 3.2 per cent in the UK. More recently, in the period 1979 to 1985, annual growth in GDP was 1.2 per cent in France and only 1 per cent in the UK (Eck, 1990).

2 France remained an agricultural society much later than the UK, with over a third of the working population still employed in agriculture at the end of World War II. In 1954, 28.4 per cent of women's employment was located in agriculture compared with 7.4 per cent in the UK (Hantrais, 1990: Table 3.2). The proportion of women employed in industry in France was also much lower than in the UK in the immediate postwar period, reflecting the UK's earlier industrial development, as too was the proportion of women employed in the services. However, the continued decrease in women's employment in French agriculture caused by the inability of the economic family holding based system to adapt to international competition after France's protectionism was dropped in the late 1950s, was matched by a growth in the numbers of women employed in the service sector, particularly after 1962, which began its expansion much later than in the UK (Bouillaguet-Bernard *et al.*, 1981). This late move into the service sector is reflected in the statistics on salaried employment for women in civilian employment which rose from 64.7 per cent to 73.5 per cent over the period 1954 to 1965. Comparative statistics for the UK over the same period are 92.6 per cent and 93.2 per cent (OECD, 1965).

3 Between 1968 and 1988, the activity rates of women aged 55 to 64 years fell from 41 per cent to 31.8 per cent in France and from only 38.1 per cent to 36.6 per cent in the UK (Bosch *et al.*, 1994: Table 6).

4 This would seem to be a continuation of the trends identified by Daric (1947). Married women's activity rates in 1931 for the non-agricultural population (active women as a percentage of the entire population; proportion of women in the active population) in France are more than double those in the UK (respectively, 19.4 per cent compared with 9.9 per cent and 39.4 per cent compared with 15.2 per cent) despite very similar marriage rates (Daric, 1947).

5 Activity levels for French women are strongly related to a number of factors: qualification levels, the partner's profession, couples' plans and the family budget (Villeneuve-Gokalp, 1994). Marry *et al.* (1995) also reveal the importance of other factors in the attachment of young women to paid employment such as their mothers' activity, their fathers' profession, the profession of their husband, the number of children and the age at which the first child was born and the woman's profession.
6 By contrast, ethnic minority women, with the exception of Pakistani and Bangladeshi women, are much more likely to work full-time across their working lives, particularly if they have a dependent child (Dale and Holdsworth, 1996).
7 This may help explain evidence for job tenure among British and French women: job tenure is considerably lower for British women than for men but is more or less the same in France (OECD, 1993).
8 For the problems of defining lone parents in Europe see Millar, 1994.
9 For recent comparative studies of lone parents in the EU see Bradshaw *et al.* (1996), Duncan and Edwards (1997) and Lefaucheur and Martin (1995).
10 For a detailed analysis of the problems of comparing unemployment data across the EU, see Glover (1994).
11 In fact the polarization of women in the face of unemployment is greater in the UK than in France see Table 2.13.

Table 2.13 Percentage unemployed by educational level for women aged 25–59 years, France and UK, 1997

	France	UK
Third level education	13.0	14.4
Upper secondary level	41.1	30.6
< upper secondary	45.9	55.0
Total	100.0	100.0

Note: for difficulties in comparing unemployment rates in France and the UK see Table 2.3.

Source: OOPEC, (1998: Table 030).

Interestingly, when the unemployment rate of those with higher education is compared with that of those without, the protection afforded by higher education to men and women in France is considerably greater than that in Britain (see Bourdon, 1995). This may help explain the race for higher qualifications in France.
12 This is born out by Eurostat figures (OOPEC, 1998: Table 107) which found that the proportion seeking part-time work in all age groups among the unemployed is significantly higher in Britain than in France (see Table 2.14). The proportion of women in involuntary part-time work (as a percentage of all economically active women) is also higher in France than in Britain (7.8 per cent compared with 4.5 per cent) (Gauvin, 1995), and the share of involuntary part-time employment

Table 2.14   Proportion of all unemployed women seeking part-time work, France and UK, 1997

	France	UK
Full-time work	78.4	45.7
Part-time work	20.9	52.8

Source: OOPEC, (1998: Table 107).

in part-time employment in France is more than double that in the UK (OOPEC, 1998: Graph 8).

13   As Hakim (1997) points out, legal definitions of part-time work display enormous variation between countries. This is also true for Britain and France in national statistics. In Britain, part-time work is defined as work for under 30 hours a week, whereas in France part-time workers are those working one-fifth shorter hours than the normal working time or the legally allowed maximum of 39 hours or any lesser number of hours specified in collective agreements. Labour Force Survey data helps us to overcome this problem as workers are asked to classify themselves as full or part-time workers according to their own definitions. However, this does not resolve all interpretation problems as norms for part-time working hours vary very considerably between Britain and France (see Hakim, 1997).

14   For a detailed comparative explanation of the growth of part-time work in Britain and France, see Garnsey (1985), Gregory (1989), Hoang-Ngoc and Lefresne (1994) and O'Reilly (1994).

15   After moves to reduce working time collectively at the beginning of the 1980s with the aim of solving the unemployment problem, pressure to improve the competitiveness of French companies in a global marketplace changed the focus in the mid-1980s to one of improving the flexibility of working time. Rising unemployment levels at the end of the 1980s, however, brought a return to the debate over work-sharing, and a series of measures starting with those seeking to increase the use of part-time work, and then to link reductions of working time to job creation and flexibility in working time (in the context of the 1993 Five year employment plan (*la loi quinquennale sur l'emploi*)). Following on from then was the *Loi Robien* of 11 June 1996 which has sought to link job creation or job maintenance in the private sector with collective reductions in working time, through the introduction of multiple forms of working-time flexibility (Girard, 1997). The recent law introducing the 35-hour week has also sought to achieve similar objectives.

16   Measures to stimulate the use of part-time work started in 1982 (edict of 26 March, 1982) when the conditions of part-time working were aligned with those of full-timers, and part-time work was encouraged in the public sector (edict of 31 March, 1982). The Socialist government then introduced measures to reduce unemployment levels (decrees of 23 March and 27 June 1984 and 5 March 1985) by subsidizing the recruitment of the unemployed on part-time contracts, or by encouraging

the transfer of full-timers to part-time contracts as part of early-retirement packages. With the aim of encouraging economic efficiency, the first Socialist government then (by the decree of 31 March 1985) gave subsidies to companies reducing working-time by the use of part-time work through its *conventions aménagement du temps de travail et modernization*. The right-wing government under Chirac then introduced more flexibility in part-time working hours (by the edict of 11 August 1986 and the law of 19 June 1987) by allowing annualized part-time working (called *le travail intermittent*) which permitted an averaging of income over the year. A return to a preoccupation with unemployment towards the end of the 1980s led to a series of measures designed to encourage workers threatened with redundancy to take up part-time work either tempo-rarily or permanently (*Conventions ADFNE mi-temps and Conventions d'aide au passage à mi-temps du FNE*). The law of 3 January 1991 saw full-time employees given the right to opt to work part-time on a voluntary basis provided the principle was agreed first through collective bargain-ing. In 1992 and 1993, deductions in employers' social security payments for employees newly working part-time (19–30 hours) were allowed (30 per cent of NI charges) provided that overall working hours in the com-pany did not fall and either a new job was created or the move to part-time working was chosen by a full-timer. The law of 31 December 1992 did, however, place limitations on the use of extra working hours for part-timers (limited to 10 per cent of their contracted hours) unless an alternative agreement was negotiated at branch level. The Five-year Employment Law (of 20 December 1993) also allowed deductions of employers' NI contributions for part-timers, widening the hours band for which the measure was applicable to 16–32 hours, and allowing the annualization of full-time work and part-time work where the business was seasonal. It also allowed more flexibility in the conditions under which NI exemptions were made and allowed the partial or full deduc-tion of employer contributions relating to family benefit payments where part-timers were in poorly paid jobs. The law also allowed companies to negotiate an increase in part-time hours by one third of their nomi-nal contract length and reduce the notice period for part-time overtime working through agreements at company level. Under the last right-wing government, the *Loi Robien* did not exclude combining incentives to reduce working time with existing incentives for part-time working as long as part-time hours were reduced in the same proportion as full-time hours. This remains a possibility as the 35 hour working week comes into application in France, although the continuation of the two is likely to be very complicated (Lebaube, 1998). Finally, and most recently, measures have been taken to improve 'working conditions' for part-timers: NI reductions are now only available for part-timers working 18–32 hours/week and are not applicable to annualized hours except when explicitly chosen by the employee. Also only one two hour break between two periods of work during the working day is now permitted (Lebaube, 1998).

17 Company-level negotiations have been increasing in importance since the introduction of the Auroux laws in 1982 which imposed annual

negotiations over working time at company level and allowed company- or sectoral-level agreements to derogate from all legislative provisions governing the flexibility in working time. The number of agreements has risen from 6754 in 1991 to 7450 in 1994, and the proportion of these relating to working time has risen from 40.6 per cent to 44.1 per cent over the same period (Bangoura *et al.*, 1995).

18 *Table 2.15* Proportion of part-time working (men and women) by sector, France and UK, 1997

	UK	France
Agriculture	18.9	15.4
Industry	7.6	5.5
Services	31.8	22.3
Total	25.3	17.6

Note: for difficulties in comparing levels of part-time work in France and the UK see footnote 13.

Source: Labour Force Survey (1997: Table 0.55).

19 The question over the degree to which part-time work is voluntary or involuntary is a problematical one. Measuring individuals' satisfaction raises an important methodological issue (see Fagan, 1998) which is that existing survey questions do not enable us to ascertain whether longer or shorter hours would be preferred: there is still room for dissatisfaction with working hours even if an individual states that they are working part-time voluntarily. As Fagan (1998: 28) points out in the Labour Force Surveys: 'it would be more helpful to ask about preferences for specified hours bands in the context that earnings would be adjusted as a result'.

20 Hantrais (1990: 149) also suggests that French women suffer from socially imposed time structures which require them to 'organize more tightly packed time schedules than their British counterparts during the smaller number of hours when they are not at their workplace'. By this Hantrais (1990) refers to the fact that importance in France is still attached to eating a cooked lunch and a cooked evening meal, which reduces time to be spent shopping and doing other chores.

21 The French institutional context provides a number of incentives for longer working hours. For example, in 1996 eligibility for sick pay and reimbursement of medical costs was dependent respectively on an average of 16 hours or 10 hours per week of paid work over three months (with additional hours minima if sick pay is to extend over six months) (PRAT, 1996). This minima has led many unions to bring in conventions for minimum weekly working hours of 16 or more, hence offering effective protection of part-timers (see Gregory, 1989 for the effect of such conventions in retailing; Maier, 1991). In addition, the various initiatives introduced by the French government to encourage the growth of part-time work in recent years have primarily stimulated the development of part-time work of over 16 hours a week (an obvious exception

to this has been the family employment (*emplois familiaux*) and local employment opportunities (*emplois de proximité*), where reductions in employers' NI contributions were initially offered to employees working eight hours a week or less and were extended to those working longer hours in 1996). The British institutional framework, by contrast, gives an incentive to shorter working hours in the form of the NI system which encourages the creation of part-time work in low-paid part-time jobs. Until recent changes in UK law achieved through a House of Lords' ruling (3 March 1994) hours thresholds were applied for the application of basic employment rights (eight hours/week continuously for five years, 16 hours/week continuously over two years) giving an additional incentive to employers to use short-time contracts. As we discuss later, the EU working-time directive (Council Directive 93/104/EC of 23 November 1993) may create some sort of pressure to reduce working hours in the UK.

22 For example those associated with economic restructuring in the public sector (*accompagnement aux restructurations – aide au passage à mi-temps/temps partiel*) and the incentives to create part-time jobs (*abattements-temps partiel*) in the private sector including special incentives for the creation of poorly paid part-time jobs.

23 Hantrais found that many highly qualified women were using part-time work as a temporary measure to help maintain their continuity in employment (Hantrais, 1990: 87).

24 In the private sector it has, for example, created incentives to employ specific groups of workers with reductions in NI charges for employers or pay rates below the minimum wage (*the Contrats de qualification* and more recently the *Crédit Formation Individualisé*) while in the public sector it has created the *Contrats Emploi Solidarité*, and more recently the *Emplois Jeunes*.

25 The measures relating to temporary work have been the following: the Law of 3 January 1979, the Edict of 5 February 1982, Law of 25 July 1985, Circular of 14 March 1986, Edict of 11 August 1986, Circular of 26 December 1986 and, finally, Circular of 26 December 1988.

26 White (1996) found that women have benefited from an increase in their skills, particularly those working part-time, over the period 1987 to 1992, but that nevertheless men continue to be asked for different skills than women, and notably a greater use of new technology compared with women's greater social skills. The growth in skills for part-timers has not been linked to increasing autonomy at work or freedom of action.

27 Further evidence of these similarities comes from comparisons of highly qualified women in Britain and France (Crompton with Le feuvre, 1996) which highlight the similar individual orientations brought to work by women in the occupations of pharmacy and finance in Britain and France, as well as the similarity in structural features of these occupations in the two countries.

28 Employees will be allowed three months unpaid parental leave when they have a baby or adopt a child after one year's service. They will also be given protection from dismissal for exerting this right. The leave can be taken up to the child's eighth birthday, full-time or part-time, in a single block or as an annual allowance (*The Times*, 1998).

Chapter 3 Women's Domestic Work

1 However, it should be noted that at the time of writing, the European Household Panel Survey was for the first time compiling comparative data from across the EU on matters internal to the household, including the division of unpaid work. This is evidence of the growing realization of the continuing importance of the family and household for economic well-being and caring functions and in terms of its impact on gender equality.

Chapter 5 Theorizing Women's Work

1 As far as unpaid work is concerned, these theorizations and explanations are usually applied simply to domestic labour but here we take them as explanations of both domestic labour and community work, given the similar gender variations in these two forms of work identified in Chapters 3 and 4 and the care-giving (or expressive) nature of much of the work undertaken under the banner of community work.

2 Criticisms of this theory deriving from cross-national comparative research have notably been made by Crompton with Le feuvre (1996) and Rubery *et al.* (1995). On the basis of their qualitative in-depth study of women in banking and pharmacy, Crompton with Le feuvre (1996) found that the patterns of work and family life of the women interviewed varied significantly by occupation. Nevertheless, the women interviewed in the two countries in the two occupations had faced very similar sets of constraints as far as combining their work with their family lives was concerned. For them, the cross-nationally systematic variation of these constraints by occupational type – and their consequences – must throw some doubt upon the assumption that variations in the patterns of women's employment reflect the existence of fundamentally different categories of women so far as work commitment is concerned. Rubery *et al.* (1995) come to question Hakim's theorization as a result of comparing the proportion of women working full-time and part-time across EU countries. They find that: 'If motherhood is associated with a low work commitment and an orientation towards a "domestic" rather than an "employment" career then this is not translated into part-time employment consistently across countries.' (Rubery *et al.*, 1995: 108). The conclusion is that reasons for working time do not simply reflect work preferences and responsibilities of motherhood. They argue that employment decisions are embedded within other social institutions and that differences in these societal systems influence how women combine employment with domestic responsibilities.

3 Duncan and Edwards (1997: 56) imply criticism of Hakim's theorization in their investigation into the factors influencing the decision of UK lone mothers to take paid work. For these authors it is 'social, *collective* [our emphasis] relations and understanding about motherhood and paid work', which they term 'gendered moral rationalities', which are the primary factors influencing this decision.

4 F. W. Taylor was the initiator of Scientific Management which was very

influential in work organization well into the twentieth century in the industrialized world. He developed new management strategy and work design in order to promote efficiency based on his observations of the armed forces and the steel industry in the 1880s. Taylor suggested three basic measures to improve efficiency based on the organizational structure, the design and measurement of work tasks and the motivation of workers: first, a type of supervision and foremanship complementary; second, a work-study method of work tasks; and third, the recruitment of a 'first-class man' for the work, who should be paid a fair wage for the job (see Dex, 1985: 25).

5 Walby (1997) points out that restructuring theories have taken forward cyclical reserve army theory and Braverman's theory in order to attempt to explain the differing employment of women in various localities. They are, however, not applicable to similarities and differences in women's paid work at national level.

6 Our description of dual-systems theorizations is based on Anglo-Saxon literature. This is because French feminist research has been relatively slow to develop such theorizations (Delphy and Kergoat, 1982). From the 1970s women's work in France began to be conceptualized in terms of the relationship between women's paid and unpaid work, the two being seen as intimately linked (see overview by Barrère-Maurisson, 1992). *Rapports sociaux de sexe* (relations between the sexes) were seen as being based on a power relationship between men and women and as leading to gendered social relations in the home and in the workplace (Kergoat, 1992).

7 It is only recently that appeals have been made for women and management perspectives to 'integrate an analysis of organizational structures and gender issues with an exploration of cultures, in relation to theorisation of power and inequality' (Green and Cassell, 1996: 171).

8 Having said this, Laufer (1993) gives evidence which suggests that French women suffer from similar problems in reaching 'top' jobs, as do British women (Davidson and Cooper, 1993).

9 For example, Craig *et al.* (1995: 3) note that payment structures and employment systems derive not just from product market or technological factors but also from 'the interaction of the economic and technological environment with institutional and social factors and, in particular, with collective organization and a differentiated or segmented labour supply'.

10 Jenson (1985: 7) uses the notion of the 'universe of political discourse' to describe the range of forces which impact on state policies. She sees the universe of political discourse as defining politics or establishing the parameters of political action by limiting the range of actors accorded the status of legitimate participant, the range of issues considered legitimate and meaningful, the policy alternatives considered feasible for implementation and the alliance strategies available for achieving change.

11 For a detailed examination of family policies in France and Britain, see Hantrais (1994) and of work/family policies, see Hantrais and Letablier (1996). For a comparison of the development of child-care policies in

Britain and France, see Moss (1988) and Lelièvre and Lelièvre (1991).

12 There is strong evidence from Jenson (1986) that the French state's intervention in mediating work and family has been influenced by a pre-existing situation by which French women have historically worked full-time more extensively than their British counterparts (a dual earner, male patriarch model prevailed well into this century). The origins of the British non-interventionist position in relation to the care of dependants came partly from a desire historically for men to continue to be financially responsible for their families in order to deter family disintegration (Jenson, 1986: 21). A partial explanation for the origins of the British non-interventionist labour market policy has been proposed by Shonfield cited in Hayward (1986). For him, in the UK, ' there is an established principle of strong unitary central power, there are other potent traditions ingrained in the political system which impede the development of active interventionist government. There is an abiding prejudice which sees it as the natural business of government to react – not to act'. By contrast, Zysman, quoted in Hayward (1986), suggests that the French state has a tradition of intervention beginning with industrialization which was managed by the state and which has prevented the market from imposing its will on society.

13 The predominance of family holdings, farms and also small shops where women were employed much later (up to the 1950s and 1960s) in France established a model of dual earning in France, while in the UK a single-earner family model was established much earlier (from about the 1850s), even if many working class families did not conform to it (Lewis, 1984; Tilly and Scott, 1987). Another contributing factor was the strong demand for women's labour in industry, commerce, banking and insurance which emerged in France from about 1870, up to and including the interwar years, when slow population growth and shortages of young people and male labour caused French employers to call on women who were cheaper to employ (Stewart, 1989).

14 Measures have tended to include mechanisms for protecting workers from the abusive use of part-time work, many requiring prior negotiation of a collective agreement at some level. For example, the edict of 11 August 1986 and the Law of 19 June 1987 introduced the notion of *le travail intermittent*: annualized part-time working with fluctuating part-time hours but an average weekly or monthly income. This form of contract could only be introduced, however, after a collective agreement at some level (company or outlet upwards) was made. Similarly, the Aubry proposals (which were not ultimately introduced because of a change of government), gave incentives for the employment of part-timers. The jobs were, however, to be accompanied by guarantees for the worker in the area of career development and in priority access to full-time jobs. Limits were also proposed on hours worked over contracted hours (from 30 per cent to 10 per cent of contracted hours) (*Le Monde*, 1992). Most recently, as discussed earlier (see Chapter 2, note 16), measures have sought to limit part-time contracts and irregular working patterns for part-timers.

15 Social security and employment-protection law has until recently made

a distinction between those working full-time and over 16 hours per week and those working below 16 hours per week. The distinction in employment law has now been removed by the House of Lords' ruling of 3 March 1994.

16 For good examples of this see INSEE-DARES (1995) and Lallement (1993).

17 For example, the edict of 16 January 1982 started a process of state disengagement from working-time questions by allowing company/sectoral level agreements to derogate from all legislative provisions governing flexibility in working time. The Law of 20 December 1993 relating to employment and training has extended to company/plant level negotiations the ability to stipulate extra working hours for part-timers (up to one third of their contract length), without there being a prior sectoral level agreement on this issue (INSEE-DARES, 1995).

Chapter 6 Gender Relations: Progress and Policy

1 The United Nations Development Project (UNDP) (Walby, 1997: 23) takes the position that 'the impact of paid employment is both large and positive for women, in that it increases women's capacities and potentials'. In its gender sensitive index of human development, the UNDP regards the extent of women's employment and their level of pay relative to men together as one of the three major indicators of the position of women (the others being education and longevity).

2 1963 saw a decree instituting mixed *Collèges d'Enseignement Secondaire* and 1975 saw the *La Loi Haby* which introduced mixed schooling for all at primary and secondary level. Under Yvette Roudy, policy sought to encourage women to choose 'unconventional' careers and the Circular of 22 July 1982 aimed at encouraging a greater awareness in education of the inequalities in training which women faced. The early 1990s saw a continuation of these policies: in 1992 three-year plans were enacted in each local education authority to encourage women into technical and scientific training. In 1996, training specifically designed to improve teachers' awareness of the inequalities in men's and women's education was introduced.

3 *Les plans d'égalité* are to be negotiated between unions and employers at company level and seek to address areas of inequality between men and women. Companies can receive subsidies by the state for the plan's application. The *Contrats pour la mixité des emplois* can also result in financial support from the state but are the result of negotiation directly between an employer and an employee. The contracts seek to give women greater access to qualifications or jobs where they are under-represented (Toutain, 1992).

4 For example, the *Sukera* project developed by the Instituto Vasco de la Mujer in the Spanish Basque country, which offers men courses in cooking, home economics and care for children and older people. At the same time women can learn carpentry, electricity or car maintenance skills. In schools, mixed groups of girls and boys attend these workshops (Commission of the European Communities, 1997).

5   However, there has been no active campaign by men in the UK for paternity or parental leave.

6   Views on the impact of the EU *per se* on women are varied. Pillinger (1992) is anxious that women will be the potential losers from European union, although Lindley (1992) points out that its effects will depend on how social cohesion is defined and whether the work and family model adopted is a sharing one.

7   Calasanti and Bailey (1994: 50) hold a very pessimistic view on the effect of sex role ideology, arguing that: 'Education and policies geared at helping men and women share domestic duties do not mean that things will "naturally" change as men and women are given more equal opportunities to engage in domestic role-sharing. It is a mistake to assume that changes which will "allow" men to be more active mean they will be, even if we socialise boys and girls more equally. Such changes are no doubt necessary but they are also insufficient, from a socialist-feminist standpoint, as they will only "naturally" work if the structural bases of power are equalised. If power is unequal, then despite policy changes it will still be men's decision as to whether or not they will participate more'. This explanation, however, is rather inadequate as Calasanti and Bailey do not address the question of what constitutes 'the power structure' outside equal opportunities, socialization and so on. It seems a pessimistic viewpoint which does not allow for change in the *status quo*.

8   Rhys Williams' 'social contract' scheme advocated a basic income which would have provided a tax-free living allowance to every man and woman whether employed or not and irrespective of relationship status (see Briar, 1997). This would have resourced domestic and caregiving work. Although not adopted the ideas have been continued and developed.

9   It has also been speculated that the process of globalization could have benefits for the gender division of labour through 'cultural globalization'. Stockman *et al.* (1995: 212) suggest that: 'Awareness of alternative ways in which women and men may arrange their work and family life might encourage a search for improvements, without taking any existing pattern as a model to be emulated. The search for better ways of living could widen internal cultural debate into inter-cultural debate'. On the other hand, Stockman *et al.* (1995) also speculate that cultural globalization could act against the interests of progress in gender relations by reinforcing 'cultural nationalism' and consolidating pre-existing gender roles.

10 A more negative scenario for the impact of globalization can be conceived, of course, if no redistribution of work is achieved while women's employment is increasingly concentrated in atypical employment at the lower end of the labour market (Stockman *et al.*, 1995; Van Hoof and Van Doorne-Huiskes, 1995).

11 This is by no means easy to achieve. Successive pieces of legislation emanating from national and supranational bodies have improved the legal status of part-time work in Britain but it is still seen predominantly as women's work. This is also true in France where part-timers have benefited from equal rights.

References

Abel, E. and Nelson, M. (eds) (1990) *Circles of Love: Work and Identity in Women's Lives*, Albany: State University of New York Press.

Acker, J. (1992) 'Reformer och kvinnor in den frantida valfardstaten', in J. Acker, A. Baude, U. Bjornberg, E. Dahlstrom, G. Forsberg, L. Gonas, H. Holter and A. Nilsson (eds) *Kvinnors och Mans Liv och Arbete*, Stockholm: SMS Forlag.

Actualités Sociales Hebdomadaires (1994) 'Enfance-famille', No. 1879, 12 May.

Afsa, C. (1996) 'L'activité féminine à l'épreuve de l'allocation parentale d'éducation', *Recherches et Prévisions*, 46: 1–8.

Anxo, D. and Daune-Richard, A-M. (1991) 'La place relative des hommes et des femmes sur le marché du travail: une comparaison en France et en Suède', *Travail et Emploi*, 8 (47): 63–78.

Arber, S. and Ginn, J. (1991) *Gender and Later Life: a Sociological Analysis of Resources and Constraints*, London: Sage.

Armstrong, P. (1982) 'If it's only women it doesn't matter so much', in J. West (ed.) *Women, Work and the Labour Market*, London: Routledge & Kegan Paul.

Bangoura, S., Folques, D., Le Corre, V. and Mabile, S. (1995) 'Reprise de la Négociation d'entreprise en 1994 et au début de l'année 1995', *Premières Synthèses*, 120: 161–70.

Barker, D. L. and Allen, S. (eds) (1976) *Dependence and Exploitation in Work and Marriage*, London: Longman.

Barnett, R. C. and Baruch, G. K. (1987) 'Determinants of fathers ' participation in family work', *Journal of Marriage and the Family*, 49: 29–40.

Barrère-Maurisson, M-A. (1992) *La division familiale du travail: La vie en double*, Paris, Presses Universitaires de France.

Barrère-Maurisson, M-A., Daune-Richard, A-M., and Letablier, M-T. (1987) 'Activité, emploi et travail des femmes: une comparaison France-Grande-Bretagne', *Actes des Journées Compaaisons Internationales en économie sociale*, Paris: Aix et CNRS-LEST.

Barrère-Maurisson, M-A., Daune-Richard, A-M. and Letablier, M-T. (1989) 'Le travail à temps partiel plus développé au Royaume-Uni qu'en France', *Economie et Statistique*, 220: 47–56.

Barron, R. D. and Norris, G. M. (1976) 'Sexual divisions and the dual labour market', in D. L. Barker and S. Allen (eds) *Dependence and Exploitation in Work and Marriage*, London: Longman.

Barthe, M. A. (1988) *L'Economie Cachée*, Paris: Syros Alternatives.

Baruch, G. K. and Barnett, R. C. (1981) 'Fathers' participation in the care of pre-school children', *Sex Roles*, 7: 1043–55.

Baumier, A. and Remy, J. (1995) 'Femmes: le sexe fort', *L'Express*, 2 March: 28–34.

Baxandell, R., Ewen, E. and Gordon, L. (1976) 'The working-class has two sexes', *Monthly Review*, 28: 1–9.

Beck, U. (1991) *The Risk Society*, London: Sage.

Beck, U. (1994) 'The reinvention of politics: towards a theory of reflexive modernisation', in U. Beck, A. Giddens and S. Lash (eds) *Reflexive Modernisation: Politics, Tradition and Aesthetics in the Modern Social Order*, Cambridge: Polity Press.

Beck, U. and Beck-Gernsheim, E. (1995) *The Normal Chaos of Love*, Cambridge: Polity Press.

Becker, G. S. (1965) 'A theory of the allocation of time revisited', *Journal of Political Economy*, 75: 493–517.

Becker, G. S. (1976) *The Economic Approach to Human Behavior*, Chicago: University of Chicago Press.

Becker, G. S. (1981) *A Treatise on the Family*, Cambridge, MA: Harvard University Press.

Beechey, V. (1977) 'Some notes on female wage labour in capitalist production', *Capital and Class*, 3: 45–66.

Beechey, V. (1978) 'Women and production: A critical analysis of some sociological theories of women's work', in A. Kuhn and A. M. Wolpe (eds) *Feminism and Materialism: Women and Modes of Production*, London: Routledge and Kegan Paul.

Beechey, V. (1989) 'Women's employment in France and Britain: some problems of comparison', *Work, Employment and Society*, 3: 369–78.

Beechey, V. and Perkins, T. (1987) *A Matter of Hours: Women, Part-time Work and the Labour Market*, Cambridge: Polity Press.

Beillan, V. (1991) 'La garde des enfants: des pratiques socialement différenciées', *Sociétés Contemporaines*, 8: 101–6.

Belloc, B. (1986) 'De plus en plus de salariés à temps partiel', *Economie et Statistique*, 193–4: 43–50.

Belloc, B. and Lagarenne, C. (1996) 'Emplois temporaires et emplois aidés', *Données Sociales*, Paris: INSEE.

Benin, M. H. and Edwards, D. A. (1990) 'Adolescents chores: the difference between dual and single-earner families', *Journal of Marriage and the Family*, 52: 361–73.

Benoit-Guilbot, O. (1989) 'Quelques réflexions sur l'analyse sociétale: l'exemple des régulations des marchés du travail en France et en Grande-Bretagne', *Sociologie du Travail*, 2: 217–25.

Benveniste, C. and Soleilhavoup, J. (1994) 'Un parent seul dans une famille sur huit' *INSEE Premiere*, no. 293, Paris: INSEE

Berk, S. F. (1985) *The Gender Factory*, New York: Plenum.

Biernat, M. and Wortman, C. B. (1991) 'Sharing home responsibilities between professionally employed women and their husbands', *Journal of Personality and Social Psychology*, 60: 844–60.

Bittman, M. (1995) 'The politics of the study of unpaid work', *Just Policy*, 2: 3–10.

Blackwell, L. (1998) *Occupational Sex Segregation and Part-time Work in Modern Britain*, unpublished PhD Thesis, London: City University.

Blair, S. L. (1991) 'The sex-typing of children's household labor: parental influence on daughters', paper presented to the meeting of the American Sociological Association, 23–27 Aug., Cincinnati, OH.

Blood, R. O. and Wolfe, D. M. (1960) *Husbands and Wives*, Glencoe, IL: Free Press.

Bock, B. and Van Doorne-Huiskes, A. (1995) 'The careers of men and women: a life course perspective', in A. Van Doorne-Huiskes, J. Van Hoof and E. Roelofs (eds) *Women and the European Labour Markets*, London: Paul Chapman.

Bock, G. (1992) 'Pauvreté féminine, droits des mères et états-providence', in G. Duby and M. Perrot (eds) *L'histoire des femmes en occident*, Paris: Plon.

Boisard, P. (1995) 'Les horaires de travail dans les pays de l'Union Européenne', *4 Pages*, no. 12, Paris: Centre D'Etudes de l'Emploi.

Borchorst, A. (1990) 'Political motherhood and child care policies: a comparative approach to Britain and Scandinavia', in C. Ungerson (ed.) *Gender and Caring: Work and Welfare in Britain and Scandinavia*, New York: Simon and Schuster.

Bosch, G., Dawkins, P. and Michon, F. (1994) *Times are Changing: Working Time in Fourteen Industrialised Countries*, Geneva: International Institute for Labour Studies.

Bouffartigue, P., de Coninck, F. and Pendariès, J-R. (1992) 'Le nouvel âge de l'emploi à temps partiel: un rôle nouveau lors des débuts de vie active des femmes', *Sociologie du Travail*, 4: 403–28.

Bouillaguet-Bernard, P., Boisard, P. and Letablier, M-T. (1986) 'Le partage du travail: une politique asexuée?', *Nouvelles Questions Féministes*, 14–15: 31–51.

Bouillaguet-Bernard, P., Gauvin-Ayel, A., and Outin, J-L (1981) *Femmes au travail, prosperité et crise*, Paris: Economica.

Bourdon, J. (1995) 'La formation contre le chomâge: une vision économique réévaluée de l'investissement économique', *Sociologie du Travail*, XXXVII, 4: 503–26.

Bradshaw, J., Kennedy, S., Kilkey, M., Hutton, S., Corden, A., Eardley, T., Holmes, H. and Neale, J. (1996) *Policy and the Employment of Lone Parents in 20 Countries, The EU Report*, York: European Observatory on National Family Policies, Social Policy Research Unit, University of York.

Brannen, J. and Moss, P. (1991) *Managing Mothers: Dual Earner Households after Maternity Leave*, London: Macmillan.

Brannen, J., Meszaros, G., Moss, P. and Poland, G. (1994) *Employment and Family Life: A Review of Research in the UK (1980–1994)*, London: Research Series no. 41, Employment Department.

Braverman, H. (1974) *Labor and Monopoly Capital: The Degradation of Work in the Twentieth Century*, New York: Monthly Review Press.

Briant, P., Rimbert, S. and Sofer, C. (1993) *Bilan: l'emploi des femmes*, Rapport présenté au Ministère du Travail. Centre de Recherche sur l'Emploi et la Production, Université d'Orléans, Faculté de Droit, d'Economie et de Gestion, July.

Briar, C. (1997) *Working for Women? Gendered Work and Welfare Policies in Twentieth-century Britain*, London: UCL Press.

Bridgwood, A. and Savage, P. (1993) *General Household Survey 1991*, London: HMSO.

Brown, C.A. (1979) 'The political economy of sexual inequality', Paper presented to the annual meeting of the American Sociological Association, Boston.

Bruegel, I. (1979) 'Women as a reserve army of labour: a note on recent British experience', *Feminist Review*, 22: 12–23.

Bruegel, I. and Hegewisch, A. (1994) 'Flexibilisation and part-time work in Europe', in P. Brown and R. Crompton (eds) *A New Europe: Economic Restructuring and Social Exclusion*, London: UCL Press.

Bryson, L. (1996) 'Revaluing the household economy', *Women's Studies International Forum*, 19(3): 207–19.

Bulletin on Women and Employment in the EU (1995) no 7. Commission of the European Communities Directorate-General for Employment, Industrial Relations and Social Affairs.

Burchell, B. and Rubery, J. (1994) 'Divided Women: labour market segmentation and gender segregation', in A. Scott (ed.) *Gender Segregation and Social Change*, Oxford: Oxford University Press.

Burchell, B. J., Dale, A. and Joshi, H. (1997) 'Part-Time Work among British Women', in H. P. Blossfeld and C. Hakim (eds) *Between Equalization and Marginalization: Women Working Part-time in Europe and the United States of America*, Oxford: OUP.

Burgess, A. (1997) *Fatherhood Reclaimed*, London: Vermillion.

Burghes, L. (1993) *One Parent Families: Policy Options for the 1990s*, York: Joseph Rowntree Foundation.

Caire, G. (1985) 'La négociation collective en France', in *Recherches Economiques et Sociales*, nouvelle série, no. 13–14 et 2e trimestre 1985, Paris: Commissariat Général du Plan Service des Etudes et de la Recherche.

Calasanti, T. and Bailey, C. (1994) 'Gender inequality and the division of household labor in the United States and Sweden: a Socialist-Feminist approach', *Social Problems*, 20: 35–53.

Cealis, R. and Zilberman, S. (1998) 'Les emplois familiaux et les organismes de services aux personnes en 1997', *Premières informations et premières synthèses*, no. 43.2.

CERC (1994) *Précarité et risque d'exclusion en France*, Documents du Centre d'étude des revenus et des coûts, no. 109, Paris: La Documentation Française.

Chabaud, D., Fougeyrollas, D. and Sonthonnax, F. (1985) *Espace et Temps du Travail Domestique*, Paris: Méridiens.

Chabaud-Rychter, D. and Fougeyrollas-Schwebel, D. (1989) 'Exchanges of services in the extended family', Paper presented to the XXVth CFR International seminar on Family, Informal networks and Social Policy, Belgrade 7–11 October.

Chadeau, A. and Fouquet, A. (1981) 'Peut-on mesurer le travail domestique?', *Economie et Statistique*, 136: 29–42.

Colvez, A. (1989) '*Aide à domicile, nouveaux dispositifs, nouvelles pratiques*', paper presented to the UNIOPSS conference, 7 November, Paris.

Comité d'information féminin (1977) *Mesures prévues en faveur de la réinsertion professionnelle des mères de famille*, Paris: Comité d'information féminin, November.

Commaille, J. (1992) *Les Stratégies des Femmes: Travail, Famille et Politique*, Paris: La Découverte.

Commission Européenne (1994) *Protection Sociale et Activité*, Brussels: Commission Européenne.

Commission of the European Communities (1993) *European Social Policy; Options for the Union*, Green Paper, Luxembourg: OOPEC.

Commission of the European Communities (1994) *European Social Policy: A Way Forward for the Union – A White Paper*, Luxembourg: OOPEC.

Commission of the European Communities (1997) Employment and Social Affairs Unit, *Equal Opportunities for Women and Men in the European Union 1996*, Luxembourg: OOPEC.

Comparaisons internationales (1989) No. spécial, 'Comparaisons franco-britanniques des trajectoires familiales et professionnelles'.

Connell, R. (1987) *Gender and Power*, Cambridge: Polity Press.

Corti, L. and Laurie, H. (1993) *Caring and Employment*, Unpublished report from ESRC Research Centre on Micro-Social Change, University of Essex.

Coutrot, L., Fournier, I., Kieffer, A. and Lelièvre, E. (1997) 'The family cycle and the growth of part-time female employment in France: boon or doom?' in H. P. Blossfeld and C. Hakim (eds) *Between Equalization and Marginalization, Women Working Part-Time in Europe and the United States of America*, Oxford: OUP.

Coverman, S. (1985) 'Explaining husbands' participation in domestic labor', *Sociological Quarterly*, 26: 81–97.

Cowan, C. P. and Cowan, P. A. (1987) 'Men's involvement in parenthood: identifying the antecedents and understanding the barriers', in P. W. Berman and F. A. Pedersen (eds) *Men's Transitions to Parenthood: Longitudinal Studies of Early Family Experience*, Hillsdale, NJ: Erlbaum.

Craig, C., Garnsey, E. and Rubery, J. (1985) *Payment Structures and Smaller Firms: Women's Employment in Segmented Labour Markets*, London: Department of Employment Research Paper no. 48.

Crompton, R. (1997) *Women and Work in Modern Britain*, Oxford: Oxford University Press.

Crompton, R., Hantrais, L. and Walters, P. (1990) 'Gender relations and employment', *British Journal of Sociology*, 41(3): 329–49.

Crompton, R., and Jones, G. (1984) *White-Collar Proletariat: Deskilling and Gender in Clerical Work*, London: Macmillan.

Crompton, R. with Le Feuvre, N. (1996) 'Paid employment and the changing system of gender relations', *Sociology*, 30(3): 427–46.

Crow, G. and Allen, G. (1994) *Community Life: An Introduction to Local Social Relations*, London: Harvester Wheatsheaf.

Dale, A. and Holdsworth, C. (1996) 'Why don't black women work part-time?', Paper presented to WZB Seminar on Part-time Employment, Berlin, September 13–14.

Dalla Costa, M. (1972) 'Women and the subversion of community', in M. Dalla Costa and S. James (eds) *The Power of Women and the Subversion of the Community*, Bristol: Falling Wall.

Dalla Costa, M. and James, S. (1972) (eds) *The Power of Women and the Subversion of the Community*, Bristol: Falling Wall.

DARES (Direction de l'Animation de la Recherche, des Etudes et des Statistiques (1993) *Dossiers Statistiques du Travail et de l'Emploi, résultats de l'enquête Conditions de Travail*, no. 98–99, Paris: Masson.

Daric, J. (1947) 'L'activité professionnelle des femmes en France. Etude statistique – évolution-comparaisons internationales', *Travaux et documents*, Cahier no. 5, INED.

Darling-Fisher, C. S. and Tiedje, L. B. (1990) 'The impact of maternal employment characteristics on fathers' participation in child care', *Family Relations*, 39: 20–6.

Daune-Richard, A-M. (1988) 'Gender relations and female labor: a consideration of sociological categories', in J. Jenson, E. Hagen and J. Reddy (eds) *Feminization of the Labour Force*, Cambridge: Polity.

Davidson, M. J. (1985) *Reach for the Top – A Women's Guide to Success in Business and Management*, London: Piatkus.

Davidson, M. J. and Cooper, C. L. (1992) *Shattering The Glass Ceiling: The Woman Manager*, London: Paul Chapman.

Davidson, M. J. and Cooper, C. L. (eds) (1993) *European Women in Business and Management*, London: Paul Chapman.

Daycare Trust and National Council for Voluntary Organisations (1992) *TECs and Childcare – Breaking New Ground*, London: Daycare Trust.

de Singly, F. (1991) 'La création politique des infortunes contemporaines de la femme mariée et salariée', in F. de Singly and F. Schultheis (eds) *Affaires de famille, Affaires d'Etat: Sociologie de la Famille*, Paris: Editions de l'Est.

Dechaux, J-H (1990) 'Les échanges économiques au sein de la parenté', *Sociologie du Travail*, 1: 73–94.

Dechaux, J-H. (1996) Les services dans la parenté: fonctions, régulation, effets, in J-C. Kaufmann (ed.) *Faire ou faire-faire? famille et services*, Rennes: Presses Universitaires de Rennes.

Delbes, C. (1983) 'Les familles des salariés du secteur privé à la veille de la retraite, 2. Les relations familiales', *Population*, 6: 22–41.

Delphy, C. (1984) *Close to Home*, London: Hutchinson.

Delphy, C. and Kergoat, D. (1982) *Les études et recherches féministes et sur les femmes en Scoiologie*, Working Paper DK - 82 - 01, Paris: GEDISST.

Delphy, C. and Leonard, D. (1992) *Familiar Exploitation*, Cambridge: Polity.

Desplanques, G. (1994) 'Concilier vie familiale et vie professionnelle', *Recherches et Prévision*, 36, CNAF, Paris, June: 11–24.

Deutsch, F. M., Lussier, J. B. and Servis, L. J. (1993) 'Husbands at home: predictors of paternal participation in childcare and housework', *Journal of Personality and Social Psychology*, 65(6): 1154–66.

Dex, S. (1985) *The Sexual Division of Work*, Brighton: Wheatsheaf Books.

Dex, S. and Shaw, L. B. (1986) *British and American Women at Work: Do Equal Opportunities Policies Matter?* London: Macmillan.

Dex, S. and Walters, P. (1989) 'Women's occupational status in Britain, France and the USA: explaining the difference', *Industrial Relations Journal*, 20(3): 203–12.

Dex, S. Walters, P. and Alden, D. M. (1993) *French and British Mothers at Work*, London: Macmillan.

Dex, S., Clark, A. and Taylor, M. (1995) *Household Labour Supply*, Sheffield: DfEE.

DfEE (Department for Education and Employment) (1996) *Work and Family: Ideas and Options for Child Care: A Consultation Paper*, London: DfEE.

DfEE (1998) *The Need for a National Childcare Strategy*, London: DfEE.

Direction de l'Animation, de la Recherche, des Etudes et des Statistiques (DARES) (1993) *Horaires de Travail en 1991, dossiers statistiques du travail et de l'emploi, résultats de l'enquête Conditions de Travail 2ᵉ partie*, Paris: Masson.

Documentation Francaise (1966) *Le Travail des Femmes en France, Notes et Etudes Documentaires*, no. 3336, 12 November.

Doeringer, P. B. and Piore, M. J. (1971) *Internal Labour Markets and Manpower Analysis*, New York: Heath.

Dominelli, L. (1991) *Women Across Continents: Feminist Comparative Social Policy*, Hemel Hempstead: Harvester Wheatsheaf.

Dubinoff, S. (1979) 'Beyond sex-typing: capitalism, patriarchy and the growth of female employment 1940–1970', Paper presented at the Eastern Sociological Society, New York.

Duncan, S. (1991) 'The geography of gender divisions of labour in Britain', *Transactions of the Institute of British Geographers*, 16(4): 420–39.

Duncan, S. (1994) 'Theorising differences in patriarchy', *Environment and Planning A*, 26(8): 1177–94.

Duncan, S. (1996) 'The diverse worlds of European patriarchy', in M. Dolors Garcia-Ramon and J. Monk (eds) *Women of the European Union: The Politics of Work and Daily Life*, London: Routledge.

Duncan, S. and Edwards, R. (1997a) 'Introduction: a contextual approach to single mothers and paid work', in S. Duncan and R. Edwards (eds) *Single Mothers in an International Context: Mothers or Workers?*, London: UCL Press.

Duncan, S. and Edwards, R. (1997b) 'Single mothers in Britain: unsupported workers or mothers?', in S. Duncan and R. Edwards (eds) *Single Mothers in an International Context: Mothers or Workers?*, London: UCL Press.

Duncan, S. and Edwards, R. (1997c) 'Single mothers: mothers versus workers, or, mothers and workers', in S. Duncan and R. Edwards (eds) *Single Mothers in an International Context: Mothers or Workers?*, London: UCL Press.

Duncan, S. and Edwards, R. (1997d) 'Lone mothers and paid work – rational economic man or gendered moral rationalities?', *Feminist Economics*, 3(2): 29–61.

Dupont, C. (1970) 'L'ennemi principal', *Partisans*, 2: 54–5.

Duriez, B. (1996) 'L'aide familiale à domicile', in J-C. Kaufmann (ed.) *Faire ou faire-faire? famille et services*, Rennes: Presses Universitaires de Rennes.

Eck, J-F. (1990) *Histoire de l'Economie Française depuis 1945*, Paris: Armand Colin.

Edmond, W. And Fleming S. (eds) (1975) *All Work and No Pay: Women, Housework and the Wages Due*, Bristol: Falling Wall.

Edmond, W. And Ronay, E. (1975) 'The housewife', in W. Edmond and S. Fleming (eds) *All Work and No Pay: Women, Housework and the Wages Due*, Bristol: Falling Wall.

Edwards, R. and Duncan, S. (1996) 'Rational economic man or lone mothers in context? The uptake of paid work', in E. Bortolaia Silva (ed.) *Good Enough Mothering? Feminist Perspectives on Lone Motherhood*, London: Routledge.

Edwards, R. C. (1979) *Contested Terrain: The Transformation of the Workplace in the Twentieth Century*, London: Heinemann.

Edwards, R. C., Reich, M. and Gordon, D. M. (eds) (1975) *Labor Market Segmentation*, Lexington MA.: D.C. Heath and Co.

Eisenstein, Z. (1978) *Capitalist Patriarchy and the Case for Socialist Feminism*, New York: Monthly Review Press.

Eisenstein, Z. (1983) The state, the patriarchal family and working mothers, in I. Diamond (ed.) *Families, Politics and Public Policy*, New York: Longman.

Elias, P. (1995) European Labor Force Survey: *Cross-tabulations, frequency distributions of employment by NACE (Rev.1) and ISCO 88 (COM) males and females by country*, Warwick: Institute for Employment Research.

Elles Voient Rouge Collective (1981) *Féminisme et Marxisme*, Paris: Ed. Tierce.

Employment in Europe (1995) Office for Official Publications of the European Communities, Luxembourg.

Engels, F. (1972) *The Origin of the Family, Private Property and the State*, London: Lawrence and Wishart.

Enjolras, B. (1995) *Le Marché Providence: aide à domicile, politique sociale et création d'emploi*, Paris: Desclée de Brower.

Equal Opportunities Magazine (1997a), 'Mainstreaming in European Community Policies', no. 1, April.

Equal Opportunities Magazine (1997b), 'A new partnership for paid and unpaid work', no. 3, December.

Equal Opportunities Magazine (1998) 'Employment. Equality in National Action Plans', August, no. 5: 4–6.

Esden, A. (1998) 'Firms fight shy of holding the baby', *The Sunday Times*, 31 May: 8.

Esping-Andersen, G. (1990) *The Three Worlds of Welfare Capitalism*, Princeton, NJ: Princeton University Press.

Estrade, M. A. and Thiesset, C. (1998) 'Des débuts de carrières moins assurés', *INSEE Première*, no. 598, July.

European foundation for the Improvement of Living and Working Conditions (1987) *Time-budget diaries: a cross-national comparison*, EFILWC, Dublin.

Eurostat (1995) *Eurostat Yearbook 1995. A statistical eye on Europe 1983–93*, Luxembourg: Eurostat.

Evandrou, M. (1990) *Challenging the Invisibility of Carers: Mapping Informal Care Nationally*, London: Welfare State Programme Discussion Paper 49, Suntory-Toyota International Centre for Economics and Related Disciplines, London School of Economics

Eydoux, A., Gauvin, A., Granie, C. and Silvera, R. (1996) *Tendances et perspectives de l'Emploi des Femmes en France au cours des années 1990*, Brussels: Rapport français du réseau 'Femmes dans l'emploi', Communauté Européenne, DGV, Bureau de l'Egalité des Chances, February.

Eyraud, F., Marsden, D. and Silvestre, J-J. (1990) 'Occupational and internal labour markets in Britain and France', *International Labour Review*, 129(4): 501–17.

Fagan, C. (1994) 'Who wants to work nine to five? 'Gendered working-time schedules in Britain', Paper presented to the Crossing Borders Conference, Center for Women's Studies, Stockholm University, May.

Fagan, C. (1998) 'Time, money and the gender order: work orientations and working time preferences in Britain', paper presented at the Gender, Work and Organization Conference, UMIST, Manchester, January 8–10.

Fagnani, J. (1995) 'L'allocation parentale d'éducation: effets pervers et ambiguités d'une prestation, *Droit Social*, 3: 287–95.

Fagnani, J. (1996) 'Family policies and working mothers: a comparison of

France and West Germany', in M. Dolors Garcia-Ramon and J. Monk (eds) *Women of the European Union: The Politics of Work and Daily Life*, London: Routledge.

Fagnani, J. (1998) 'Helping mothers to combine paid and unpaid work – or fighting unemployment? The ambiguities of French family policy', *Community, Work and Family*, 1(3): 297–311.

Favrot-Laurens, G. (1996) 'Soins familiaux ou soins professionnels? La construction des catégories dans la prise en charge des personnes agées dépendantes', in J-C. Kaufmann (ed.) *Faire ou faire-faire? Famille et services*, Rennes: Presses Universitaires de Rennes.

Ferree, M. M. (1990) 'Beyond separate spheres: feminism and family research', *Journal of Marriage and the Family*, 52: 866–84.

Ferree, M. M. (1991) 'The gender division of labor in two-earner marriages: dimensions of variability and change', *Journal of Family Issues*, 2: 158–80.

Ferri, E. and Smith, K. (1996) *Parenting in the 1990s*, London: Family Policy Studies Centre/Joseph Rowntree Trust.

Finch, J. (1989) *Family Obligations and Social Change*: Cambridge: Polity Press.

Finch, J. and Groves, D. (1983) (eds) *A Labour of Love: Women, Work and Caring*, London: Routledge.

Finch, J. and Mason, J. (1993) *Negotiating Family Responsibilities*, London: Routledge.

Flipo, A. (1996) 'Les services de proximité de la vie quotidienne', *INSEE Première*, no. 491, Paris: INSEE.

Flipo A. and Olier, L. (1996) 'Faire garder ses enfants: ce que les ménages dépensent', *INSEE Première*, no. 481, Paris: INSEE.

Foudi, R., Stankiewicz, F. and Vanecloo, N. (1982) 'Chômeurs et économie informelle', *Cahiers de l'observation du changement social et culturel*, no. 17, Paris: CNRS.

Fougeyrollas, D. (1994) 'Entraide familiale: de l'universel au particulier', *Société Contemporaine*, 17: 51–73.

Fraser, N. (1994) 'After the family wage: gender equity and the welfare state', paper presented at Crossing Borders Conference, Stockholm, 27–29 May.

Freely, M. (1998) 'Getting the boys on board', *The Guardian*, 12 May: 4–5.

Gabrielle David, M. And Starzec, C. (1996) 'Aisance à 60 ans, dépendance et isolement à 80 ans', *INSEE Première*, no. 447, Paris: INSEE

Gallie, D. (1978) *In Search of the New Working Class: Automation and Social Integration Within the Capitalist Enterprise*, Cambridge: Cambridge University Press.

Gallie, D. (1985) 'Directions for the future', in B. Roberts, R. Finnegan and D. Gallie (eds) *New Approaches to Economic Life: Economic Restructuring, Unemployment and Social Divisions of Labour*, Oxford: Oxford University Press.

Galtier, B. (1998) 'Salariés du privé à temps partiel: multiplicité des situations', Centre d'Etudes de l'Emploi, *4 pages*, no. 27, May.

Gardiner, J. (1975) 'Women's domestic labour', *New Left Review*, 89: 47–58.

Gardiner, J. (1976) 'The political economy of domestic labour in capitalist society 'in D. Barker and S. Allen (eds) *Dependence and Exploitation in Work and Marriage*, Harlow: Longman.

Gardiner, J. (1997) *Gender, Care and Economics*, Basingstoke: Macmillan.

204   *References*

Garnsey, E. (1985) 'A comparison of part-time employment in Britain and France', Paper presented at International Working Group conference on Labour Market Segmentation, Santiago de Compostelle, July.

Gauthier, A. and Lelièvre, E. (1995) 'L'emploi des femmes en Europe: inégalités, discontinuité, politiques sociales', in A. M. Guillemart (ed.) *Comparer les systèmes de protection sociale en Europe, Vol 1, rencontres d'Oxford*, Paris: MIRE.

Gauvin, A. (1995) 'Le sur-chômage féminin à la lumière des comparaisons internationales: chômage, sous emploi et inactivité', *Les Cahiers du Mage*, 3–4: 25–36.

Gershuny, J. (1978) *After Industrial Society? The Emerging Self-service Economy*, London: Macmillan.

Gershuny, J. (1992) 'Change in the domestic division of labour in the UK, 1975–87: dependent labour versus adaptive partnership', in N. Abercrombie and A. Warde (eds) *Social Change in Contemporary Britain*, Cambridge: Polity.

Gershuny, J. and Jones, S. (1986) *Time Use in Seven Countries 1961–1984*, Shankill: European Foundation for the Improvement of Living and Working Conditions.

Gershuny, J., Godwin, M. and Jones, S. (1994) 'The domestic labour revolution: a process of lagged adaptation', in M. Anderson, F. Bechhofer and J. Gershuny (eds) *The Social and Political Economy of the Household*, Oxford: Oxford University Press.

Giddens, A. (1991) *Modernity and Self-Identity*, Cambridge: Polity Press.

Giddens, A. (1994) 'Living in a post-industrial society', in U. Beck, A. Giddens and S. Lash (eds) *Reflexive Modernisation: Politics, Tradition and Aesthetics in the Modern Social Order*, Cambridge: Polity Press.

Ginn, J. and Arber, S. (1991) 'Gender, class and income inequalities in later life', *British Journal of Sociology*, 42(3): 369–96.

Ginn, J. and Arber, S. (1993) 'Pension penalties: the gendered division of occupational welfare', *Work, Employment and Society*, 7(1): 47–70.

Ginn, J. and Arber, S. (1995) 'Moving the goalposts: the impact on British women of raising their state pension age to 65', in J. Baldock and M. May (eds) *Social Policy Review*, no. 7, London: Social Policy Association.

Ginn, J. and Sandell, J. (1997) 'Balancing home and employment: stress reported by social services staff', *Work, Employment and Society*, 11(3): 413–34.

Ginn, J., Arber, S., Brannen, J., Dale, A., Dex, S., Elias, P., Moss, P., Pahl, J., Roberts, C. and Rubery, J. (1996) 'Feminist fallacies: a reply to Hakim on women's employment', *British Journal of Sociology*, 7(1): 167–74.

Girard, D. (1997) '33. 000 salariés bénéficient de la loi Robien', *La Tribune*, 27 March: 9.

Gissot, C. and Meron, M. (1996) 'Chômage et emploi en mars 1996', *INSEE Première*, no. 427, Juin.

Glaude, M. and de Singly, F. (1986) 'L'organisation domestique: pouvoir et négociation' Economie et Statistique, 187: 125–141.

Glover, J. (1994) 'Concepts of Employment and Unemployment in Labour Force data' in M-T. Letablier and L. Hantrais (eds) *The Family–Employment Relationship*, Cross-National Research Papers, Fourth Series: Concepts and Contexts in International Comparisons of Family Policies in Europe, No.

2, Loughborough University: Cross-National Research Group.

Glover, J. (1996) 'Studying working women cross-nationally', *Work, Employment and Society*, 9: 22–41.

Glover, J. and Arber, S. (1995) 'Polarization in mothers' employment', *Gender, Work and Organization*, 2(4): 165–79.

Glucksmann, M. (1995) 'Why "work"? Gender and the "Total Social Organisation of Labour" ', *Gender, Work and Organization*, 2(2): 63–75.

Godchau, J-F. (1970). 'Lutte de sexes ou de classes', *Partisans*, 54–55: 230–77.

Godwin, D. D. (1991) 'Spouses' time allocation to household work: a review and critique', *Lifestyles: Family and Economic Issues*, 12: 253–94.

Gokalp, C. and David, M. G. (1982) 'La garde de jeunes enfants', *Population et Société*, 161: 22–32.

Goldscheider, F. K. and Waite, L. J. (1991) *New Families, No Families? The Transformation of the American Home*, Berkeley CA: University of California.

Gordon, D. M. (1972) *Theories of Poverty and Underemployment: Orthodox, Radical and Dual Labor Market Perspectives*, Lexington MA.: Lexington Books.

Green, E. and Cassell, C. (1996) 'Women manager, gendered cultural processes and organizational change', *Gender, Work and Organization*, 3(3): 168–78.

Greenstein, T. N. (1996) 'Husband's participation in domestic labor: interactive effects of wives' and husbands' gender ideologies', *Journal of Marriage and the Family*, 58: 585–95.

Gregory, A. (1987) 'Le travail à temps partiel en France et en Grande-Bretagne', *Revue Française des Affaires Sociales*, 3: 53–60.

Gregory, A. (1989) *A Franco-British Comparison of Patterns of Working Hours in Large-scale Grocery Retailing, with Specific Reference to Part-time Work*, unpublished PhD thesis, Birmingham: Aston University.

Gregory, A. (1995) 'Patterns of working hours large-scale grocery retailing. Convergence after European Union?', in P. Cressey and B. Jones (eds) *Work and Employment in Europe: A New Convergence?*, London: Routledge.

Gregory, A. and O'Reilly, J. (1996) 'Checking out and cashing up: the prospects and paradoxes of regulating part-time work in Europe', in R. Crompton, D. Gallie and K. Purcell (eds) *Changing Forms of Employment: Organisations, Skills and Gender*, London: Routledge.

Gregson, N. and Lowe, M. (1994) *Servicing the Middle Classes: Class, Gender and Waged Domestic Labour in Contemporary Britain*, London: Routledge.

Grief, G. L. (1985) 'Children and housework in the single father family', *Family Relations*, 34: 353–57.

Hagen, E. and Jenson, J. (1988) 'Paradoxes and promises: work and politics in the postwar years', in J. Jenson, E. Hagen and C. Reddy, (eds) *Feminization of the Labour Force: Paradoxes and Promises*, Oxford: Polity Press.

Haicault, M. (1984). 'La gestion ordinaire de la vie en deux', *Sociologie du Travail*, 3: 268–77.

Hakim, C. (1991) 'Grateful slaves and self-made women: fact and fantasy in women's work orientations', *European Sociological Review*, 7: 101–21.

Hakim, C. (1995) 'Five feminist myths about women's employment', *British Journal of Sociology*, 46(3): 429–55.

Hakim, C. (1996) 'The sexual division of labour and women's heterogeneity', *British Journal of Sociology*, 47(1): 178–88.

Hakim, C. (1997) 'A sociological perspective on part-time work', in H.-P. Blossfield and C. Hakim (eds) *Between Equalization and Marginalization: Women Part-time Workers in Europe and the USA*, Oxford: Oxford University Press, 22–70.

Hakim, C. (1998) *Social Change and Innovation in the Labour Market*, Oxford: OUP.

Hantrais, L. (1985) 'Leisure lifestyles and the synchronisation of family schedules: a Franco-British perspective', *World Leisure and Recreation*, 3: 18–24.

Hantrais, L. (1990) *Managing Professional and Family Life*, Aldershot: Dartmouth.

Hantrais, L. (1993) 'Women, Work and Welfare in France', in J. Lewis, (ed.) *Women and Social Policies in Europe*, Aldershot: Edward Elgar: 116–137.

Hantrais, L. (1994) 'Comparing family policy in Britain, France and Germany', *Journal of Social Policy*, 23(2): 135–60.

Hantrais, L. and Letablier, M-T. (1995) *Familles, travail et politiques familiales en Europe*, Paris: Cahiers du Centre d'Etudes de l'Emploi. no. 35, Presses Universitaires de France.

Hantrais, L. and Walters, P. (1994) 'Making it in and making out: women in professional occupations in Britain and France', *Gender, Work and Organisation*, 1 (1): 23–32.

Hantrais, L., Clark, P. A. and Samuel, N. (1984) 'Time-space dimensions of work, family and leisure in France and Britain', *Leisure Studies*, 3: 301–17.

Harris, C. C. (1983) *The Family and Industrial Society*, London: Allen and Unwin.

Harris, C. C. (1987) *Redundancy and Recession in South Wales*, Oxford: Basil Blackwell.

Harrop, A. and Moss, P. (1995) 'Trends in parental employment', *Work, Employment and Society*, 9(3): 421–44.

Hartmann, H. (1979) 'Capitalism, patriarchy and job segregation by sex', in Z. R. Eisenstein (ed.) *Capitalist Patriarchy*, New York: Monthly Review Press.

Hartmann, H. and Bridges, A. (1981) 'The unhappy marriage of marxism and feminism: towards a more progressive union', in L. Sargent (ed.) *Women and Revolution: A Discussion of the Unhappy Marriage of Marxism and Feminism*, Boston: South End Press.

Haskey, J. (1994) 'Estimated numbers of one parent families and their prevalence in Great Britain 1991', *Population Trends*, 78, London: HMSO.

Hatchuel, G. (1989) 'Acceuil des jeunes enfants: la course à la débrouille', *Consommation et Mode de Vie*, 41: 1–4.

Hatchuel, G. (1991) *Activité féminine et jeune enfant*, Paris: CREDOC.

Hawkins, A. J. and Roberts, T-A (1992) 'Designing a primary intervention to help dual-earner couples share housework and child care', *Journal of Family Relations*, 41: 169–77.

Hayward, J. (1986) *The State and Market Economy: Industrial Patriotism and Economic Intervention in France*, Brighton: Wheatsheaf Books.

Hegewish, A. (1995) 'A mi-chemin entre l'Amérque et l'Europe. Les femmes et le chômage en Grande-Bretagne', *Les Cahiers du Mage*, 3–4: 11–24.

Hewitt, P. (1993) *About Time: The Revolution in Work and Family Life*, London: IPPR/Rivers Oram Press.

Hill, M. (1987) *Sharing Childcare in Early Parenthood*, London: Routledge and Kegan Paul.

Hiller, D. V. (1984) Power, dependence and division of family work, *Sex Roles*, 10: 1003–19.

Hilton, J. M. and Haldeman, V. A. (1991) 'Gender differences in the performance of household tasks by adults and children in single-parent and two-parent, two-earner families', *Journal of Family Issues*, 12: 114–30.

Hirata, H. and Senotier, D. (eds) (1996) *Femmes et partage du travail*, Paris: Syros.

Hirschmann, J. (1975) 'Organising on the second job', in W. Edmond and S. Fleming (eds) *All Work and No Pay: Women, Housework and the Wages Due*, Bristol: Falling Wall.

Hoang-Ngoc, L. and Lefresne, F. (1994) 'Les règles d'utilisation du temps partiel dans les régimes d'accumulation français et britannique', *Revue de l'IRES*, 14: 144–72.

Hobson, B. (1994) 'Solo mothers. Social policy regimes and the logics of gender', in D. Sainsbury (ed.) *Gendering Welfare States*, London: Sage

Hochschild, A. (1989) *The Second Shift: Working Parents and the Revolution at Home*, New York: Viking Press.

Hogg, C. and Harker, L. (1992) *The Family-Friendly Employee: Examples from Europe*, New York: Day Care Trust.

Holtermann, S. (1995) 'The costs and benefits to British employers of measures to promote equality of opportunity 'in J. Humphries and J. Rubery (eds) (1995) *The Economics of Equal Opportunites*, Manchester: Equal Opportunities Commission.

Hood, J. and Golden, S. (1979) 'Beating time/making time: the impact of work scheduling on men's family roles', *The Family Co-Ordinator*, 28: 575–82.

Horrell, S. and Rubery, J. (1991) 'Gender and working time: an analysis of employers' working-time policies', *Cambridge Journal of Economics*, 15, 373–91.

Huber, J. and Spitze, G. (1981) 'Wives' employment, household behaviors and sex-role attitudes', *Social Forces*, 60: 150–69.

Husson, M. (1996) 'L'emploi des femmes en France. Une comptabilité en temps de travail (1980–1990)', in H. Hirata and D. Senotier, (eds) *Femmes et partage du travail*, Paris: Syros, 138–147.

inforMISEP (1996) 'Création d'emplois', no. 54, Summer: 9–10.

INSEE (1992) *Les enfants de moins de 6 ans*, Paris: INSEE.

INSEE (1994) *Les familles monoparentales*, Paris: INSEE.

INSEE (1995) *Les Femmes: contours et caractères*, Paris: INSEE.

INSEE (1997) *Les immigrés en France: contours et caractères*, Paris: INSEE.

INSEE-DARES (1995) *Le travail à temps partiel*, Les Dossiers thématiques, no. 2, Paris: Editions Liaisons.

Ironmonger, D. (1996) 'Time use and satellite accounts for modelling the household economy', International Association for Research into Income and Wealth 24th Conference, Lillehammer, Norway.

James, S. (1975) *Sex, Race and Class*, Bristol: Falling Wall.

James, S. (1994) 'Women's unwaged work: the heart of the informal sector', in M. Evans (ed.) *The Woman Question* (2nd edition), London: Sage.

Jay, M. (1998) *Delivering for Women: Progress so Far*, London: DfEE.

Jeder-Madiot, F. and Ponthieux, S. (1996) 'Embauches, métiers et conditions d'emploi des jeunes débutants', *Premières Synthèses*, no. 96-07-29-1, Paris: Ministère du Travail et des Affaires Sociales.

Jenkins, S. and O'Leary, N. (1996) 'Household income plus household production and the distribution of extended income in the UK', *Review of Income and Wealth*, 42(4): 26–41.

Jenson, J. (1984) 'The problem of women', in M. Kesselman (ed.) *The French Workers' Movement*, London: Allen and Unwin.

Jenson, J. (1985) 'Struggling for Identity: The Women's Movement and the State in Western Europe' *West European Politics*, 8(4): 5–18.

Jenson, J. (1986) 'Gender and reproduction: or, babies and the state', *Studies in Political Economy*, 20: 9–45.

Jenson, J. (1987) 'Changing discourse, changing agendas: political rights and reproductive policies in France', in M. Katzenstein and C. Mueller (eds) *Changing Paradigms: New Theoretical Perspectives from the Women's Movement in Western Europe and the USA*, Philadelphia, PA: Temple UP.

Jenson, J. (1988) 'The limits of "and the" discourse: French women as marginal workers', in J. Jenson (ed.) *Feminization of the Labour Force: Paradoxes and Promises*, New York: OUP.

Jenson, J. (1990) 'Labour market and family policy in France: an intersecting complex for dealing with poverty', in G. Goldberg and E. Kremen (eds) *The Feminization of Poverty Only in America?*, Westport, CT: Greenwood.

Jenson, J. (1993) 'Représentations des rapports sociaux de sexe dans trois domaines politiques en France', in A. Gautier and J. Heinen (eds) *Le Sexe des Politiques Sociales*, Paris: Côté-femmes.

Jenson, J. and Sineau, M. (1995) *Mitterrand et les Françaises: un rendez-vous manqué*, Presses de Sciences Po: Paris.

Johnson, G. E. and Stafford, F. P. (1974) 'The earnings and promotion of women faculty', *American Economic Review*, 64(6): 888–903.

Jordan, B., James, S., Kay, H. and Redley, M. (1992) *Trapped in Poverty*, London: Routledge.

Joshi, H. and Davies, H. (1992) *Childcare and Mothers' Lifetime Earnings: Some European Contrasts*, CEPR Discussion Paper 600, London: Centre for Economic Policy Research.

Joshi, H. and Hinde, A. P. R. (1993) 'Employment after childbearing in post-war Britain: cohort-study evidence on contrasts within and across generations', *European Sociological Review*, 9(3): 203–27.

Joshi, H. Davies, H. and Land, H. (1996) *The Tale of Mrs Typical*, London: Family Policy Studies Centre.

Junter-Loiseau, A. and Guilloux, P. (1979) 'Réflexions sur la formation professionnelle continue des femmes à la recherche d'un travail', *Droit Socio*, 11: 435–46.

Juster, T. and Stafford, F. (1985) (eds) *Time, Goods and Well-Being*, Michigan: Institute for Social Research, University of Michigan.

Kamerman, S. B. and Kahn, A. J. (eds) (1978) *Family Policy: Government and Families in Fourteen Countries*, New York: Columbia University Press.

Kamerman, S. B. and Kahn, A. J. (1989) 'Child care and privatisation under

Regan', in S. B. Kamerman and A. J. Kahn (eds) *Privatisation and the Welfare State*, Princeton: Princeton University Press.

Kanter, M. R. (1977) *Men and Women of the Corporation*, New York: Basic Books.

Kergoat, D. (1992) 'A propos des rapports sociaux de sexe', *Revue M*, 53–54: 16–19.

Kerr, C. (1954) *Labor Markets and Wage Determination, the Balkanization of Labor Markets, and other Essays*, Berkeley: California University Press), reprinted 1977.

Kerr, C., Dunlop, J. T., Harbison, H. H. and Myers, C. A. (1960) *Industrialism and Industrial Man*, Cambridge, MA: Harvard University Press.

Kiernan, K. (1992) 'The roles of men and women in tomorrow's Europe', *Employment Gazette*, October: 491–9.

Kluwer, E. S., Heesink, J. A. M. and Van de Vliert, E. (1996) 'Marital conflict about the division of household labor and paid work', *Journal of Marriage and the Family*, 58: 958–69.

Kluwer, E. S., Heesink, J. A. M. and Van de Vliert, E. (1997) 'Marital dynamics of conflict over the division of labor', *Journal of Marriage and the Family*, 59: 635–53.

Kolberg, J. E. (1991) 'The gender dimension of the welfare state', *International Journal of Sociology*, 21(2): 119–48.

Kornhaber, A. (1996) *Contemporary Grandparenting: A Comprehensive Textbook*, London: Sage.

Kuhn, A. and Wolpe, A. M. (1978) *Feminism and Materialism: Women and Modes of production*, London: Routledge and Kegan Paul.

Lallement, M. (1993) 'France – the case of retail trade', Paper presented at the meeting on 'Flexible Working Time Arrangements: The Roles of Bargaining and Government Intervention', Paris: OECD, 3–4 May.

Lane, C. (1993) 'Gender and the labour market in Europe: Britain, Germany and France Compared', *Sociological Review*, 41(2): 274–301.

Laufer, J. (1993) 'Women in Business and Management – FRANCE', in M. J. Davidson, and C. Cooper (eds) *Women in Business and Management*, London: Paul Chapman, 107–132.

Le Corre, V. (1995) 'Le recours croissant des entreprises au temps partiel', *Premières Synthèses*, no. 97, DARES, 4 Juillet.

Le Gall, D. (1996) 'Faire garder les enfants dans les familles à beau-parent', in J-C. Kaufmann (ed.) *Faire ou faire-faire? famille et services*, Rennes: Presses Universitaires de Rennes.

Le Monde (1992) 'Mme Martine Aubry présente un dispositif pour développer le travail à temps partiel', 6 August: 15.

Le Monde (1997) 'Les allocations familiales seront placées sous plafond de ressources', 21 June: 14.

Le Nouvel Observateur (1990) Spécial Femmes, No. 1361, 6–12 December.

Lebaube, A. (1998) 'Le travail à temps partiel concurrencé par les 35 heures', *Le Monde*, Supplément Initiatives, 8 August: 1.

Lefaucheur, N. and Martin, C. (1995) *Qui doit nourrir l'enfant dont le père est 'absent'?* Rapport de recherche sur les fondements des politiques familiales européennes (Angleterre-France-Italie-Portugal), Travaux de Recherche et d'Analyse du Social et de la Sociabilité, Paris.

210   *References*

Lefaucheur, N. and Martin, C. (1997) 'Single mothers in France: supported mothers and workers', in S. Duncan and R. Edwards (eds) *Single Mothers in an International Context: Mothers or Workers?*, London: UCL Press.

Leira, A. (1992) *Welfare States and Working Mothers*, Cambridge: Cambridge University Press.

Leira, A. (1994) 'Concepts of caring: loving, thinking and doing', *Social Service Review*, June: 85–201.

Lelièvre, F. and Lelièvre C. (1991) *Histoire de la Scolarisation des Filles*, Paris: Nathan.

Lemel, Y. (1996) 'La rarete relativé des aides à la production domestique', in J-C. Kaufmann (ed.) *Faire ou faire-faire? famille et services*, Rennes: Presses Universitaires de Rennes.

Lemmenicier, B. (1980) 'La spécialisation des rôles congugaux. Les gains du mariage et la perspective du divorce', *Consommation*, 1: 27–72.

Lemmenicier, B. (1988) *Le marché du mariage et de la famille*, Paris: Presses Universitaires de France.

Lemmenicier, B. and Levy-Garboua, L. (1981) 'Arbitrage autarcie-marché: une explication du travail féminin', *Consommation*, 2: 41–74.

Leonard, D. (1984) 'Preface 'in C. Delphy, *Close to Home*, London: Hutchinson.

Leonard, M. (1994) *Informal Economic Activity in Belfast*, Aldershot: Avebury.

Leprince, F. (1991) 'Day care for young children in France', in P. Moss and E. Melhuish (eds) *Day Care for Young Children*, London: Routledge.

Leslie, L. A., Branson, M. and Anderson, E. A. (1989) 'The impact of couples' work profile on husbands' and wives' performance of childcare tasks', *Family Perspective*, 22: 327–44.

Letablier, M-T. (1995) 'Women's Labour Force participation in France: the paradoxes of the 1990s', *Journal of Area Studies*, 6: 108–16.

Letablier, M-T. (1996) *L'activité professionnelle des femmes en France sur fond de pénurie d'emploi*, Working Paper 96/51, Paris: Centre d'études de l'emploi.

Lettre de Matignon (1986) 'Nouvelle politique familiale: priorité au 3ᵉ enfant', no. 201, 12 November.

Lettre-CAP (1997) 'La famille au coeur des débats', no. 72, February–March: 10–11.

Lewis, J. (1984) *Women in England 1870–1950, Sexual Divisions and Social Charge*, Brighton: Wheatsheaf Books.

Lewis, J. (1992a) *Welfare States and Working Mothers*, Cambridge: Cambridge University Press.

Lewis, J. (1992b) *Women in Britain since 1945*, Oxford: Blackwell.

Lewis, J. (1992c) 'Gender and the development of welfare regimes', *Journal of European Social Policy* 2(3): 159–74.

Lewis, J. (1993) (ed.) *Women and Social Policies in Europe*, Aldershot: Edward Elgar.

Lewis, J. (1997a) 'Introduction', in J. Lewis (ed.) *Lone Mothers in European Welfare Regimes: Shifting Policy Logics*, London: Jessica Kingsley.

Lewis, J. (1997b) 'Lone mothers: the British case', in J. Lewis (ed.) *Lone Mothers in European Welfare Regimes: Shifting Policy Logics*, London: Jessica Kingsley.

Lewis, S. (1997) '"Family friendly" employment policies: a route to changing organizational culture or playing about at the margins?', *Gender, Work and Organization*, 4(1): 13–23.

Liaisons Sociales (1993) 'Politique familiales, Rapport Codaccioni', Supplement to number 11 562, 11 November.

Liaisons Sociales (1997) 'Pour une politique globale de la famille. Rapport du comité de pilotage de la Conférence de la famille ("rapport Gisserot")', no. 20/97, 21 February.

Liaisons Sociales (1998) 'Travail à temps partiel. 'Directive européenne', no. 7807, 5 February.

Libération (1994) 'Simone Veil veut adapter 'les allocs' à la crise', 5.

Libération (1998) Enquête sur le travail, 'Les principales dispositions du projet de loi le 19 mai 1998', http://www. liberation. fr/travail/index. html.

Liff, S. and Cameron, I. (1997) 'Changing equality cultures to move beyond "Women's Problems" ', *Gender, Work and Organization*, 4(1): 35–46.

Lindley, R. (1992) *Women's Employment: Britian in the Single European Market*, London: HMSO.

Lister, R. (1990) *The Exclusive Society*, London: Child Poverty Action Group.

Lister, R. (1997) *Citizenship: feminist perspectives*, London: Macmillan.

Lloyd, C. B. and Niemi, B. T. (1979) *The Economics of Sex Differentials*, New York: Columbia University Press.

Lutzel, H. (1989) 'Household production and national accounts', *Statistical Journal of the United Nations Economic Commission for Europe*, 6: 337–48.

Luxton, M. (1986) 'Two hands for the clock: changing patterns in the gendered division of labour in the home', in M. Luxton and H. Rosenberg (eds) *Through the Kitchen Window: The Politics of Home and Family*, Toronto: Garamond Press.

Luxton, M. (1997) 'The UN, women and household labour: measuring and valuing unpaid work', *Women's Studies International Forum*, 20(3): 431–9.

Macran, S., Joshi, H. and Dex, S. (1996) 'Employment after childbearing: a survival analysis', *Work, Employment and Society*, 10(2): 273–96.

Madinier, H. and Mouillard, M. (1984) 'La perception du travail au noir par les jeunes', *Consommation*, no. 4: 21–9.

Maier, F. (1991) 'The regulation of part-time work: a comparative study of six EC-countries', Discussion paper FSI 01-9, Berlin: Wissenschaftzentrum Berlin für Sozialforschung.

Mallier, T. and Rosser, M. (1980) 'Part-time workers and the economy', *International Journal of Manpower*, 1(2): 2–7.

Marpsat, M. (1991) 'Les échanges au sein de la famille: l'héritage, aides financières, garde des enfants et visites aux grands parents', *Economie et Statistique*, 239: 59–66.

Marry, C., Fournier-Mearelli, I. and Kieffer, A. (1995) 'Activité des jeunes femmes: héritages et transmissions', *Economie et Statistique*, 3(4): 67–79.

Marsden, D. (1989) 'Institutions and labour mobility: occupation and internal labour markets in Britain, France, Italy and West Germany', in R. Brunetta and C. Dell Aringa (eds) *Markets, Institutions and Cooperation*, London: Macmillan.

Marsh, A. and McKay, S. (1993) 'Families, work and the use of childcare', *Employment Gazette*, 101(8): 361–70.

Martin, C. (1996) *L'après-divorce. Rupture du lien familial et vulnérabilité*, Rennes: Presses Universitaires de Rennes.

Martin, J. and Roberts, C. (1984) *Women and Employment: A Lifetime Perspective*, report of the 1980 DE/OPCS Women and Employment Survey, London: HMSO.

Maruani, M. (1979) *Les syndicats à l'épreuve du syndicalisme*, Paris: Syros.

Maruani, M. (1985) *Mais qui a peur du travail des femmes?*, Paris: Syros.

Maruani, M. and Decoufle, A-C. (1987) 'Pour une sociologie de l'emploi', *Revue française des affaires sociales*, 41(3): 7–29.

Maruani, M. and Nicole, C. (1989) *La flexibilité à temps partiel – conditions d'emploi dans le commerce*, La Documentation Française, collection Droits des femmes, Paris.

Marx, K. (1954) *Capital*, Vol. 1, London: Lawrence and Wishart.

Matthews, V. (1998) 'Flexibility is a friend to higher profits', *The Times*, August 12: 25.

Maurice, M., Sellier, F. and Silvestre, J-J. (1982) *Politique d'éducation et organisation industrielle en France et en Allemagne*, Paris: PUF.

McDowell, L. (1991) 'Life without father and Ford: the new gender order of post-Fordism', *Transactions of the Institute of British Geographers*, 16(4): 400–19.

McDowell, L. and Massey, D. (1984) 'A woman's place', in D. Massey and J. Allen (eds) *Geography Matters! A Reader*, Cambridge: Cambridge University Press.

McInnes, J. (1998) 'Analysing patriarchy, capitalism and women's employment in Europe', paper presented at the Gender, Work and Organisation Conference, January 10th, UMIST, Manchester.

McKee, L. (1987) 'Households surviving unemployment: the resourcefulness of the unemployed', in J. Brannen and G. Wilson (eds) *Give and Take in Families: Studies in Resource Distribution*, London: Unwin Hyman.

McMahon, M. (1995) *Engendering Motherhood: Identity and Self-transformation in Women's Lives*, New York: Guildford Press.

McRae, S. (1991) 'Occupational change over childbirth', *Sociology*, 24(4): 589–606.

McRae, S. (1995) *Part-time Work in the EU: The Gender Dimension*, Dublin: European Foundation for the Improvement of Living and Working Conditions.

Meilland, C. (1996) 'Le temps de travail dans l'Union Européenne: une analyse sexuée dans six pays', *La revue de l'IRES*, 22: 121–62.

Meillassoux, C. (1981) *Maidens, Meal and Money*, Cambridge: Cambridge University Press.

Meron, M. and Minni, C. (1996) 'L'emploi des jeunes: plus tardif et plus instable qu'il y a vingt ans', *Données Sociales*, Paris: INSEE.

Merritt, R. and Rokkan, S. (1966) *Comparing Nations: The Use of Quantitative Data in Cross-national Research*, New Haven: Yale University Press.

Michon, F. (1994) 'Les grands paradigmes de l'économie du travail', in M. Lallement (ed.) *Travail et emploi. Le temps de métamorphoses*, Paris: L'Harmattan.

Milkman, R. (1976) 'Women's work and economic crisis: some lessons of the Great Depression', *Review of Radical Political Economy*, 8(1): 21–32.

Millar, J. (1994) 'Defining lone parents: family structures and social relations', in L. Hantrais and M-T. Letablier (eds) *Conceptualising the Family*, Cross-National Research Papers, Fourth Series: Concepts and Contexts in

International Comparisons of Family Policies in Europe, no. 1, Loughborough University: the Cross-National Research Group.

Ministre du Travail (1978) *Note à l'attention des membres de la commission 'harmonisation vie familiale – vie professionnelle*, Comité du Travail Féminin, Note 11-5Cm 1 September.

Monk, J. and Garcia Ramon, M-D (1996) 'Placing women of the European Union', in M-D. Garcia-Ramon and J. Monk (eds) *Women of the European Union*, London: Routledge.

Morris, L. (1990) *The Workings of the Household*, Cambridge: Polity.

Morris, L. (1995) *Social Divisions: Economic Decline and Social Structural Change*, London: UCL Press.

Morrow, V. (1996) 'Rethinking childhood dependency: children's contributions to the domestic economy', *The Sociological Review*, 23: 34–52.

Mósesdóttir, L. (1995) 'The state and the egalitarian, ecclesiastical and liberal regimes of gender relations', *British Journal of Sociology*, 46(4): 623–43.

Mosesdóttir, L. (1998) 'Transformation and reproduction of gender relations in Sweden, Germany and the United States', paper presented at the Gender, Work and Organization Conference, Manchester, January 9–10.

Moss, P. (1988) *Childcare and Equality of Opportunity*, Consolidated Report to the Commission of the European Communities, Brussels.

Moynot, J-L. (1978) 'La force du travail féminine dans la production et la société', in Centre d'Etudes et de recherches marxistes, *La condition féminine*, Paris: Editions Sociales.

Murgatroyd, L. and Neuberger, H, (1997) 'A household satellite account for the UK', *Economics Trends*, 527: 32–39.

Myrdal, A. and Klein, V. (1970) *Women's Two Roles: Home and Work*, London: Routledge.

National Council for One Parent Families (1994) *Annual Report 1993–94*, London: National Council for One Parent Families.

National Economic Development Office (NEDO) (1986) *Changing Working Patterns: How Companies Achieve Flexibility to Meet New Needs*, London: National Economic Development Office.

Nelson, P. (1994) 'Family day care providers: dilemmas of daily practice', in E. Nankano Glenn, G. Chang and L. Rennie Forcey (eds) *Mothering: Ideology, Experience and Agency*, London: Routledge.

Network of Experts on the Situation of Women in the Labour Market (1996) *Bulletin on Women and Employment in the EU*, no. 9, Commission of the European Communities, October.

Nicole-Drancourt, C. (1989) 'Stratégies professionnelles et organisation des familles', *Revue française de sociologie*, 30(1): 57–80.

Nicole-Drancourt, C. (1996) 'Rapport à l'activité et insertion professionnelle', *Les Cahiers du Mage*, nå. 1, Egalité, discrimination: hommes et femmes sur le marché du travail, 37–8.

O'Brian, M. (1995) 'Fatherhood and Family Policies in Europe', *The Family in Social Policy and Family Policy*, Cross-National Research Papers, 4(3): 48–56.

Office of Population Censuses and Surveys (OPCS) (1996) *Living in Britain: Results from the 1994 General Household Survey*, London: HMSO.

Office for Official Publications of the European Communities (OOPEC) (1998) *Labour Force Survey, Results 1997*, Luxembourg: OOPEC.

O'Reilly, J. (1994) *Banking on Flexibility*, Aldershot: Avebury.

O'Reilly, J. (1995) 'Le temps partiel dans les deux Allemagne. 'Vers un 'modèle sociétal et sexué', Différences de sexe sur le marché du travail, *Les Cahiers du Mage*, 2: 39–51.

O'Reilly, J. and Fagan, C. (eds) (1998) *Part-Time Prospects: An International Comparison of Part-time Work*, London: Routledge.

Oakley, A. (1974) *The Sociology of Housework*, Oxford: Martin Robinson.

OECD (1965) *Manpower Statistics 1954–1964*, Paris: OECD.

OECD (1985) *The Integration of Women into the Economy*, Paris: OECD.

OECD (1993) *Employment Outlook*, Paris: OECD.

OECD (1994) *Women and Structural Change: New Perspectives*, Paris: OECD.

OECD (1996) *Labour Force Statistics 1974–94*, Paris; OECD.

OECD (1997) *Framework for the Measurement of Unrecorded Economic Activities in Transition Economies* (OCDE/GD (97)177), Paris : OECD.

OPCS (1992) *General Household Survey: Carers in 1990*, OPCS Monitor SS92/2, OPCS, London.

Orloff, A. (1993) 'Gender and the social rights of citizenship: state policies and gender relations in comparative research', *American Sociological Review*, 58(3): 303–28.

Pahl, R. E. (1984) *Divisions of Labour*, Oxford: Basil Blackwell.

Pahl, R. E. (1995) *After Employment*, Oxford: Blackwell.

Parker, G. (1988) 'Who cares? A review of empirical evidence from Britain', in R. E. Pahl (ed.) *On Work*, Oxford: Blackwell.

Parsons, T. (1955) *Family Socialization and Interaction Process*, Glencoe: The Free Press.

Perrons, D. (1997) 'Gender as a form of social exclusion: gender inequalities in the regions of Europe', in P. Lawless, R. Martin and S. Hardy (eds) *Tackling Unemployment and Social Exclusion: Landscapes of Labour Inequality*, London: Jessica Kingsley.

Peters, S. (1997) 'Feminist strategies for policy and research – the economic and social dynamics of families', in M. Luxton (ed.) *Feminism and Families: Changing Policies and Critical Practices*, Halifax: Fernwood Books.

Pfau-Effinger, B. (1993) 'Modernisation, culture and part-time employment: the example of Finland and West Germany', *Work, Employment And Society*, 7(3): 383–410.

Pillinger, J. (1992) *Feminising the Market: Women's Pay and Employment in the European Community*, London: Macmillan.

Piore, M. J. (1975) 'Notes for a theory of labor market stratification', in R. C. Edwards, M. Reich and D. M. Gordon (eds.) *Labor Market Segmentation*, Lexington MA.: D. C. Heath.

Pitrou, A. (1990) 'Des carrières de femmes 'solidaires', *Femmes Info*, 75/76: 18–20.

Pitrou, A. (1996) 'Le mythe de la famille et du familial', in J-C. Kaufmann (ed.) *Faire ou faire-faire? famille et services*, Rennes: Presses Universitaires de Rennes.

Pittman, J. F. and Blanchard, D. (1996) 'The effects of work history and timing of marriage on the division of household labor: a life-course perspective', *Journal of Marriage and the Family*, 58: 78–90.

Pleck, J. H. (1985) *Working Wives / Working Husbands*, Beverley Hills: Sage.

Polachek, S. W. and Siebert, W. S. (1993) *The Economics of Earnings*, Cambridge: Cambridge University Press.

Potuchek, J. L. (1992) 'Employed wives' orientations to breadwinning: a gender theory analysis', *Journal of Marriage and the Family*, 54: 548–58.

PRAT (1996) *Le Guide de vos droits et avantages*, Paris: Editions PRAT.

Pratt, G. and Hanson, S. (1993) 'Women and work across the life course: moving beyond essentialism', in C. Katz and J. Monk (eds) *Full Circles: Geographies of Women over the Life Course*, London: Routledge.

Premier Ministre (1969) *L'emploi féminin et le VIème plan*, Paris: Secrétariat général du Comité Interministériel de la formation professionnelle et de la promotion sociale.

Presser, H. B. (1994) 'Employment schedules among dual-earner spouses and the division of household labor by gender', *American Sociological Review*, 59: 348–64.

Procter, I. and Ratcliffe, P. (1992) 'Employment and domestic work: a comparison of samples of British and French Women', in S. Arber and N. Gilbert (eds) *Women and Working Lives: Divisions and Change*, Basingstoke: Macmillan.

Qureshi, H. and Walker, A. (1989) *The Caring Relationship: Elderly People and their Families*, London: Macmillan.

Radin, N. (1982) 'Primary caregiving and sole-sharing fathers', in M. E. Lamb (ed.) *Nontraditional Families: Parenting and Child Development*, Hillsdale, NJ: Erlbaum.

Rogerat, C. and Senotier, D. (1996) 'De l'usage du temps de chômage' in H. Hirata and D. Senotier (eds) *Femmes et partage du travail*, Paris: Syros.

Rosenberg, S. (ed.) (1989) *The State and the Labor Market*, New York: Plenum Press.

Rosenfeld, L. B., Bowen, G. L. and Richman, J. M. (1995) 'Communication in three types of dual-career marriages', in M. A. Fitzpatrick and A. L. Vangleslisti (eds) *Explaining Marital Interactions*, Thousand Oaks, CA: Sage.

Rothschild, J. (ed.) (1983) *Machina ex dea: feminist perspectives on technology*, Oxford: Pergamon.

Roussel, L. and Bourguignon, O. (1979) *La famille Après le Mariage et les Enfants*, Paris: Presses Universitaires de France.

Roy, C. (1991) 'Les emplois du temps dans quelques pays occidentaux', *Données Sociales*, 3: 223–25.

Royal Society of Arts (1996) *Towards a New Definition of Work*, London: Royal Society of the Arts.

Rubery, J. (1978) 'Structured labour-markets, worker organization and low pay', *Cambridge Journal of Economics*, 2, March.

Rubery, J. (1988) 'Women and recession: a comparative perspective', in J. Rubery (ed.) *Women and Recession*, London: Routledge and Kegan Paul.

Rubery, J. (1989) 'Precarious forms of work in the UK', in G. and J. Rodgers (eds) *Precarious Jobs in Labour Market Regulation: the Growth of Atypical Employment in Western Europe*, Geneva: International Institute for Labour Studies, ILO.

Rubery, J. (1992) 'Productive systems, international integration and the single European market', in A. Castro, P. Mehaut and J. Rubery (eds) *International Integration and Labour Market Organisation*, London: Academic Press.

Rubery, J. and Fagan, C. (1996) 'Le temps partiel en Grande-Bretagne', Egalité équité, discrimination: hommes et femmes sur le marché du travail', *Les Cahiers du Mage*, 2: 55–76.

Rubery, J. and Grimshaw, D. (1994) *Changing Patterns of Work and Working Time: Towards the Integration or the Segmentation of the Labour Market in the UK*, UMIST, April.

Rubery, J., Fagan, C. and Humphries, J. (1992) *Occupational Segregation of Men and Women in the UK*, Manchester School of Management: UMIST.

Rubery, J., Smith, M. and Fagan, C. (1995) *Changing Patterns of Work and Working-time in the European Union and the Impact on Gender Divisions*, Report for the Equal Opportunities Unit, DGVV, Brussels: European Commission.

Rubery, J., Smith, M., Fagan, C. and Grimshaw, D. (1996) *Les femmes et le taux d'emploi en Europe, European Network on the Situation of Women in the Labour Market*, Report for the Equal Opportunities Unit, DGV, of the European Commission, Manchester School of Management, August.

Rubery, J. Smith, M. and Fagan, C. in collaboration with Almond, P. and Parker, J. (1996a) *Trends and Prospects for Women's Employment in the 1990s, European Network of Experts on the Situation of Women in the Labour Market*, Report for the Equal Opportunities Unit, DGV, of the European Commission, Manchester School of Management, UMIST, November.

Rubery, J. and Tarling, R. (1988) 'Women's employment in declining Britain', in J. Rubery (ed.) *Women   and Recession*, London: Routledge and Kegan Paul.

Rubin, J. Z., Pruitt, D. G. and Kim, S. H. (1994) *Social Conflict: Escalation, Stalemate and Settlement*, New York: McGraw-Hill.

Ruggie, M. (1984) *The State and Working Women: A Comparative Study of Britain and Sweden*, Princeton, NJ: Princeton University Press.

Russell, G. (1982) 'Shared caregiving families: an Australian study', in M. E. Lamb (ed.) *Nontraditional Families: Parenting and Child Development*, Hillsdale, NJ: Erlbaum.

Russell, G. and Radin, N. (1983) 'Increased paternal particpation and child development outcomes', in M. E. Lamb and S. Sagi (eds) *Fatherhood and the Family*, Hillsdale, NJ: Erlbaum.

Sachs, C. E. (1983) *The Invisible Farmers: Women in Agricultural Production*, Totowa, NJ: Rowman and Allanheld.

Sainsbury, D. (ed.) (1994) *Gendering Welfare States*, London: Sage.

Scanzoni, J. and Fox, G. L. (1980) 'Sex roles, family and society: the seventies and beyond', *Journal of Marriage and the Family*, 42: 743–55.

Schmid, G. (1991) *Women and Empoyment Restructuring: Women in the Public Sector*, OCDE/GD(91)213, Paris: Organisation for Economic Cooperation and Development.

Schmid, G. (1992) 'Is the state a model employer for women?', Paper presented at the Annual Conference of the European Association of Labour Economists, 3–6 September.

Schmid, G. (1994) *Competition and Cooperation between the Sexes, Institutional Alternative for the Fair and Efficient Organisation of Labour Markets*, unpublished paper, Berlin: Wissenshaftszentrum Berlin für sozialforschung WZB.

Segal, L. (1990) *Slow motion*, London: Virago.

Servis, L. J. and Deutsch, F. M. (1992) 'Paternal particpation in childcare and its effects on children's self-esteem', Eastern Psychological Association Meeting, Boston, April.

Shelton, B. E. (1992) *Women, Men and Time*, New York: Greenwood Press.

Short, P. (1996) 'Kinship, reciprocity and vulnerability', *Australian Journal of Social issues*, 31(2): 127–45.

Siim, B. (1990) 'Women and the welfare state: between private and public dependence: a comparative approach to care work in Denmark and Britain', in C. Ungerson (ed.) *Gender and Caring: Work and Welfare in Britain and Scandinavia*, New York: Simon and Schuster.

Singly de, F. and Maunaye, E. (1996) 'Le rôle et sa délégation', in J-C. Kaufmann (ed.) *Faire ou faire-faire? famille et services*, Rennes: Presses Universitaires de Rennes.

Singly, F. de (1993) *Parents Salariés et Petites Maladies d'Enfant*, Paris: La Documentation Française.

Sly, F. (1995) 'Ethnic groups and the labour market: analyses from the spring 1994 Labour Force Survey', *Employment Gazette*, June: 251–61.

Sly, F. (1996) 'Ethnic minority participation in the labour market: trends from the Labour Force Survey 1984–1995', *Labour Market Trends*, June, 259–70.

Sofer, C. (1985) *La division du travail entre hommes et femmes*, Paris: Economicas.

Sofer, C. (1986) *La production d'enfants, une production domestique essentielle des femmes*, Working Paper 18, Paris: Club Flora Tristan.

Sokoloff, N. (1980) *Between Money and Love: The Dialectics of Women, Work and the Family*, New York: Praeger.

Sorge, A. and Warner, M. (1986) *Comparative Factory Organisation: An Anglo-German Comparison of Manufacturing Management and Manpower*, Aldershot: Gower.

South, S. J. and Spitze, G. (1994) 'Housework in marital and nonmarital households', *American Sociological Review*, 59: 327–47.

Spitze, G. (1988) 'Women's employment and family relations: a review', *Journal of Marriage and the Family*, 50: 595–618.

Steil, J. M. and Turetsky, B. A. (1987) 'Is equal better? The relationship between marital equality and psychological symptomatology', in S. Oskamp (ed.) *Family Process and Problems: Social Psychological Aspects*, Beverley Hills, CA: Sage.

Stewart, M. L. (1989) *Women, Work and the French State Labour Protection and Social Patriarchy 1879–1919*, Kingston, Montreal, London: McGill-Queen's University Press.

Stockman, N., Bonney, N. and Xuewen, S. (1995) *Women's Work in East and West: The Dual Burden of Employment and Family Life*, London: UCL Press.

The Times (1998) Budget 1998: 12 page Special Section, 18 March: 15.

The Times (1998a) 'Irvine calls for an end to "macho" working culture', 10 July: 9.

Thompson, L. and Walker, A. J. (1991) 'The place of feminism in family studies , *Journal of Marriage and the Family*, 57: 847–65.

Thurow, L. C. (1975) *Generating Inequality*, New York: Basic Books.

Tilly, L. A. and Scott, J. W. (1987) *Women, Work and Family*, London: Holt, Reinhart and Winston.

Timmer, S. G., Eccles, J. and O'Brien, K. (1985) 'How children use time', in T. F. Juster and F. P. Stafford (eds) *Time, Goods and Well-being*, Ann Arbor, MI: Institute for Social Research, University of Michigan.

Tomasini, M. (1994) 'Hommes et femmes sur le marché du travail 1973–1993', *INSEE Première*, no. 324, June.

Toutain, G. (1992) *L'emploi au féminin: pour une méthode de la mixité professionnelle*, Paris: La Documentation Française.

Turner, R., Bostyn, A. M. and Wight, D. (1985) 'The work ethic in a Scottish town with declining employment', in B. Roberts, R. Finnegan and D. Gallie (eds) *New Approaches to Economic Life: Economic Restructuring, Unemployment and the Social Division of Labour*, Manchester: Manchester University Press.

Umberson, D., Warton, C. B. and Kessler, R. C. (1992) 'Widowhood and depression: explaining long-term gender differences in vulnerability', *Journal of Health and Social Behaviour*, 33: 10–24.

United Nations (1995) *The Declaration and the Platform for Action of the Fourth World Conference on Women*, Beijing, China, September.

United Nations Development Programme (1995) *Human Development Report 1995*, Oxford: Oxford University Press.

Van der Uppe, T. and Roelofs, E. (1995) 'Sharing domestic work', in A. Van Doorne-Huiskes, J. Van Hoof and E. Roelofs (eds) (1995) *Women and the European Labour Markets*, London: Paul Chapman.

Van Doorne-Huiskes, A. and Van Hoof, J. (1995) 'Gendered patterns in institutional constraints: an attempt at theoretical integration', in A. Van Doorne-Huiskes and J. Van Hoof (eds) *Women and the European Labour Markets*, London: Paul Chapman.

Van Hoof, J. and Van Doorne-Huiskes, (1995) 'Epilogue: emancipation at the cross-roads', in A. Van Doorne-Huiskes, J. Van Hoof and E. Roelofs (eds) *Women and the European Labour Markets*, London: Paul Chapman.

Villeneuve-Gokalp, C. (1985) 'Incidences des charges familiales sur l'Organisation du Travail Professionnel des Femmes', *Population*, 40(2): 267–98.

Villeneuve-Gokalp, C. (1994) 'Garder son emploi, garder ses enfants: une analyse par catégorie sociale', in H. Léridon and C. Villeneuve-Gokalp (eds) *Constance et inconstances de la famille*, Paris: INED/PUF.

Volling, B. L. and Belsky, J. (1991) 'Parent, infant and contextual characteristics related to maternal employment decisions in the first year of infancy', *Family Relations*, 42: 4–12.

Walby, S. (1990) *Theorising Patriarchy*, Oxford: Blackwell.

Walby, S. (1997) *Gender Transformations*, London: Routledge.

Ward, L. (1998) 'Workplace revolution for women', *The Guardian*, 5 November: 1.

Warde, A. (1990) 'Production, consumption and social change: reservations regarding Peter Saunders & "sociology of consumption"', *International Journal of Urban and Regional Research*, 14(2): 228–48.

Warde, A. and Hetherington, K. (1993) 'A changing domestic division of labour?', *Work, Employment and Society*, 7(1): 23–45.

Wareing, A. (1992) 'Working arrangements and patterns of working hours in Britain', *Employment Gazette*, March: 88–100.

Watson, G. (1992) 'Hours of work in Great Britain and Europe', *Employment Gazette*, November: 539–557.

Watson, G. and Fothergill, B. (1993) 'Part-time employment and attitudes to part-time work', *Employment Gazette*, May: 213–20.

West, C. and Zimmerman, D. H. (1987) 'Doing gender', *Gender and Society*, 1: 125–51.

White, M. (1983) *Long-term Unemployment and Labour Markets*, London: Policy Studies Institute.

White, M. (1996) 'Compétences et qualité de la vie professionnelle: différences de sexe en Grande Bretagne', *Les Cahiers du Mage, Egalité, Equité, Discrimination: Hommes et Femmes sur le Marché du Travail*, 2: 25–40.

Wilkinson, F. (1987) 'Deregulation, structured labor markets and unemployment' in P. J. Pedersen and R. Lund (eds) *Unemployment: Theory, Policy and Structure*, Berlin: Walter de Gruyter.

Wilkinson, H. (1994) *No Turning Back: Generations and the Gender Quake*, London: Demos.

Wilkinson, H. (1995) 'Has love been lost to labour?' *Independent*, 5 October: 21.

Willemsen, T., Frinking G. with Vogels, R. (1995) *Work and Family in Europe: The Role of Family Policies*, Tilburg: Tilburg University Press.

Williams, C. C. (1988) *Examining the Nature of Domestic Labour*, Aldershot: Avebury.

Williams, C. C. and Windebank, J. (1998a) *Informal Employment in the Advanced Economies: Implications for Work and Welfare*, London: Routledge.

Williams, C. C. and Windebank, J. (1998b) 'Household survival strategies' in G. Haughton (ed.) *Community Economic Development: From the Grassroots to Regional Economic Development*, London: Jessica Kingsley.

Williams, C. C. and Windebank, J. (1999) 'The Formalisation of Work Thesis: a critical evaluation', *Futures*, 31(6): 547–558.

Windebank, J. (1991) *The Informal Economy in France*, Aldershot: Avebury.

Windebank, J. (1996) 'To what extent can social policy challenge the dominant ideology of mothering? A cross-national comparison of Sweden, France and Britain', *Journal of European Social Policy*, 6(2): 147–61.

Windebank, J. (1999) 'Political motherhood and the everyday experience of mothering: a comparison of the child care strategies of French and British working mothers', *Journal of Social Policy*, 28(1): 1–25.

Working Mothers Association (1994) *UK Employer Initiatives, Working Examples of Family Friendly and Equal Opportunities Policies*, London: Parents at Work.

Young, M. and Wilmott, P. (1975) *The Symmetrical Family: A Study of Work and Leisure in the London Region*, Harmondsworth: Penguin.

Zick, C. D. and Allen, C. R. (1996) 'The impact of parents' marital status on the time adolescents spend in productive activities', *Journal of Family Relations*, 45: 65–71.

Zvonkovic, A. M., Greaves, K. M., Scmiege, C. J. and Hall, L. D. (1996) 'The marital construction of gender through work and family decisions: a qualitative analysis', *Journal of Marriage and the Family*, 58: 91–100.

Index